The War
Everyone Lost
—And Won

Indochina

Regional
Boundary
National
Boundaries

CHINA

VIET BAC
TONKIN
TAY BAC
NORTH VIET NAM
• Dienbienphu   • Hanoi

BURMA
• Haiphong

• Luang Prabang
PLAIN OF JARS

LAOS

• Vientiane

A N N A M

HO CHI MINH TRAIL

DEMILITARIZED ZONE
Tchepone •   • Hue
MILITARY REGION I
(I CORPS)
• Danang

THAILAND

CENTRAL HIGHLANDS

MILITARY REGION 2
(II CORPS)

• Bangkok

CAMBODIA

Mekong River

Tonle Sap

SOUTH VIET NAM

Phnom Penh •
• Tay Ninh
• Saigon
MILITARY REGION 3
(III CORPS)
Kampong Som •

COCHINCHINA
Can Tho •   MEKONG DELTA

MILITARY REGION 4 (IV CORPS)

Map courtesy of Cartographic Section, School of Geoscience, Louisiana State
University

TIMOTHY J. LOMPERIS

The War
Everyone Lost
—And Won

AMERICA'S INTERVENTION IN
VIET NAM'S TWIN STRUGGLES

LOUISIANA STATE UNIVERSITY PRESS
BATON ROUGE AND LONDON

LIBRARY OF CONGRESS CATALOGING IN PUBLICATION DATA

Lomperis, Timothy J., 1947–
   The war everyone lost—and won.

   Bibliography: p.
   Includes index.
   1. Vietnamese Conflict, 1961–1975.   2. Vietnam—
History.   I. Title.
DS557.7.L65   1984   959.704'3   83-11989
ISBN 0-8071-1104-X

To
ANA MARIA
for her love and support

In memoriam
WILLIAM C. GAUSMANN
1918–1977
my mentor on Viet Nam
and other matters

CONTENTS

ACKNOWLEDGMENTS

This study could never have been written without the help and encouragement I received, and I would like to settle my accounts, partially, by providing some recognition. The lion's share of the responsibility for this book belongs to my wife, Ana María. Her love and support sustained me and gave me the time and the peace so vital to such an endeavor. Her concern for and participation in this enterprise extended to a partnership of endless listening, clearheaded counsel, editorial resuscitation, and basic confidence in the value of this project. Dedicating this book to her, then, is the very least I can do.

I met Bill Gausmann, a Hanoi watcher at the embassy in Saigon, through our common denominational connection, the Lutheran Church. Our friendship grew rapidly, and his brilliant mind exposed me to most of the intellectual issues undergirding the war in Viet Nam. As I wrote, memories of conversations with Bill were constantly on my mind. My one sorrow is to have been denied his counsel in this project; but to acknowledge his critical role, I have written this in his memory.

A very special thank you is also due my parents, Clarence and Marjorie Lomperis, who passed on to me the spirit of critical inquiry and who instilled in me at least a shadow of a characteristic family determination to see things through to completion. What has sustained me most over the years, however, has been their faith in me, often despite overwhelming contradictory evidence. The rest of my family's understanding has been nothing short of heroic. A special vote of thanks is also due my in-laws, Daymond and Irma Turner—Irma for her kind hospitality and Daymond for the spur of the dreaded question, "How's your book coming"?

That the book came out at all is in no small measure due to the substantive help of some very special persons at Duke University. The friendship of Ole Holsti has been invaluable, and I appreciate and respect the rapid responses and the priority he gave to my work. Meg McKean's special interest, even while in Japan, has left me greatly in her debt. Her constructive comments improved the quality of the work.

I would also like to thank Al Eldridge for his help on conceptual and theoretical points. Bruce Kuniholm and Ralph Braibanti rendered valuable assistance with the historical background and developmental aspects of the study.

Most of life's enterprises cost money, and this book has been no exception. The United States Army provided me free transportation, board, and room for a tour in Viet Nam that furnished the background and impetus for this work. Upon my return from Viet Nam, the G.I. Bill made graduate school possible. The Earhart Foundation provided me with generous fellowships for much of my graduate education as well as one of two critical summer research fellowships in Baton Rouge. The other fellowship came from the Louisiana State University Graduate School and enabled me to turn the manuscript in on time. The typing skills and enthusiasm of Janice Walker were an inspiration.

Finally, the folks at Louisiana State University Press have shown great depths of understanding in handling my manuscript. Les Phillabaum and Beverly Jarrett showed great tact and professionalism; Martha Hall supervised the revisions with patience and encouragement; and Catherine Barton, my copy editor, polished the remaining roughage with finesse and forbearance. Ellis Sandoz, of the Political Science Department at LSU, is responsible for getting us all together in the first place.

For all this help, I am deeply grateful.

The War
Everyone Lost
—And Won

INTRODUCTION

In November of 1967 two officers from an American
division visited the senior adviser to the district
which abutted their division headquarters in order to
be briefed on the local situation. The adviser said the
situation was terrible, with the VC in control and the
GVN unsure even of the district town. So bitter was
the adviser that the visiting officers grumbled about
his "negativism," pointing out that their division had
the NVA units in the hills on the run and had killed
over 500 of them in the past month. The adviser
replied: "Colonel, that's your war, not mine."

F. J. WEST, JR.
Area Security: The Need, the Composition,
and the Components

In Viet Nam a five-mile walk can take one through two totally different
worlds. But if during the American involvement Viet Nam presented a
picture of highly variegated hues, since the end of the American involvement in 1975, hindsight has simplified the picture and rendered
the experience globally applicable. Thus, in the last several years "Viet
Nam" has managed to crop up just about everywhere.

In the congressional debates over American aid to Angola in 1975,
during its postindependence civil war, aid opponents repeatedly warned
that the United States was sliding into another Viet Nam. Later, during
1977 and 1978, when President Carter faced the crisis of Soviet intervention in Ethiopia and Somalia as well as the May, 1978, massacre of
whites in Congo's Shaba Province, he complained that he was handicapped in Africa by the Viet Nam legacy of congressional restraints.
Closer to home, in the summer of 1979 the specter of Viet Nam loomed
large in American thinking during the successful Sandinista campaign
to drive Anastasio Somoza out of Nicaragua. And in his trip to Lebanon

in September, 1979, civil rights leader Jesse Jackson saw another Viet Nam in the making. The continually effervescing memories of Viet Nam were not helpful to President Carter's attempt to put together a rapid deployment force for the Middle East as the centerpiece of his Carter Doctrine. Seeking to put some distance between the crises of his administration and Viet Nam, he warned that "not every instance of the firm application of power is a potential Vietnam."[1] More recently, during the Reagan administration, any contemplation of the "application of force" in El Salvador has immediately brought forth comparisons with Viet Nam. Everything in the threadbare script of the Indochina debacle has seemingly come to haunt the United States once again: elusive guerrillas, American advisers, a land reform program that is too little-too late, a bungled State Department white paper, controversial elections, and perpetual rumors of negotiations.

Just as the Munich appeasement of 1938 became a benchmark historical lesson and analogy for American policy makers of the 1950s and 1960s, Viet Nam appears destined to play a similar role for those of the 1980s. However, if it is clear that Viet Nam will be an important signpost along the path of American policy, it is by no means clear what this sign should say. As the story of the officers and the adviser illustrates, a close look at the American involvement in Viet Nam can render two, or more, entirely different readings.

Despite the different readings, confusion, and even frank unwillingness of many Americans to confront the implications of Viet Nam, the Communist victors, their fraternal Socialist patrons, and their Western well-wishers have shown no such reluctance. To them, the message of Viet Nam is plain. Prophesying in his testament shortly before his death in 1969, North Viet Nam's President Ho Chi Minh said, "We, a small nation, will have earned the signal honor of defeating, through heroic struggle, two big imperialisms—the French and the American—and of making a worthy contribution to the world national liberation movement." The lesson, Ho had stated earlier, was simple. It demonstrated the Marxist-Leninist truth that "imperialist aggressive wars are bound to be defeated, national-liberation revolutions are bound to be successful." This only confirmed what the North Vietnamese military leader

1. "Arms Policy: Farewell to Nixon Doctrine," Washington *Post*, December 13, 1979, Sec. A, p. 33.

General Vo Nguyen Giap had declared at the beginning of the war: "If it proves possible to defeat the 'special war' tested in South Viet Nam by the American imperialists, this will mean that it can be defeated everywhere else as well." However controversial the domino theory was in the United States, there was no debate about its validity among Vietnamese Communists.[2]

This faith was seconded by the Chinese, who saw the struggle of the Vietnamese as the most convincing contemporary example of a successful Marxist, people's war—a struggle that they felt confident would produce a global chain reaction. Western well-wishers were also quick to make this point right after the Communist triumph. One such admirer was Australian journalist Denis Warner, who intoned: "They [the Vietnamese] are the only people in the world who have ever engaged the U.S. in a major war—and won. . . . They borrowed from the teaching of Mao and improved his technique beyond recognition. When Giap and Dung claim they have made a new development in the art of leading a revolutionary war, none can contradict them."[3]

Clear as the significance of Viet Nam may be to the Communists, the ambiguity of the Americans toward their intervention persists. In fact, one American writer, Leslie Gelb, has argued that ironically, despite the Communist triumph, the United States did achieve its objectives.[4] With such contradictory conclusions, if Viet Nam is to play the role of a benchmark analogy for American policy makers in the 1980s similar to the role Munich played for their counterparts of the 1950s and 1960s, then a semblance of the clarity of the meaning of Munich needs to be established for Viet Nam.

Part of the confusion surrounding the lessons of the conflict in Viet Nam is due to its complexity. It was a massive, even global undertaking that cut across a variety of issues and affected many countries, agencies, institutions, and the social classes or strata within them. The effects on all these parties were varied, to say the least, and resulted in a multitude of perspectives on the war. For example, an examination of

2. Ho Chi Minh, *Selected Writings (1920–1969)* (Hanoi, 1973), 361, 277; Chalmers A. Johnson, *Autopsy on People's War* (Berkeley, Calif., 1973), 30–31.

3. Denis Warner, *Certain Victory: How Hanoi Won the War* (Kansas City, Kan., 1978), 275.

4. Leslie H. Gelb, with Richard K. Betts, *The Irony of Vietnam: The System Worked* (Washington, D.C., 1979), 1–6, 352–54.

the Pentagon papers might reveal several truths and lessons of the war from the perspective of the American foreign-policy making establishment. Numerous theologians and social moralists have denounced or supported the war from an ethical perspective. Among politicians and writers are those who view the war in the context of its effects on the international system and the struggle between the two superpowers and their opposing ideologies. And others analyze the impact of such a prolonged and disruptive war on the crisis of political and economic development. With such diversity, perhaps it is sufficient to settle for each faction deriving its own lessons rather than to hope for comprehensive lessons accommodating all these issues, constituencies, and perspectives.

Still, for everyone who writes on Viet Nam, there is almost an irresistible imperative to proclaim its lessons. Indeed such early critics as Marvin Gettleman offered lessons even as the war was just getting underway.[5] Ironically, with a reputation for being singularly ignorant of history, Americans nevertheless have an obsession with drawing historical lessons. And it is easier and quicker to draw these lessons if the information can be kept meager. Delving into anything as complex as Viet Nam is likely to cause confusion. Thus, many Americans appear content to remember Viet Nam either as an unmitigated disaster or as a noble crusade, and they draw their simple lessons accordingly.

Although the question of Viet Nam's lessons hovers over almost every page, this is not so much a study of those lessons as it is an examination of what happened there, specifically from two vantage points: national legitimacy and revolutionary legitimacy. Once we can grasp what happened in Viet Nam, then we can cast the wider net for its general lessons and properly assess whether the crises of today are comparable to it.

As Edgar Furniss has pointed out, the war played to two attentive audiences: the national audience of the Vietnamese people, over whose welfare the war was ostensibly being fought, and the international audience of concerned groups and nations.[6] Members in both audi-

5. Marvin E. Gettleman, (ed.), *Vietnam: History, Documents, and Opinions on a Major World Crisis* (New York, 1965), 6–10.
6. Edgar S. Furniss, Jr., *Counterinsurgency: Some Problems and Implications* (New York, 1966), 12.

ences had developed a stake, and become participants to some degree, in the outcome. Their interests, however, were often different. For the Vietnamese, the focus was on the struggle for national legitimacy. This meant more than just a struggle for power between the non-Communists and the Communists; the drama centered on the question of whose power and rule was right for Viet Nam. While this struggle was not uninteresting to members of the international audience, their attention was directed toward the action over the more general or global claims of the actors. The Communists declared their revolution to be a demonstration of the revolutionary strategy of people's war. For the Americans, who intervened in behalf of the non-Communists, the question was whether the United States foreign policy of containment, coupled with the latest counterinsurgency strategies and technologies, could prevent this people's war from succeeding. The issue for the international audience, then, was the revolutionary legitimacy of the Vietnamese Communists' application of people's war.

With respect to these two vantage points, it is my conclusion that Viet Nam was the war that everyone lost—and won. Certainly the prize of political power belonged to the Communists. But the struggle was for more than power. It was for legitimacy, or rightful rule, as well. With the postliberation impoverishment of the Socialist Republic of Viet Nam and the mass exodus of Vietnamese from the fatherland in historically unprecedented numbers, the Mandate of Heaven has yet to settle very comfortably or securely on the shoulders of the Lao Dong (Communist) party. It is in light of what has happened after "liberation" that the former Saigon government can perhaps claim something of a moral victory. The *ancien regime* did make some strides in bringing South Viet Nam into the modern world. For all their failings, the various South Vietnamese governments supported by the United States were not appreciably worse than a host of other governments in the Third World to which the Americans committed themselves.

Nevertheless, the failings of South Viet Nam were abundant. Although not all these failings can be blamed on the United States, it had become so involved in the fate of Viet Nam that the South Vietnamese government had trouble in maintaining its separate identity in the eyes of its own people. In fact, American support had become such an opium that one simple explanation for the collapse of Saigon in just two years, from 1973 to 1975, is that the withdrawal of much of this support proved too much of a shock for an almost completely addicted society. As committed as the United States had been to South Viet Nam, those two years did not secure the "decent interval" with which Henry Kissinger had sought to distance the United States from the fate of South Viet Nam. The collapse of Saigon, therefore, was also an American defeat.

In shifting the vantage point to a focus on the struggle for revolutionary legitimacy, however, it is the Communists who had a problem with a "decent interval." In their case the problem was the indecently long interval between the time when they proclaimed they were using a strategy of people's war and the time when they actually stopped using it. They claimed they were fighting a people's war all the way through 1975, when in fact they had abandoned this form of struggle in the rubble of the Tet offensive in 1968. Thus, as a people's war the triumph of 1975 was a fraud, and the United States, perhaps surprisingly, deserves recognition for discrediting this strategy. But the manner in which the United States succeeded was something like swatting a fly with a sledgehammer, and after such an effort, one hesitates to get enthusiastic about recommending future applications. Accepting these conclusions depends upon an understanding of national legitimacy and a recognition of the importance of a revolutionary faithfulness to the strategy of people's war in assessing the significance of the Communist victory.

National Legitimacy

Legitimacy is one of those central political concepts that lie at the foundation of any political order. As such, a clear definition of it is necessary for an understanding of the order itself. Yet providing a clear definition often proves to be an elusive task, largely because the term acquires concrete meaning only in a specific setting. Generally speaking, though, to attain legitimacy a political regime must guarantee the well-being, physically and economically, of its citizens or subjects. These facets are relatively easy to measure. Are a ruler's charges safe in their persons? Can they live out their lives unmolested by invading armies? Can they make a decent living for their families, after taxes and various other levies that governments typically exact from their citizenry?

More is required of legitimacy, however, than the provision of physical and economic security. At best these provisions will only guarantee a *passive* legitimacy, one based on a calculation of mutual interests. A calculation of interests is continuous and can easily be reversed by a regime's missteps. Such a form of legitimacy has no surplus margins. Something more is required to make legitimacy *active*, whereby the subjects grant their rulers some measure of voluntary support, freeing the ruler from the constant pressure of accommodating each calculation of his subjects' interests.[7]

Without this extra or active dimension to legitimacy, a government is liable to either open rebellion or more subtle impediments. Among those impediments are political *attentisme*, a term used particularly during the French phase of the war to describe those who adopted a fence-sitting, wait-and-see attitude, and the slightly different "free rider phenomenon," a phrase Samuel Popkin borrowed from economic theory to refer to the large proportion of a population that sits back and lets the government do everything for them. Eqbal Ahmad defines active legitimacy as "that crucial and ubiquitous factor in politics which invests power with authority." He further explains that this authority comes to a government or other institution of power when its constituents, subjects, or citizens recognize its power as deriving from some principle or source that is outside the power-holding body and that provides it with an operative ideological justification. Such principles as the divine right of kings and the Mandate of Heaven have served this purpose in the past, and democratic constitutionalism and the dictatorship of the proletariat perform the same duty in the present. For the subjects to recognize this authority and thereby invest it with legitimacy, this ideological justification must provide them with valued societal goods. These goods are subject to standards that provide indicators of the relative justice and, hence, legitimacy of power holders.[8]

An application of such a general definition of legitimacy to a particular country requires a deep look into the historical developments and patterns that have shaped its culture. Whether a grant of legitimacy

7. For the concept of these two types of legitimacy, I am indebted to David Easton. He calls them legitimacy of interest and legitimacy of belief. See David Easton, *A Systems Analysis of Political Life* (New York, 1965), 278–89.

8. Samuel L. Popkin, *The Rational Peasant: The Political Economy of Rural Society in Vietnam* (Berkeley, Calif., 1979), 14; Eqbal Ahmad, "Revolutionary War and Counter-Insurgency," *Journal of International Affairs*, XXV, No. 1, p. 5.

comes from a moral or a rational calculation, the calculation will be rooted morally and rationally in the society's particular experiences in fashioning its political order.[9] For some countries, external entanglements in domestic politics have been an important part of their history and have even yielded beneficial results. Thus, the presence of large numbers of foreign troops may not adversely affect the legitimacy of a ruler requesting this assistance. Greece, for example, owes its independence to external intervention, and the presence of large numbers of British troops later in its civil war in the 1940s did not tarnish the legitimacy of the Greek government. The Vietnamese historical experience has not resulted in a benign attitude toward large numbers of foreign troops, who in fact, the Vietnamese regard with anathema. A definition of active legitimacy in Viet Nam, then, can only emerge from an understanding of its particular historical components.

Revolutionary Legitimacy

While each side of the contest for national legitimacy—the Communists and the nationalists—must be evaluated according to the standards of Vietnamese legitimacy, the Communists, as the revolutionary group seeking to impose a new political order and type of legitimacy, must also be evaluated by their even more demanding standards of revolutionary legitimacy. This is in recognition of the fact that in embracing a Marxist, people's war as a revolutionary strategy, the Vietnamese Communists had an additional criterion of legitimacy in following the beat of this very different drummer. Revolutions consist of both strategies and goals, and, as such, are as much concerned with revolutionary means as revolutionary ends. Thus, how much of a chain reaction the Vietnamese revolution will ultimately produce depends, in part, on how closely the script or strategy of people's war was being followed.

The relative adherence of the Communists to this script, then, held the attention of a far wider audience than the national one in Viet Nam.

9. A debate rages between advocates of moral economy and rational legitimacy. The moral economy approach is advanced by James C. Scott, *The Moral Economy of the Peasant* (New Haven, Conn., 1976). On the other side is Ronald Rogowski, *Rational Legitimacy: A Theory of Political Support* (Princeton, N.J., 1974). Popkin applies the latter approach to Viet Nam, in *The Rational Peasant*.

American concern over the threat of people's war emerged as part of a two-tracked confrontation that developed between communism and the Western democracies after World War II. The first track consisted of usually direct and sharp clashes of interest between the United States and the Soviet Union. The second traced a less threatening course involving a campaign of winning over the untutored minds of the Third World to the American way of progress, democracy, and development. In the first track, initial postwar American foreign policy toward the Soviet Union was ambivalent, as the United States sought to continue the wartime alliance with Britain and the Soviet Union in the United Nations. The stubbornness of the Soviets in the four-power occupation of Germany, however, proved that the alliance was going to be difficult to maintain. The gains the Soviets made in eastern Europe and Manchuria, and the difficulty in securing the withdrawal of Soviet troops from Iran in 1946, caused uneasiness in the West, however much the Soviets contended they were only seeking to establish security corridors. By 1948 Americans began to take the Communist revolutionary rhetoric seriously, and the Truman administration forged a bipartisan foreign policy of containment that lasted until the Tet offensive of 1968.

The first component of this policy was the Truman Doctrine of 1947, which provided aid to Greece to suppress externally supported guerrillas and to Turkey to withstand Soviet pressure for special rights to the Dardanelles. George Kennan's "X" article of July, 1947, warned that the Soviet regime was basically expansionist but was more patient than the Nazis and would be continually probing for soft spots in a long-term effort. Thus, he suggested, the United States policy should be one of firm and vigilant containment dealing with the Soviets from a position of strength.[10]

The most vital area where the Soviets needed to be contained was Europe. In 1948 Congress passed the second component of its containment policy, the Marshall Plan, which provided reconstruction aid to rebuild the shattered western European economy and turn aside the appeal of communism. Containment continued with the North Atlantic Treaty Organization pact of 1949 and the secret National Security Council study of 1950, which warned that for a foreign policy of con-

10. X [George F. Kennan], "Sources of Soviet Conduct," *Foreign Affairs*, XXV (July, 1947), 566–82.

tainment to be credible, taxes had to be raised, defense expenditures increased, and troops sent to Europe. This need for a credible defense was further emphasized by the Korean War, which lasted from 1950 to 1953. Following the Korean War, Secretary of State John Foster Dulles put together a string of treaties (Central Treaty Organization, Southeast Asia Treaty Organization, and mutual defense treaties with Taiwan and South Korea) to contain the Communists throughout the world. In 1957 the Eisenhower Doctrine was proclaimed to ward off Soviet intervention in the Middle East. In the next two years the United States intervened once in Jordan and once in Lebanon. Throughout this period, crises over Berlin flared up continually. These direct confrontations with the Soviets culminated in the thirteen-day Cuban Missile Crisis of October, 1962, which brought the world to the brink of a nuclear exchange. At this time the administration of John F. Kennedy was much enamored with "brush-fire wars" and counterinsurgency theories, and with the Soviet retreat in Cuba, it expected that the next probe for a soft spot would be via a guerrilla, people's war. By the mid-1960s the next challenge to the policy of containment appeared to lurk in the jungles and deltas of Laos and South Viet Nam.

The other track also led to Viet Nam. Following the stunning success of the Marshall Plan, Truman thought the program could be extended to the Third World as well, to convince those countries that political and economic progress is possible through liberalism, democracy, and free enterprise rather than through the revolutionary violence of the Communists. Thus, a rather lavish program of military, economic, and technical assistance, so far amounting to more than $150 billion, became the centerpiece of American foreign policy toward the Third World. Weighed against the Marshall Plan, the program quickly proved disillusioning, yet it did provide an effective tool for retaining American influence, as well as a vehicle for projecting "the American way."

One of the problems of development the program confronted was the lack of internal legitimacy accorded to the regimes of many underdeveloped countries, to the point that the regimes were often too weak and unstable even to manage the assistance, let alone cope with internal rebellions or guerrilla movements supported from the outside. Thus, as a companion piece to its foreign assistance program, the Pentagon and its "think tanks" (Rand and Stanford Research Institute, among others) developed counterinsurgency programs and theories to assist "friendly governments" beset by insurgent elements. Weapons were liberally dispensed, nationals were brought to the United States for special training at police academies and military installations, and training missions were set up in the countries and supplemented by a network of political and military advisers. Counterinsurgency operations were aimed at separating active guerrillas from the mass of the people. The important thing to avoid was adding to peasant grievances and thereby fueling the mobilization of the peasantry by the guerrillas.

These modern theories of revolution and counterinsurgency achieved a wide currency in the United States during the early 1960s, as·American policy makers sought to fashion a global strategy for containing this latest type of Communist probe for free-world soft spots. All too often these theories started from a general set of deductive principles to which all cases were expected to conform. Unfortunately, these principles were seldom scrutinized with respect to their relevance to the internal realities of each particular case. In Viet Nam, as in other cases, the thwarting of the Communist bid for power via a Marxist, people's war relied crucially on the incumbent regime's ability to preserve its hold on the mantle of national legitimacy against the competing claims of the Communists. The final test of any Western intervention in such a struggle, then, depended on the effect this intervention had on the legitimacy of the regime being helped—that is, legitimacy as it was defined in that specific country. What made such an intervention even more delicate was the fact that in Viet Nam, as well as in other countries, the very terms and standards of this legitimacy were subjected to the conflicting pulls of traditional identity and the demands for modern development.

Again, though, beyond these general principles, a conception of the grounds of the struggle for legitimacy in Viet Nam must emerge from a thorough grasp of the development of the Vietnamese political tradition and culture. Only after more inductive investigation can general conclusions about the war emerge.

PART I

National Legitimacy

CHAPTER ONE

Before the
American Involvement

For the Vietnamese the idea of legitimacy is most clearly subsumed under the Chinese concept of the Mandate of Heaven, which embodies
several time-honored duties. The principal task of any holder of the
Mandate of Heaven in Viet Nam has been the preservation of Vietnamese identity. The Vietnamese have always been borrowers from
other cultures, but the borrowing has had to be, in some way or other,
Vietnamized by the ruling establishment so that the people would not
lose their identity as Vietnamese. More tangibly, it has always been the
almost sacred charge of Viet Nam's rulers to rid the country of foreign
invaders and meddlers. The longest tradition in this respect was the
struggle against the one thousand years of Chinese domination (*ca.* 100
B.C. through 900 A.D.). After the Vietnamese finally secured their independence from the Chinese, this imperative continued against the Portuguese, Dutch, French, and, finally, the Americans. Part of this striv-
ing for independence drove the Vietnamese south for space in a long
march to the Camau Peninsula (at Viet Nam's southern tip) that began
in the fifteenth century. The march added regional variants to their
identity and gave the Vietnamese a well-deserved reputation in Southeast Asia as both a giant slayer and a military bully.

While protecting the Vietnamese culture and fatherland from external adversaries was one of their charges, Vietnamese rulers further

gained legitimacy by dispensing justice internally. In a predominantly agrarian society this meant ensuring an equitable distribution of land so that the peasants on whom the social order was based not only had enough to provide for their families but also had a place to cultivate the memory of their ancestors and a communal place to keep alive the traditions of their villages.

This, then, was traditional Viet Nam; however, as Viet Nam moved into the modern world, the nature of this traditional legitimacy changed. The French came, and the dual economy and dual political system they imposed shook the Confucian order to its foundations. As Vietnamese nationalists struggled with Western ideas, values, economics, and institutions, they were handicapped by the lack of anything in their own history potent and cogent enough to counter this Western challenge. The last Vietnamese dynasty, the Nguyens, had permanently sullied their mandate by their disastrous cooperation with the French. But the French found it increasingly difficult to stay on, and if World War II meant just one thing in Asia, it was that the mandate of the white man was fast ending. In this uncertainty the Communists stepped in to offer an entirely different political order with which to re-create Vietnamese society.

Still, until the revolution was complete, the Communists had to justify their claims for an active legitimacy in the Vietnamese context, that is, in terms that squared with rightful rule as it was traditionally understood and as it was evolving under the shocks of the twentieth century. Herein lay (and still lies) the struggle in Viet Nam for legitimacy.

Traditional Viet Nam

Early Vietnamese history is dotted with legends of genies, dragons, and fairies. The founding myth of the Vietnamese people is that they are the offspring of the mating, 4,000 years ago, of a male dragon from the sea and a female fairy from the land. However fanciful, the early legends helped the Yueh, or Giao Chi—the people of the Red River Delta—develop a sense of their distinctive identity as Vietnamese. Developing this distinct identity early was fortuitous, because the descent into recorded history landed the Vietnamese under the yoke of the early Han

dynasty of China in 111 B.C., scarcely 150 years after An Zuong had finally united the warring mountain and plains people under the Vietnamese kingdom of Au Lac in 258 B.C. An Zuong's achievement attracted the attention of a Chinese general who annexed Au Lac into his
kingdom of Nam Viet, centered in Canton; in turn, the Hans, who ruled
all of China, intervened.[1]

The thousand years of Chinese domination left a profound impression on Vietnamese culture. Nevertheless, the period was punctuated
by revolts whose leaders are remembered today as Viet Nam's first heroes and heroines. The most venerated were the Trung sisters, who
ended their short-lived rebellion (from 40 A.D. to 42 A.D.) by jumping
into the Red River rather than submitting to the reconquering Chinese
army. Another heroine, Trieu Au, rose up in 248 A.D. And in 542 A.D. Ly
Bon, a man, waged an unsuccessful campaign for independence.[2]

Rebellions began again in the early tenth century, and Ngo Quyen
finally secured Vietnamese independence in 939 after trapping and
burning a large Chinese fleet in the shallow waters of Haiphong. Three
short-lived dynasties struggled to maintain this freedom until power
was stabilized with the accession of the Ly dynasty (lasting from 1009
to 1224). The Lys moved the capital to Thang Long (Hanoi), where it
remained until 1802. Early in the dynasty, in 1075, Emperor Ly Thuong
Kiet beat back a Chinese attempt at reconquest. The Lys developed
government administration at provincial and district levels and built
the famous dikes of the Red River Delta under a system of corvée labor.
The Ly dynasty was followed by another strong dynasty, the Tran,
which lasted until 1400. Its great hero was Tran Hung Dao, the military
strategist who, during the years 1282 to 1289, defeated three land attempts at reconquest by the Mongol Kublai Khan and pulled off a repeat performance of Ngo Quyen's fleet burning. The Trans raised a
conscript national army directly responsibile to the emperor and extended the royal administrative machinery to the village level.[3]

During this period the Confucians and the Buddhists both helped

1. Joseph Buttinger, *Vietnam: A Political History* (New York, 1968), 21–22;
Nguyen Khac Vien, "Traditional Vietnam: Some Historical Stages," *Vietnamese
Studies*, XXI [1969?], 18–22.

2. Buttinger, *Vietnam*, 30–33.

3. *Ibid.*, 38–39; Nguyen Khac Vien, "Traditional Vietnam," 35–36, 39–48; David G. Marr, *Vietnamese Anticolonialism 1885–1925* (Berkeley, 1971), 11.

the imperial court to establish its sway over the people, but they soon quarreled over official court favor. The Confucians gradually won out, because, as Thich Nhat Hanh points out, "the Tran Dynasty realized that while Buddhism contained a powerful inner life, Confucianism had a political philosophy and a code of conduct necessary for the development of the kingdom."[4] From the Confucians the dynasties adopted competitive examinations, based on classical Confucian texts, to select mandarins for their bureaucracy, and they seized on the notion of the Mandate of Heaven to legitimize their rule. In the villages, on the other hand, the peasants adopted the Confucian worship of ancestors, but they clung to their own genies, added a few Buddhist and Taoist ones, and went regularly to Buddhist pagodas. This mixture formed the value base of Vietnamese society.

With the collapse of the Tran dynasty in 1400, the ever-present threat of Chinese intervention came to life in the Ming reoccupation from 1407 to 1427. Once again a hero rose up to drive the Chinese out. After a successful ten-year guerrilla campaign, Le Loi founded a new Vietnamese dynasty and crowned himself the Prince of Pacification. To secure the Mandate of Heaven, Le Loi promptly redistributed land to the peasants. The dynasty lasted until 1788 and reached its apogee under Le Thanh Tong, whose reign from 1461 to 1497 is remembered as the golden age of Viet Nam. He launched a major land reform program that directly intervened in village life by redistributing communal land to all, by rank, every six years. His conquest of the Indic kingdom of Champa in 1471 paved the way for Viet Nam's famous march to the South, a slow-motion version of America's westward movement, with villagers sending their surplus population to start pioneer settlements in the South. These settlements produced a chain that finally reached the Camau Peninsula in 1757. Inevitably, differences in geography and experience brought forth regional distinctions among the Tonkinese, Annamese, and the southerners of the Mekong Delta and Gia Dinh (Saigon), but they were not enough to destroy their essential identity as Vietnamese.[5]

4. Thich Nhat Hanh, *Vietnam: Lotus in a Sea of Fire* (New York, 1967), 8.
5. Buttinger, *Vietnam*, 15, 45–56, 50; Truong Buu Lam, "Patterns of Vietnamese Response to Foreign Intervention: 1858–1900," *Yale University Southeast Asia Studies*, XI (1967), 55; Nguyen Khac Vien, "Traditional Vietnam," 78.

However glorious for the Vietnamese, the march to the South was not a happy experience for their neighbors. The Communist historian Nguyen Khac Vien admits that the attempts of the Les to extend their control over the *montagnards* (the many tribal peoples living in the mountains and plateaus of the Indochinese Peninsula) inaugurated a long tradition of revolt against Vietnamese rule.[6] In addition, the Chams were literally wiped out in the Vietnamese conquest of Champa, and the Khmers (the forebears of the people of Kampuchea) were pushed westward from the Mekong Delta. The memory of these experiences still serves to keep relations between Vietnamese and Cambodians, and ethnic Vietnamese and tribal highlanders, distant.

The classical political order of the Les was undergirded by a Confucian ideology, which bestowed legitimacy on an emperor by the Mandate of Heaven. To the Vietnamese there were two components to this concept of the Mandate of Heaven. They were embodied in the two Vietnamese words for ruler. One term was *hoang de* (emperor), which reflected the Confucian and Chinese emphasis on hierarchy and correct social relations. The other word was *vua* (king), the term used by the peasants for the protector who was close to them. On a cultural level, this meant the emperor's mandate was to introduce Chinese culture but at the same time to Vietnamize it. The emperor ruled the villages through his mandarins, whose power he always tried to curtail in order to prevent warlordism and insurrection. Meanwhile, the villages retained the essential autonomy of relatively self-sufficient communities. The Vietnamese language lends itself to pithy epigrams, and one of the most famous is, The laws of the emperor yield to the customs of the village. The villagers themselves decided how their village would meet such external obligations as the census, taxes, corvée labor, and conscription. It is important to remember that when there were peasant rebellions, they were directed against mandarin officials, not against the village elites.[7]

6. Nguyen Khac Vien, "Traditional Vietnam," 82–83.
7. Alexander B. Woodside, *Vietnam and the Chinese Model: A Comparative Study of Nguyen and Ch'ing Civil Government in the First Half of the Nineteenth Century* (Cambridge, Mass., 1971), 10; Samuel L. Popkin, *The Rational Peasant: The Political Economy of Rural Society in Vietnam* (Berkeley, Calif., 1979), 112; Alexander B. Woodside, *Community and Revolution in Modern Vietnam* (Boston, 1976), 117.

By the early sixteenth century, the Les could no longer hold the centripetal forces of their expanded kingdom in check. Baronial families fought for real control under nominal Le rule. In 1592 one family in the North won out, but shortly thereafter in 1620 the southern governor revolted. From 1627 to 1673 the northerners tried unsuccessfully to bring the southerners to heel in a bitter civil war. Both sides called in foreign advisers and support, the northerners from the Dutch and the southerners from the Portuguese. Finally, they agreed upon a truce that lasted for one hundred years and divided the country at the sixteenth parallel.[8]

The Tay Sons and the Nguyens

Onto this scene burst the revolt of the three Tay Son brothers from central Viet Nam's Binh Dinh Province. Seizing the provincial capital in 1773, the Tay Sons were masters of the entire South by 1788, having twice defeated the southern ruler, Nguyen Anh, and forcing him to flee to Thailand. In 1786 they turned their attention to the North. In 1788, just as victory was in their grasp, the Le emperor appealed to the Ch'ing dynasty in China for help. Undaunted, Nguyen Hue, the leader of the three, proclaimed himself emperor, quietly celebrated the New Year (Tet) a month early, and then later surprised the Chinese in the midst of their celebrations. In their brief rule the Tay Sons acted in defiance of accepted conventions. They gave precedence to military leaders over mandarin bureaucrats and overthrew classical Chinese as the language of the court. Despite Marxist attempts to paint them as forerunners of modern socialism, what they put into effect was little more than a military dictatorship.[9]

Whatever his ultimate intentions, Nguyen Hue died in 1792, and his son and brothers were unable to hold on to power. This faltering was what Nguyen Anh had been waiting for. When he returned from Thai-

8. Bernard B. Fall, *The Two Viet-Nams: A Political and Military Analysis* (2nd rev. ed.; New York, 1968), 18; Buttinger, *Vietnam*, 48–49.

9. Nguyen Khac Vien, "Traditional Vietnam," 117–25; Woodside, *Vietnam and the Chinese Model*, 2–3; Fall, *The Two Viet-Nams*, 19.

land with French military advisers, he launched a campaign against the Tay Sons that resulted in their final defeat in 1802. Nguyen Anh then moved the imperial capital to Hue, took the regnal name Gia Long in 1802, and established Viet Nam's last royal dynasty, the Nguyen, which lasted until 1884.[10] His choice of the name Gia Long signified that he wanted posterity to remember him for his unification of the country from north to south. *Gia* was from Gia Dinh (Saigon), and *Long* from Thang Long (Hanoi).

The Nguyens came to power riding a wave of conservative reaction to the social protest of the Tay Sons, and their first order of business was to reestablish Confucian orthodoxy in the realm. Another prime objective of the court was a centralized government over an extended territory having a large population of seven to eight million. The task proved difficult. Even under Gia Long, the great unifier, power was dispersed, with the court's direct sway confined to the central reign of Annam. The North and South were under the effective control of military overlords. Under the reign of Minh Mang, from 1820 to 1841, however, the desired centralization was achieved, and this made him the only Vietnamese emperor ever to rule the area of Viet Nam from the Red River Delta in the North to the Mekong Delta in the South. Despite this consolidation, the Nguyen court never gained the fundamental legitimacy that was accorded the Les. Its writ was most tenuous at the village level. Peasant uprisings in the 1840s and 1850s inspired the construction of Vauban-styled fortresses. Unfortunately, these fortress towns only increased the regime's isolation from the peasantry. In the bureaucracy, the numerous circumventions of the examination system and the gross underrepresentation of southerners seriously undermined the traditional respect for mandarins. Further, within the dynasty itself, Tu Duc, who reigned from 1847 to 1883, had to contend with a continuing challenge to his succession from the royal family, obliging him to execute his elder brother in 1854 and kill the rest of his family in 1866.[11] It was at this inopportune time that the struggling Nguyens confronted another challenge—the French.

10. Donald Lancaster, *The Emancipation of French Indochina* (London, 1961), 27–30.
11. Marr, *Vietnamese Anticolonialism*, 22–25; Woodside, *Vietnam and the Chinese Model*, 159, 219–20.

Arrival of the French

Actually, the first Westerners to arrive were Portuguese traders, who established a trading post in 1540 and controlled all Western trade with Viet Nam for the rest of the century. They called the country Cochinchina because it was midway between the Indian coast of Cochin and China. By the end of the century, the Dutch and the British appeared in the Far East and broke the Portuguese monopoly. The Dutch established themselves in both the South and the North, but the British, who appeared in 1672, confined themselves to the North.

Finding Viet Nam unprofitable, the British and Dutch withdrew by 1700, the latter also because they had backed the wrong side in the civil war. The eighteenth century provided a breathing spell for the Vietnamese, while the British and French struggled for supremacy in India. The Portuguese, however, remained, not so much for mercantile reasons as for religious ones. They took seriously Pope Alexander II's 1493 edict granting them the exclusive mandate to convert Asia. The missionaries who arrived regularly from the early sixteenth century onward were more successful in Viet Nam than anywhere else except the Philippines. Perhaps the most energetic missionary was the Frenchman Alexandre de Rhodes, who arrived in 1627. In his zeal to convert the Vietnamese, Rhodes devised a Roman script for the Vietnamese language to make the translation of religious materials easier. Seizing upon this as an opportunity to declare a form of cultural independence from the Chinese and their character writing, the Vietnamese adopted Rhodes's invention and called it *quoc ngu* (national writing).

Frustrated by the lack of support from his Portuguese superiors, Rhodes turned to the French for sponsorship of his evangelical plans. After his death, the Vatican granted the French the evangelization rights to Indochina, and in 1664 the French Society of Foreign Missions was established. A close cooperation soon developed between French merchants and apostolic vicars. By the middle of the eighteenth century some 300,000 Vietnamese had converted to Christianity. The Vietnamese court, however, grew suspicious of this Western religion and began to expel the missionaries. Persecution became harsher under the rigidly orthodox Nguyens, who promptly forgot the earlier help of their French advisers. This was especially true under Thieu Tri, who, during his reign from 1841 through 1847, began to kill Christian converts and seize French bishops.[12]

This sequence of events finally led to armed intervention. Ironically, it was the Americans who fired the first shots. In 1845 the USS *Constitution*, under the command of John Percival, sailed into Danang Harbor, seized the local mandarins, and demanded the release of a French bishop. When the mandarins refused, Percival eventually released them and sailed away. Then the French tried to free their hapless bishop in 1847. They leveled the town but were no more successful than the Americans.[13]

The French, however, did not just sail away. In 1858 they returned and bombarded both Danang and Gia Dinh. The next year a French naval expedition enroute to China failed to negotiate religious liberty for the Christians and left a force of one thousand men in Gia Dinh, which fell under a nine-month siege until relieved by a French admiral in 1861. By 1862 the enterprising admiral had seized three provinces, and in 1867 the emperor Tu Duc ceded the remaining three provinces of Cochinchina.

The rest of the French conquest is a story of both Vietnamese and French vacillation between hesitation and compulsive action. In 1873 Jean Depuis proved the navigability of the Red River as a possible trade route to China's Yunnan Province. The French governor of Cochinchina promptly dispatched Captain Francis Garnier north with two hundred men to secure the route. After taking the Hanoi citadel, Garnier was killed in a subsequent action for the surrounding Red River Delta. The French withdrew and did nothing for almost ten years. When in 1882 the French learned that Chinese troops had arrived in the Red River Delta as part of a secret Vietnamese embassy to Peking, however, Captain Henri Riviere was sent, along with four hundred men, on the second French mission to the north. After he seized Hanoi, Riviere met with the same fate as Garnier and was killed by Chinese

12. Buttinger, *Vietnam*, 55–56; Lancaster, *The Emancipation of French Indochina*, 27; Truong Buu lam, "Patterns of Vietnamese Response," 4.
13. Truong Buu Lam, "Patterns of Vietnamese Response," 4.

soldiers in May, 1883. This time, though, the French did not withdraw. Instead, they sent a major expedition to shell Hue in August, 1883 (one month after Tu Duc's death), and completed the conquest of the Red River Delta in 1884. On June 6, 1884, the Patenotre–Nguyen Van Tuong Treaty established a French protectorate over Annam and Tonkin in a public ceremony in which the court disavowed the camel's seal that had symbolized its tributary relationship with China.[14] Despite a three-year revolt in the name of the boy emperor, Ham Nghi, and a brief incursion by a Chinese army, the Nguyens had irrevocably lost the Mandate of Heaven.

The French accomplished the conquest of Indochina with a force of only three thousand men. Aside from the general technological and military superiority of the Occidentals over the Orientals during this period, it is worth recounting some of the reasons offered by Truong Buu Lam for the French victory. Tu Duc's court was deeply disturbed by the French encroachments; issues were hotly debated, with some arguing for immediate action against the French and others arguing for holding out until the advent of more propitious circumstances. The result was paralysis. This was compounded by Tu Duc's personality and situation. He was a sensitive poet in chronic ill health, he was guilt ridden over the executions of his brother and family, and he faced rebellion after rebellion throughout his reign. While Hue could appeal to nationalistic loyalties, every imperial act of conciliation toward the French drove a greater wedge between the court and the populace. The most serious breach occurred in 1873, when the court suppressed an anti-French revolt in Annam's Nghe An and Ha Tin provinces. Subsequent uprisings against the French in Tonkin, in 1883 and 1884, did not even bother to invoke the emperor's name. Thus, in 1884 when the Can Vuong faction of the Nguyen court tried to rally around Ham Nghi in an effort to drive the French out, the Nguyens could not even count on the support of their own people. Truong Buu Lam concludes that while the continuity of resistance to foreign domination gave definition to Vietnamese nationalism, interventions were successful when the people were divided.[15]

French rule lasted until March 9, 1945. Its effect was to create half a

14. *Ibid.*, 23–25.
15. *Ibid.*, 16–21, 33–34.

revolution, which destroyed the traditional order but failed in the crucial task of replacing it with a legitimate new one. Through an unusually large colonial bureaucracy, the French fashioned a society of "structural dualism" in both the economic and political spheres.[16] Economically, they created a modern sector made up of cosmopolitan urban centers, agricultural plantations-for-export in the Mekong Delta and Central Highlands, and mining and fledgling industries in Tonkin, which grew out of, and away from, the surrounding traditional agricultural and poor rural sectors in Annam and Tonkin. Politically, they ruled the colony through two administrative structures. Cochinchina they ruled directly, but in the protectorates of Annam and Tonkin the Vietnamese court was allowed to keep its mandarin bureaucracy, while the French *resident superieur* maintained his own *residents* and officials in the provinces.[17] This system naturally exacerbated traditional regional differences.

The French success at maintaining a dualistic society in Viet Nam served to further discredit the imperial court and its mandarin bureaucracy. The traditional civil service exams were abandoned, and new ones based on French education were instituted in 1911. The continued cooperation of the mandarins in their own destruction made them dispensable; indeed, their services were dispensed with altogether in 1920. The loss of the mandarins produced no great outcry in the villages, but the direct intervention of French rule in village life was another matter. French "reforms" began in 1921 and consisted of measures to control village budgets directly, to provide for popularly elected village councils to replace the traditional hierarchical councils of notables, and to make the traditional head tax progressive. The latter two actions were especially resisted, and most reforms were repealed in 1927 and 1941.[18] Thus, the French also discovered that their rule could not penetrate the customs of the village. On the national level, the

16. By the 1930s the French bureaucracy numbered 4,500 to 5,100 Frenchmen and 20,000 to 28,000 indigenous personnel ruling a population of 17 million. See John T. McAlister, Jr., *Viet Nam: The Origins of Revolution* (New York, 1969), 262. This was more than three times the number of British civil servants required to rule India, with over ten times the population, in 1937. See Dennis J. Duncanson, *Government and Revolution in Vietnam* (New York, 1968), 103.

17. Woodside, *Community and Revolution in Modern Vietnam*, 21.

18. Popkin, *The Rational Peasant*, 134, 137–41.

French, unlike the British in India, tried rigidly suppressing all expressions of nationalistic sentiment. In this, too, they were unsuccessful.

The Three Waves of Nationalism

Modern Vietnamese nationalism grew out of a three-waved resistance to French rule. Those supporting the resistance were the traditionalists, represented by the Can Vuong scholar-patriots; the transitionalists, who split into those wanting to overturn the feudal regime in Hue and those wanting to restore the court by throwing out the French; and the moderns, both Communist and non-Communist, who sought to put forward a modern equivalent or substitute for Confucianism.[19]

The class most displaced by French rule was the mandarin scholar-gentry, who led the traditional phase of the revolt.[20] After the capture and execution of the boy emperor, Ham Nghi, in 1888, the Can Vuong continued to resist, most notably under the scholar Phan Dinh Phung, whom the French finally hunted down and executed in 1896. Also, a nationalistic bandit, De Tham, held out against the French from 1893 to 1903 in an effective guerrilla campaign. The Buddhists got into the act as well, with the monk Vo Tru leading an uprising in 1898 in Tonkin's Phu Yen Province.

The first two decades of the twentieth century were the era of the transitionalists, centering around Phan Chu Trinh and Phan Boi Chau. Phan Chu Trinh, a philosopher-patriot much enamored with Western ideas (but increasingly less so of Westerners themselves), sought to rid his countrymen of Confucianism and the trappings of the imperial court. In 1906 the Eastern Capital Non-Tuition School was established in Hanoi by scholars under his influence. It was an intellectual challenge to the Confucian court and opened Vietnamese intellectuals to Western ideas. Although the school had nothing to do with the 1908 tax revolt, suspicious French authorities closed it down and arrested Phan Chu Trinh. He continued to write during his exile abroad and was finally allowed to return to Saigon in 1925. There he was able to attract

19. William John Duiker, *The Rise of Nationalism in Vietnam, 1900–1941* (Ithaca, N.Y., 1976), 290.
20. Woodside, *Community and Revolution in Modern Vietnam*, 8, 234–36.

followers with his stirring addresses until his death in March, 1926. His ideas survived via the medium of the Constitutionalist party and its journals. This was the only party to be granted any sort of sanction from French authorities, and it spent its time in the 1920s and 1930s competing with ever-diminishing success against the Communists and Trotskyites in Saigon municipal elections.[21]

By far the better known of the two transitionalists, Phan Boi Chau is still regarded by many Communists and non-Communists as the father of modern Vietnamese nationalism. As a young boy, Ho Chi Minh met and admired him. Phan's one objective was to rid the country of the French, but despite some wavering, he also sought to restore the imperial court. He began his career as a revolutionary in 1900 with a three-part strategy. First, he sought popular, domestic support among the Can Vuong remnants and guerrilla mountain bands. Second, he enlisted the support of Prince Cuong De as a titular leader in order to attract support from the royal family. Finally, he looked for foreign assistance in restoring Vietnamese independence. From 1900 to 1905 he worked on the domestic part of his program. In 1905 he brought students over to Japan as the centerpiece of his Exodus to the East movement. There he became leader of the Reformation Society. His efforts to secure Japanese help, however, were disappointing, and he subsequently turned to the Chinese for aid and inspiration.[22]

The failure to launch a general uprising (*khoi nghia*) in the 1908 tax revolt was a blow, but the 1911 revolution in China galvanized Phan Boi Chau into action. In February, 1912, he founded the Restoration Society, and despite a last-minute balk by Sun Yat Sen in delivering assistance, Phan launched a program of assassinating French officials which lasted until 1913. In June, 1915, he attempted unsuccessfully to organize an uprising of Vietnamese border guards. The last two gasps of transitionalist revolt, with Phan playing a role in both, were the Duy Tan uprising of May, 1916, and the August, 1917, revolt in which Hanoi was briefly seized from the French by rebellious Vietnamese colonial militiamen. French forces were able to thwart these two revolts with a total

21. Marr, *Vietnamese Anticolonialism*, 163–84, 194; Duiker, *The Rise of Nationalism*, 135–49.
22. Marr, *Vietnamese Anticolonialism*, 98–119; Duiker, *The Rise of Nationalism*, 38–47.

of only two thousand men. Imprisoned by the French for his efforts, Phan was released in 1917 and thereafter confined his activities to writing. A suggested accommodation between Ho and Phan in 1924 never materialized because of Phan's arrest in 1925.[23] Spending the rest of his life under house arrest, Phan played the role of elder statesman for the modern Nationalists; but his sympathies essentially lay with the Viet Nam Quoc Dan Dan (VNQDD), or Nationalist party.[24]

The modern wave of nationalism flowed out of the intellectual and spiritual ferment that gripped Viet Nam in the mid-1920s much as it had gripped China during the May Fourth movement from 1914 to 1920. Alarmed by all the activity, the French outlawed all political groups. Religious groups, however, were not disturbed, and Confucianism and Buddhism in particular began revivals in the late 1920s. Two new religious groups arose, though, both with distinctly political overtones—the Cao Dai and the Hoa Hao. The Cao Dai (Great Way) was started by a group of civil service spiritualists who began meeting in 1925. They believed in an all-seeing cosmic eye whose "way" was revealed by such worthies as Lao Tzu, Victor Hugo, and Jesus Christ. The Cao Dai built a holy see in Tay Ninh, and they organized themselves into an effective church along Roman Catholic lines. They numbered 100,000 in 1932 and 300,000 by 1938. The Hoa Hao was started in 1939 by Huynh Phu So, the "mad bonze," who was an apostle of nationalism and reform Buddhism. It quickly attracted a wide following in the Mekong Delta. These two groups, along with the Catholics and Communists, were the only ones to achieve any success in mobilizing the peasantry. Popkins observes that in their efforts to create new rural societies they not only were anticolonial but were also against the Confucian "golden past."[25]

To continue their activities in the late 1920s, the explicitly political groups had to go underground. The largest and best organized of these was the VNQDD, which was similar to China's Kuomintang (National-

23. Duiker, *The Rise of Nationalism*, 69–85; Virginia Thompson, *French Indo-China* (New York, 1937), 90. Joseph Buttinger, in *Vietnam*, 159, recounts the story that Ho Chi Minh was persuaded by his subordinates to let Phan Boi Chau be arrested in order to provoke nationalist opposition to French rule. Ho's intermediary was bribed 150,000 piastres by the French Sûreté in effecting the arrest. Communist sources vigorously dispute this account.
24. Duiker, *The Rise of Nationalism*, 91.
25. Buttinger, *Vietnam*, 194–95; Popkin, *The Rational Peasant*, 184–85.

ist) party. Its strategy was one of a military takeover followed by a period of political tutelage that would lead eventually to a constitutional government. It was the first party to organize around an appeal to key social groups, specifically the noncommissioned officers of the colonial militia. In fact, the Communists picked up their emphasis on military proselyting from the VNQDD. The party was started in 1927 by a schoolteacher, Nguyen Thai Hoc. By 1929 it boasted 1,500 members in 120 cells, mostly in the Red River Delta. Initially it was a bloody-minded group. Its first act was a campaign of assassination in February, 1929, netting it a hated French labor "recruiter." Two hundred twenty-nine party members were promptly arrested. Undaunted, Hoc prepared an elaborate uprising against the French, starting with a mutiny of the Vietnamese militia. The plan erupted, prematurely, into the famous Yen Bay mutiny of February 9, 1930. Genuinely alarmed, the French were ruthless in their reprisals. Hoc was executed, and even though the party became more moderate, it was suppressed in 1931 and 1932. The remnants fled to China.[26]

The baton then passed to the Communists and Ho Chi Minh, or Nguyen Ai Quoc (Nguyen the patriot), as he was known at the time. In their continuous, unbending struggle for political power, the Communists were fortunate to have Ho Chi Minh as their leader. Neither an intellectual like Phan Boi Chau or Phan Chu Trinh nor a hothead like Nguyen Thai Hoc, Ho was tactically flexible, an astute organizer, a unifying conciliator, and sure of his ultimate goal. He was born to a poverty-stricken but prestigious mandarin family in Nghe An Province, a hotbed of the Can Vuong movement. In 1911 he left for France, where he subsisted by menial jobs and began his career as a revolutionary. In 1920 he joined the French Communist party and went to Moscow, and in 1925 he arrived in Canton as the Communist International (Comintern) representative for Viet Nam.

In February, 1930, Ho convened a meeting in Hong Kong and persuaded the three quarreling Vietnamese Marxist groups to unite into the Vietnamese Communist party. Under Comintern pressure the party was renamed the Indochinese Communist party (ICP) six months

26. Duiker, *The Rise of Nationalism*, 156–65; McAlister, *Viet Nam*, 88–91; Douglas Pike, *History of Vietnamese Communism, 1925–1976* (Stanford, Calif., 1978), 25–27; Woodside, *Community and Revolution in Modern Vietnam*, 62–63.

later, to give it a more internationalist orientation. The party received an annual Comintern stipend, and throughout the crucial years of the 1930s it acknowledged the "wholehearted assistance of Soviet, Chinese and French Communist parties." The ICP's founding strategy was the orthodox Marxist two-staged revolutionary thesis. According to the thesis, Socialist revolution was to be preceded by the bourgeois democratic revolution to overthrow the imperialist and feudal leaders through a worker-peasant alliance led by the proletariat. To initiate this revolution and alliance, the ICP began with 1,500 party members and perhaps 100,000 sympathizers.[27]

Before the Communists could get very far, the peasant uprisings that produced the Nghe-Tin Soviets erupted in June, 1930. Although Communist organizers were everywhere, the party could only take partial credit. Beginning in Annam's Nghe An and Ha Tin provinces, the uprisings soon spread to both deltas and for a brief moment became truly national in scale. French repression was bloody. In all, 10,000 Vietnamese were killed, 50,000 exiled, and 100,000 jailed. While the uprisings provided the ICP with solid revolutionary experience, the party could not decide on its target—the French, the mandarins, or the landlords. Consequently, the party's violence was excessive and their strategy poorly organized. The party's line was that the Communists of the Nghe-Tin Soviets provided a dress rehearsal for the August revolution but that they were impetuous.[28]

In 1935 the party swung to an urban strategy, obeying the "front policy" enunciated by the Comintern's seventh Congress in July of that year. Under Leon Blum's "democratic front" in France, the party was allowed to function in the open. In the South the party found itself in a losing battle with the Trotskyites. Begun in 1933 under gifted leadership, the Trotskyites scored telling blows on the ICP for its subservience to the Comintern and for its attempts at a multi-class united front. Despite an internal split, the Trotskyites won the elections for the

27. Duiker, *The Rise of Nationalism*, 216; Jean Chesneaux, "The Historical Background of Vietnamese Communism," *Government and Opposition*, IV (Winter, 1969), 118–41; Pike, *History of Vietnamese Communism*, 12, 155–3; Commission for the Study of the History of the Viet Nam Workers' Party, *An Outline History of the Viet Nam Workers' Party (1930–1975)* (Hanoi, 1976), 16, 21.

28. Pike, *History of Vietnamese Communism*, 18–21; Commission for the Study of the History of the Viet Nam Workers' Party, *An Outline History of the Viet Nam Workers' Party*, 19.

Saigon Municipal Council from 1933 to 1939, and in the Cochinchina Council election of 1939 they garnered 80 percent of the votes. However, with the collapse of the democratic front in September, 1939, the French ordered a halt to political parties and suppressed the Trotskyites' urban activities. Both groups went underground. The Communists resurfaced; the Trotskyites, essentially, did not. In addition to having allegedly set up the house arrest of Phan Boi Chau, the Communists may have further tarnished their national legitimacy by cooperating with the French in effecting the demise of the Trotskyites through the provision of membership lists to the Sûreté. That the party had no scruples in destroying the Trotskyites was clear from its belief that "with the Trotskyites, there should be absolutely no compromise."[29]

As the only ones left in the field, for all practical purposes, the Communists resurfaced at the eighth session of the ICP Central Committee, convened by Ho from May 10 to 19, 1941. This session marked the first time Ho had met with party leaders since the founding conference in 1930. The meeting signaled a key shift in the struggle. In perforce rediscovering the countryside, the Communists switched the ground of the revolution from a class struggle against feudalism to a national struggle for independence against imperialism. To broaden its appeal they created a political front, the Viet Nam Doc Lap Dong Minh Hoi (Viet Nam Independence League, or Viet Minh for short), and an even broader mass association for "national salvation," the Viet Nam Cuu Quoc Hoi. These factions were held together and controlled by the cells of the ICP. In emerging victorious against their rivals, the Communists could be thankful for the tactical adroitness that allowed them to make this shift to the countryside, the mistakes of the other nationalists, their political organizational abilities, the invaluable tool of their Marxist-Leninism as an ideological icon, and the extreme repression of the French, who polarized the struggle and squeezed out any middle ground. In 1941, then, "The movement, the man and the moment converged."[30]

29. Woodside, *Community and Revolution in Modern Vietnam*, 201–202, 214–15; Buttinger, *Vietnam*, 181–82; Pike, *History of Vietnamese Communism*, 37; Commission for the Study of the History of the Viet Nam Workers' Party, *An Outline History of the Viet Nam Workers' Party*, 25.
30. McAlister, *Viet Nam*, 136–39; Pike, *History of Vietnamese Communism*, 38–40; Duiker, *The Rise of Nationalism*, 292.

Impact of World War II

World War II was a crucial time of side-choosing for the competing Nationalist groups in Asia. Those who sided with the Japanese generally wound up losers in the postwar grants of independence. Indochina was the only part of Japan's Greater East Asia Co-Prosperity Sphere that was not conquered or ruled directly. Instead, the Japanese tolerated a continued French administration in exchange for the use of the colony's resources and facilities for their war machine. Politically, the Japanese undermined the French rule by imposing numerous curbs on French troops, stationing their own soldiers in the colony, and intriguing among the Cao Dai and Hoa Hao as well as establishing two revolutionary parties in the North.[31]

The Viet Minh chose to oppose both the French and the Japanese. They spent the early war years building their organization around their new strategy. The "land to the tiller" theme of the 1930s was replaced by an emphasis on confiscating the land of imperialists and traitors. Like the Communist Chinese at Yenan, the Viet Minh started to carve out a guerrilla zone in the Tay Bac (the mountainous area along Viet Nam's border with Laos). If the Viet Minh were not too energetic against the French, it was because, despite the tenuousness of their situation, the French were hardly paper tigers. During the war, the French commanded a force of 99,000 in Indochina, including 20,000 Europeans. The Japanese maintained an averge troop strength of 35,000, although in February, 1945, they built it up to 62,000. Nevertheless, in the South, the characteristically independent Communist leader Tran Van Giau launched an uprising, against party orders, in December, 1940, in the Mekong Delta, but it was totally suppressed by the French. Prior to the uprising, the party was actually stronger in the South, but the French reprisals decimated the southern cadres. Thus the center of activity shifted to, and remained in, the North, where Vo Nguyen Giap began organizing the Viet Nam National Salvation Army from Tho tribesmen recruits. After two disappointing skirmishes with the militia, they withdrew to the Tay Bac in February, 1942.[32]

31. Buttinger, *Vietnam*, 195–96.
32. McAlister, *Viet Nam*, 110, 122–23, 132, 141.

The real boost to the Viet Minh during the war came from abroad. In October, 1942, the Chinese organized the Viet Nam Revolutionary League to form sabotage and espionage networks against the Japanese. The Viet Minh was only one of the league's ten members, but since it had the only effective force inside Viet Nam, the Chinese reluctantly asked Ho to be chairman. It was also for this reason that both the American Office of Strategic Services and the French dropped small arms and equipment to Viet Minh guerrillas. With these weapons, Giap built his forces up to 5,000 by the war's end. Suspicious of all this activity, the Japanese on March 9, 1945, staged a lightning coup de force, granted the Vietnamese independence under a puppet regime, and disarmed and interned all French troops, except for 6,000 who fled to China.[33] With the French rendered impotent, the Japanese on the verge of defeat, and everyone else quite literally out of the country, the Communists decided to seize the moment.

The August Revolution and the Return of the French

During the very week of the Japanese coup, the party, in a meeting convened by Truong Chinh, decided to prepare for a general uprising and quickly began to take action. In April the Viet Minh divided the country into seven military zones and christened their force the Viet Nam Liberation army. In June they proclaimed the six provinces of the Viet Bac along the Chinese border to be a free zone while they more quietly deployed their first battalion-sized unit. At another meeting in early August, chaired by Truong Chinh, the party decided to strike before any Allied armies of occupation could enter Viet Nam. On August 17 a rally organized by the imperial delegate in Hanoi to celebrate the fall of Japan grew unruly and was taken over by Viet Minh agitators. Two days later the Viet Minh staged a rally of their own. One thousand Communist troops entered Hanoi, and 30,000 armed Japanese and 750 local militia offered no resistance. The imperial delegate fled. At the same time demonstrations broke out in Hue as well as in Saigon, although in Saigon Giau's followers got out of hand and attacked Frenchmen. Os-

33. Buttinger, *Vietnam*, 200–201; McAlister, *Viet Nam*, 114, 161–62.

tensibly from students in Hanoi, a call came for the emperor Bao Dai's abdication and the establishment of a provisional government under the Viet Minh. On August 25 Bao Dai complied, handing over the seal of the kingdom to the Communists. As head of the provisional government, Ho Chi Minh entered Hanoi and addressed a rally of a half million on September 1.[34]

The only step remaining in securing the mandate of the people for the provisional government was to hold elections for a national assembly. The elections were held on January 6, 1946, with the Communists and their allies winning all but 70 of the 380 seats. Beneath this facade of democracy lay some back-room deals and chicanery. Under pressure from the occupying Chinese generals (who arrived in October), the Viet Minh offered to give the VNQDD 50 seats and the Dong Minh Hoi 20 if they would not compete in the elections. The two parties agreed, figuring that with the Viet Minh in control of the government machinery they couldn't do better in the elections anyway. While the Viet Minh could have won the elections fairly, it didn't. First, contrary to its propaganda that the elections were nationwide, they were not held in the South, except clandestinely in a few constituencies. Second, elections were not held in towns controlled by the Dong Minh Hoi and VN-QDD, yet Viet Minh representatives were seated from them. Finally, the size of the Viet Minh vote, 92 percent in the country and 97 percent in the cities, cast grave suspicions. This inaugurated an ignoble tradition of fraudulent elections in postwar Viet Nam, which continued in both Viet Nams after the 1954 Geneva accords.[35]

Well before the elections were held however, the brief idyll of independence was fading. The Potsdam Conference called for the British to reoccupy Viet Nam south of the sixteenth parallel and for the Chinese north of it to receive the Japanese surrender until "proper" authority could be reestablished (after some wavering by the Americans, this was accepted as meaning French). The first to arrive were the British, with elements of the 20th Indian Division arriving on September 13. Its

34. Woodside, *Community and Revolution in Modern Vietnam*, 228–29; McAlister, *Viet Nam*, 158–59, 188, 192–93, 204–206.
35. Fall, *The Two Viet-Nams*, 65; Commission for the Study of the History of the Viet Nam Workers' Party, *An Outline History of the Viet Nam Workers' Party*, 46; McAlister, *Viet Nam*, 237–38.

1,500 men faced the unenviable task of disarming nearly 20,000 Japanese and keeping apart the 4,000 interned French and 15,000 armed Viet Minh around Saigon. Initially, the British tried to play an even hand, but with the mounting disorder, the British commander was persuaded to rearm 1,900 Frenchmen. With both sides then attacking civilians, matters became even worse. On September 25 and 26 the Viet Minh assaulted in force, but the British, French, and 5,000 rearmed Japanese under British command drove them out. In early October French troop ships arrived; by the end of the month they had unloaded 25,000 troops, and by December French forces reached 50,000. This was enough to reoccupy the country up to the sixteenth parallel at month's end, although, except for the coastal cities, the French never really reoccupied Annam.[36]

The Chinese troops sent into the North in October to supervise the surrender of 48,000 Japanese came in such numbers (150,000) and behaved in such a way as to give the Viet Minh and the French a common interest in securing their prompt departure. As for the French, the Chinese did not let them participate in the formal Japanese surrender ceremonies, did not permit the escaped French troops in China to return, and did not release the 4,000 French soldiers imprisoned in the Hanoi citadel. As for the Viet Minh, the Chinese openly supported the VNQDD and Dong Minh Hoi against them, allowing the two parties to control the towns along the Chinese army's routes of march. Both parties were given a substantial press in their vilifications of the Viet Minh as a mere front organization for the ICP. In fact, as a tactical maneuver, the Viet Minh announced on November 11, 1945, that the ICP had been disbanded.[37]

After difficult wrangling in which the French had to agree to give up all their Chinese concessions, the Chinese consented to withdraw their troops by April, 1946. Determined to destroy all nationalist competition after the Chinese left, the Viet Minh helped the French suppress the northern areas controlled by the Dong Minh Hoi and VNQDD. In the

36. McAlister, *Viet Nam*, 199, 211–13; George McTurnan Kahin and John W. Lewis, *The United States in Vietnam* (New York, 1967), 24; Popkin, *The Rational Peasant*, 233.
37. McAlister, *Viet Nam*, 225–30, 233–35.

South, from August, 1945, to December, 1946, the Communists assassinated forty key nationalist political leaders, including future President Ngo Dinh Diem's brother.[38]

Negotiations between the French and the Viet Minh on the future of Viet Nam began in the fall of 1945, but they only became serious after the January elections. On March 6, 1946 the French and Ho's coalition government reached an accord on a joint French–Viet Minh reoccupation and disarmament of Japanese in the North following the Chinese withdrawal. In the summer and early fall, Vietnamese and French negotiators tried to work out, first at Dalat and later at Fontainebleau, a *modus vivendi* on the future status of Viet Nam. The efforts of the diplomats, however, were continually undermined by rising tensions in the field. The French high commissioner Thierry d'Argenliu, for example, did everything in his power to torpedo the negotiations.[39]

Despite a vague agreement on September 16, no accord was reached on political issues. Fundamentally, the two views of the future could not be squared. In October 1946, the French adopted a constitution that did not provide for full independence for the colonies, and the November constitution of the Ho government made no mention of Viet Nam being part of the French Union. At the root of the differences in the two constitutions lay two divergent military perceptions: the Viet Minh thought it could throw the French into the sea, and the French were confident they would decimate the Viet Minh.[40]

The period of negotiations gave the two sides time to marshal their forces. By the time hostilities broke out in December, 1946, both sides commanded armies of 100,000. The Viet Minh had clearly pulled off a remarkable feat in expanding its forces from the time of the August revolution. To the initial 5,000 veterans, they added, in less than a year and a half, 4,000 Japanese deserters, who set up and ran the Viet Minh arsenals as well as trained new recruits; 3,000 Vietnamese who had served with the French in Europe; 24,000 Vietnamese who had served with the French militia; and 55,000 Vietnamese who had served with the French colonial army.[41]

38. Buttinger, *Vietnam*, 256; McAlister, *Viet Nam*, 206–208.
39. McAlister, *Viet Nam*, 380–81, 306–307.
40. Fall, *The Two Viet-Nams*, 74–75.
41. McAlister, *Viet Nam*, 251–52, 298–301; Fall, *The Two Viet-Nams*, 74–75; Buttinger, *Vietnam*, 261.

The War with France

The agreement, lacking a political concord, could do nothing to allevi-
ate the rising tensions, leaving open warfare the only avenue of relief. It
was not long in coming. Even before the agreement was signed, d'Argenliu, on September 10, ordered the reestablishment of French customs authority in Tourane (Danang) and Haiphong. When a French patrol boat stopped a contraband-laden junk in Haiphong Harbor on
November 20, the Viet Minh fired on the patrol boat and attacked
French forces in the city. The next day a truce was arranged, but on
November 22 a French burial detail was ambushed in the mountain
town of Lang Son. Enraged, the French commander in chief, General
Jean Valluy, ordered his forces to teach the Viet Minh a hard lesson. On
November 23 the Viet Minh were given two hours to evacuate Haiphong's China Quarter. They asked for more time. The deadline and a
45-minute extension passed. General fighting erupted. Mistaking a
mass of fleeing civilians for an attack on Cat Bi Airfield, the French
heavy cruiser *Suffren* opened fire, slaying 6,000 (the Viet Minh claimed
20,000). Jean Sainteny was sent to negotiate on December 2, but the
talks fell apart when three days later d'Argenliu reoccupied Danang.
On the evening of December 19, according to a prearranged signal, the
Viet Minh pulled the switch on Hanoi's electricity supply, and the war
was on. The first phase was a fierce contest in the North for the cities.
At a cost of nearly 2,000 deaths between December 19 and February 7,
the French pushed the Viet Minh back into the hills.[42]

Defeated in the cities, the Viet Minh retreated to their traditional
strongholds in Annam, the Mekong Delta, and the six provinces of the
Viet Bac. The Viet Bac was the heart of the Viet Minh resistance, and
the provisional government installed all its government departments in
the limestone caves surrounding the town of Thai Nguyen. In the Viet
Bac, the Viet Minh actually governed. It ran a literacy campaign, provided food, collected taxes and land rent, distributed land, and built up
its strength so that in 1949 it could announce a general mobilization of
the area (at no pay). At this point the Viet Minh were turning out their
forces in companies and battalions, and by December, 1950, it had

42. Buttinger, *Vietnam*, 265–66; Fall, *The Two Viet-Nams*, 75; McAlister, *Viet
Nam*, 307, 314–15.

formed three operational divisions. Maintaining control over the struggle in Annam, and especially in Cochinchina, was difficult from the Viet Bac, but representatives from the Central Committee were present in both places to ensure that party instructions were followed. By the end of the war nearly ten million people lived in Viet Minh zones.[43]

In the war against the French, the Communists sought to wage a three-phased war of guerrilla attack, attrition, and movement, according to the model of Mao Tse-tung. Official party sources say the second phase of attrition began after the unsuccessful French campaign, in the winter of 1947, to wipe out the Viet Minh forces and destroy their Viet Bac base area. Regardless of the stage, George K. Tanham asserts that the French retained the initiative until the first major attacks of the Viet Minh in late 1949. By the end of the war, the North had definitely moved to stage three, but the Communist effort in the South never left the first stage of hit-and-run guerrilla attacks. Whoever had the initiative and whatever the stage of strategy, it is probably accurate to characterize the war until late 1949 as a stalemate, since, in contradiction of their original perceptions, the Viet Minh could not drive the French into the sea, and the French could not decimate the Viet Minh.[44]

Much like the American effort twenty years later, in the early stages of the war French opinion was united on the general policy goal of retaining Indochina. But a division soon developed over tactics, with the Right demanding a military solution and the Left favoring the political approach of negotiations. Throughout the war, French authorities trod both paths simultaneously.[45]

Militarily, in addition to bringing in their own regular forces and foreign legionnaires from Europe, the French recruited substantial numbers of Vietnamese into the Expeditionary Corps and militia to defend static positions and thereby free French forces for offensive actions. Capitalizing on Communist excesses in the South, the French were able to bring the three sects (Cao Dai, Binh Xuyen, and Hoa Hao) over to their side. They underwrote the sect armies' payrolls and assigned them regions of control in the Mekong Delta. By 1952 the sects fielded

43. Lancaster, *The Emancipation of French Indochina*, 418–28.
44. Commission for the Study of the History of the Viet Nam Workers' Party, *An Outline History of the Viet Nam Workers' Party*, 55; George K. Tanham, *Communist Revolutionary Warfare: From the Viet-Minh to the Viet-Cong* (New York, 1961), 15, 17.
45. Buttinger, *Vietnam*, 279.

armies totaling 32,000. The Communists had only themselves to blame for this loss. Tran Van Giau's ruthless scorched-earth policies against the French and indiscriminate assassinations of nationalist leaders forced his recall to Hanoi in January, 1946. Giau's replacement, Nguyen Binh, however, was hardly less ruthless. While abandoning the scorched-earth tactics, he formed a "security service" that began a thorough program of selective terror. His main effort was directed at destroying the sects, but it had the unintended effect of driving them into the arms of the French. Binh's biggest blunder was his treacherous ambush and execution of Huyn Phu So, the revered leader of the Hoa Hao, in 1947. Thus, despite intensive Communist activity in the Mekong Delta, the party was only able to control and organize one-third of the delta's population. Out of a total party membership of 180,000 in 1948, only 23,000 were from Cochinchina.[46]

Another tactic the French employed was the use of *montagnard* commando groups. Begun in late 1951 and modeled after the French *maquis*, the commando groups operated behind enemy lines in the Viet Bac and Central Highlands. By 1954 they numbered 15,000. While these groups tied down at least ten regular Viet Minh battalions, they failed in their objective of interrupting Viet Minh supply movements.[47] With the French need for more conventional forces rapidly expanding, the Elysée Agreement (March, 1949) called for the creation of a separate Vietnamese army in 1950 that would reach four divisions by 1952. Even though thirty-five battalions were formed, only one division was organized. Because of intense American pressure the program subsequently speeded up.[48] The heart of this problem was the political dilemma of Vietnamese unwillingness to join such an army without meaningful independence, and the continued French resistance in fully granting it.

Politically, the formula the French hit upon was to grant Indochina "independence within the French Union" and to deny a role for the Viet

46. Duncanson, *Government and Revolution in Vietnam*, 195; Buttinger, *Vietnam*, 259; Lancaster, *The Emancipation of French Indochina*, 132, 139; McAlister, *Viet Nam*, 206; Popkin, *The Rational Peasant*, 230–32, 242.
47. Bernard B. Fall, *Street Without Joy* (New York, 1972), 267–76. A similar tactic by the Americans against the Ho Chi Minh Trail yielded similar results; however, CIA efforts in Laos among Meo tribesmen were more successful.
48. Lancaster, *The Emancipation of French Indochina*, 247–50.

Minh through the "Bao Dai solution." In the case of the former, French moves always came too slowly and always fell too short of real independence; and in the case of the latter, pinning their hopes on the puppet Nguyen emperor Bao Dai and ignoring the Communists without a real grant of independence were totally unrealistic approaches. The Bao Dai solution began in February, 1947, when, with French blessings, the VNQDD and Dong Minh Hoi formed the United National Front and appealed to Bao Dai to return to Viet Nam. It was not until September that Bao Dai was even willing to talk to the French. On December 7, 1947, he conferred with them on a warship along the northern Viet Nam coast. In 1948 Bao Dai, a tragic figure beset by competing pressures, vacillated, like his predecessors, between coming to terms with the French and holding aloof. Finally, on March 8, 1949, the Elysée Agreement between Bao Dai and the French president formally conferred "independence" to Viet Nam as an Associated State of the French Union. Despite repeated subsequent agreements on the details, the continual failure of the French to grant genuine sovereign independence remained a crucial stumbling block to a political solution. On July 3, 1953, the French said the time had come to "perfect the independence of the Associated States." This was not done until April 28, 1954. By then, it was too late.[49]

Tired of the military stalemate, but claiming the situation was under control, the French announced their intention to withdraw 9,000 troops in early 1950. Seeing the situation from a diametrically opposite perspective, Giap announced in February, 1950, that the war of attrition was over and that the time was ripe for Mao's third stage, the war of movement. Throughout the war the French had maintained a string of border posts along the Chinese frontier that were obviously a major source of irritation to the Viet Minh, particularly since late 1949 when friendly Chinese Communist troops began to arrive at the border. In a series of lightning attacks from May to October, Giap forced the French to abandon these posts. At the last one, Cao Bang, the garrison attempted to break out and link up with a 3,500-man relief force. It was never effected, and in a major military disaster, 7,000 French forces were routed. French withdrawal plans were quietly shelved.[50]

To fill the breach, the French summoned the colorful General Jean de

49. Buttinger, *Vietnam*, 297–311.
50. Lancaster, *The Emancipation of French Indochina*, 216–18.

Lattre de Tassigny, the commander of French forces in Europe, to command the Expeditionary Corps. He arrived on December 17, 1950. General Giap, enthusiastic over the appointment, said, "The French are sending against the People's Army an adversary worthy of its steel. We will defeat him on his own ground." In December Giap led his men out of the Viet Bac, and in January, 1951, threw a total of thirty battalions at Vinh Yen, on the fringes of the Red River Delta. He was thrown back with 6,000 casualties. Two other attacks were equally costly. Giap then withdrew to the Viet Bac, warning the French and the population to expect a protracted guerrilla war. He had lost one-third of his regular army. General de Lattre, however, was not able to savor his victories for very long. He died within a year.[51]

While Giap rebuilt his forces, the Communist party, reportedly upon Chinese Communist advice, came out of the cold.[52] In March, 1951, the Viet Minh radio station announced that the Viet Nam Lao Dong (Communist) party had been formed in February and had held a second national Congress for its 760,000 members. It also announced the merger of the broader based Lien Viet front (formed in May, 1946, to attract nationalist parties and groups) with the Viet Minh.[53] The Lao Dong party, of course, was nothing but a resurfacing of the never-disbanded Indochina Communist party (ICP). Many non-Communist nationalists felt bitterly betrayed by this merger, particularly Catholics who had joined the Lien Viet in considerable numbers. This betrayed group helped form the core of anticommunism in the subsequent regime in South Viet Nam.

Both sides, perceiving that they were in a stalemate, sought a breakthrough in international support. For the Viet Minh, the arrival of Chinese Communist troops along the border in December, 1949, provided timely support for the launching of stage two. The French, realizing after Giap's offensives that a greater effort was required than they were themselves capable of, sent General de Lattre to Washington in September, 1951. He successfully secured substantial American aid by portraying the Indochina War as an anti-Communist crusade.[54]

51. *Ibid.*, 224–27; Buttinger, *Vietnam*, 327.
52. Lancaster, *The Emancipation of French Indochina*, 227.
53. Commission for the Study of the History of the Viet Nam Workers' Party, *An Outline History of the Viet Nam Workers' Party*, 63–67.
54. Jean Lacouture, *Vietnam: Between Two Truces*, trans. Konrad Kellen and Joel Carmichael (New York, 1965), 9.

Whether or not the Viet Minh would have been able to launch stage two without Chinese help, as Robert F. Turner argues, the Military Trade Agreement of January 18, 1950, between the Viet Minh and the People's Republic of China provided the Vietnamese Communists with a total of 80,000 tons of military supplies, arriving at a rate of 4,000 tons per month by 1954. Douglas Pike estimates the value of this aid at $700 million—$500 million military and the rest economic.[55]

Chinese aid was not confined to logistics. Although George M. Kahin and John W. Lewis concede that only the heavy artillery used by the Viet Minh at Dienbienphu came from China, King C. Chen, Donald Lancaster, and Pike, among others, aver that the Chinese had 7,000 to 8,000 technicians and advisers stationed in Viet Minh areas. Both Chen and Dennis J. Duncanson contend that some 40,000 Viet Minh troops received training from the Chinese, both in China and in Viet Nam. Thus, China served as an essential rear base and safe haven for Communist troops. Lancaster specifically charges that the troops Giap used for his offensive in 1952 and 1953 were outfitted and trained by the Chinese, and Duncanson adds the allegation that Chinese artillery units took part in the siege of Dienbienphu as actual combatants. Whether the real picture of Chinese aid is confined to that of Kahin and Lewis or extended to that of Duncanson, China did play a considerable role in the Viet Minh victory and did much to offset the larger amount of American aid. This contribution was best summed up by Le Duan, the Lao Dong (Labor) party secretary, in 1960: "The great victory of the Chinese Revolution in 1949 and the inestimable help of the Chinese people to our people's resistance war made an extremely important contribution to the success of the resistance war."[56]

In the early postwar years, United States policy toward the French in Indochina was ambivalent. President Roosevelt was not keen on a French return to Indochina, and after the Yalta conference he proposed the idea of a trusteeship for the colony. Roosevelt was never specific about this trusteeship, and when Ambassador Patrick Hurley and Gen-

55. Robert F. Turner, *Vietnamese Communism: Its Origins and Development* (Stanford, Calif., 1975), 81; King C. Chen, *Vietnam and China, 1938–1954* (Princeton, N.J., 1969), 261, 276, 278; Pike, *History of Vietnamese Communism*, 106.

56. Kahin and Lewis, *The United States in Vietnam*, 271; Chen, *Vietnam and China*, 273; Lancaster, *The Emancipation of French Indochina*, 254–55; Pike, *History of Vietnamese Communism*, 75; Duncanson, *Government and Revolution in Vietnam*, 177; quoted in Turner, *Vietnamese Communism*, 86.

eral Albert C. Wedemeyer in China pressed for a clarification of United States policy toward Indochina and the notion of a trusteeship, they met with frustration. The idea of a trusteeship faded away during the United Nations San Francisco conference (April to June, 1945), not so much, Chester Cooper contends, because the Truman administration was against it, but because no one privy to Roosevelt's idea felt inclined to push it after his death.[57] The only agency within the United States government that supported Ho was the OSS. Due to concerns in Europe, the other government agencies were solidly behind the French. In 1946 the Truman administration decided not to impede the French return. The United States then displayed very little interest in Indochina until late 1949, when the Communist triumph in China radically altered the picture. Until this point, Bao Dai had inspired very little enthusiasm in Washington, but with the China debacle he began to be depicted as a staunch patriot. In February, 1950, the United States extended recognition to his government. Thirty other states quickly followed suit.

This inaugurated an American decision to increase military and economic assistance to the French effort while at the same time urging a grant of real independence to the Vietnamese government. General de Lattre's trip to Washington helped to ensure that the emphasis remained on the former. The aid began to flow in mid-1950 and by year's end had reached $150 million. In 1954 the annual rate was $1 billion. This was one-third of the entire American foreign aid program, larger by far than the portion assigned to the other big recipient, India. From 1950 to 1954 the United States contributed $2.6 billion, which by 1954 underwrote 78 percent of the French war effort. As in the case of the Chinese, the American war effort was not confined to logistics. In January, 1954, the United States finally agreed to send 1,200 ground personnel to maintain American equipment. Also, in the latter stages of the war, American contract pilots flew transports for French operations, most notably at Dienbienphu.[58]

57. Chester L. Cooper, *The Lost Crusade: America in Vietnam* (New York, 1970), 34–39, 44.
58. William P. Bundy, "Path to Viet Nam: Ten Decisions," *Orbis*, XI (Fall, 1967), 648–49; Kahin and Lewis, *The United States in Vietnam*, 30–31; Russell H. Fifield, "The Thirty Years War in Indochina: A Conceptual Framework," *Asian Survey*, XVII (September, 1977), 862; Lancaster, *The Emancipation of French Indochina*, 289; Fall, *Street Without Joy*, 263.

With both sides successful in securing external assistance, the war on the ground heated up considerably. To better consolidate their pacification efforts, the French withdrew from the southern Red River Delta in February, 1952, entrusting its defense to Catholic militias. In October, Giap launched his second major offensive by attacking French positions in the highlands of Tonkin. Withdrawing under heavy attack, the French finally held the line at Na Son in December. Although Giap lost 7,000 men, he had the run of northwest Tonkin. More ominously, in January, 1953, the Viet Minh attacked French positions in the Central Highlands, marking the first large-scale action in the South. By threatening the nearby Viet Minh stronghold of Binh Dinh, however, the French forced the Communists to withdraw.[59]

When Henri Navarre became the French commander in chief in the spring of 1953, both sides were feverishly building up their forces. In May, the French could count some 463,800 men on their side, while the Viet Minh had 350,000. In this balance the French did enjoy complete air superiority, although this advantage was limited by the range of the planes and the fact that Indochina had only five major airfields. However, Navarre was appalled that the bulk of the French forces were tied down in static defense (100,000 in the Red River Delta alone), which left fewer troops for offensive operations than were available to the Viet Minh. Realizing their resources had been strained to their limits, the French put the Navarre plan into effect; it was designed to augment offensive forces by raising a much larger Indochinese army to take over the role of static defense and by avoiding major engagements until this new strike force was ready. (Fifteen years later this plan was reincarnated as "Vietnamization".)[60]

What was overlooked in the Navarre plan was the termitelike way in which the whole structure of French power was being eaten away in the villages. In 1952, of the Red River Delta's 2,700 villages, 600 were under Viet Minh control. In July, 1953, the figure had more than doubled to 1,486. Lancaster asserts that in the whole of the North the Viet Minh controlled 5,000 of 7,000 villages and hamlets, and Kahin and Lewis cite reports that in the South 60 percent of the villages outside of sect areas were under Communist sway.[61]

59. Lancaster, *The Emancipation of French Indochina*, 254–58.
60. *Ibid.*, 264–65; Tanham, *Communist Revolutionary Warfare*, 105.
61. Buttinger, *Vietnam*, 323; Lancaster, *The Emancipation of French Indochina*, 264–65; Kahin and Lewis, *The United States in Viet Nam*, 102.

But something more dramatic was required to convince the French they were finished. Part of the Navarre plan was to lure the Viet Minh into a major set-piece battle wherein French air and artillery power could be used to best advantage. Remote Dienbienphu on the Laotian border appeared to be the perfect place to block Viet Minh columns invading Laos and to trap them into a fight. In November, French paratroops landed and reactivated the camp. Mountains three miles distant were deemed too far away for Viet Minh artillery. Meanwhile, according to party history, the Central Commitee decided in December, 1953, to launch a major attack on Dienbienphu, and it gave Giap direct command of the battlefield. By March the Viet Minh had surrounded the camp and placed it under a 55-day siege lasting until May 7, when their pennant finally flew over the command bunker. The French had committed 16,000 crack troops, which were overwhelmed by a besieging force of 40,000 men.[62]

The Chinese made an important contribution at Dienbienphu. One source even contends that a Chinese general was in actual command of the battlefield. While this is unlikely, Chinese heavy weaponry and tactical advice, along with some actual partipation, did make a crucial difference in the battle. Edgar O'Ballance concludes, "Without Red Chinese aid General Giap could not have fought at Dienbienphu." Yet it is wishful thinking to ascribe the Viet Minh victory solely to the Chinese. Even without Dienbienphu the French had reached an untenable position in 1954, suffering equally disastrous defeats in the Red River Delta and Annam.[63]

The Americans did not make an important contribution at Dienbienphu. A French attempt to get the United States to provide a crucial air raid (Operation VULTURE) did not succeed. Admiral Arthur W. Radford, chairman of the Joint Chiefs of Staff, and Vice-President Richard Nixon were enthusiastic, but Secretary of State Dulles equivocated. President Eisenhower rejected the French request on April 5, when he could not get an endorsement from the British or congressional leaders. Among those opposed were Senator John F. Kennedy and Senate Ma-

62. Commission for the Study of the History of the Viet Nam Workers' Party, *An Outline History of the Viet Nam Workers' Party*, 70–71; Duncanson, *The Emancipation of French Indochina*; Buttinger, *Vietnam*, 356.

63. Hoang Van Chi, *From Colonialism to Communism: A Case History of North Vietnam* (New York, 1965), 65; Edgar O'Ballance, "Sino-Soviet Influence on the War in Vietnam," *Contemporary Review*, CCX (February, 1967), 70.

jority Leader Lyndon Johnson. Thus the French learned, as the South Vietnamese, too, learned twenty-one years later, that the escalation ladder of their American allies did not have as many rungs as that of their Communist adversaries.[64]

While fighting continued elsewhere until July, Dienbienphu had unquestionably convinced the French to divest themselves of their Indochinese burden. The war had cost French forces 92,707 dead, 76,369 wounded, and 30,861 missing. The Viet Minh did not publish their casualties, but Bernard B. Fall estimates them in excess of a half million killed. Total civilian casualties were approximately a quarter million.[65]

The Geneva "Accords"

Even before Dienbienphu, the war had reached such intensity that both sides began to explore the possibility of a negotiated settlement. On November 29, 1953, a Swedish newspaper leaked a statement by Ho Chi Minh that expressed his willingness to study cease-fire proposals. An idea for a forum came when, on January 25, the Soviet Union announced its acceptance of an old Western proposal for a Big Four conference on Germany. Two days later Ho made his earlier statement official, and British and Soviet diplomats steered the agenda toward a discussion of Indochina. When the conference convened on April 26, the focus had switched from Germany to a discussion of the problems of superpower relations with the underdeveloped world, especially Korea and Indochina.[66]

A variety of concerns acted to bring the conference into being. As the degree of American involvement increased, the Russians and Chinese became worried that the Americans might become directly involved and establish a permanent military presence in the region—a worry doubtless shared by the Viet Minh. Principally, three factors led the French to the negotiations. First, despite the substantial increases in American aid, the costs to the French continued unabated. Second, the mounting criticism of the war by early 1954 had won over the Socialist

64. Fall, *The Two Viet-Nams*, 225–26; Guenter Lewy, *America in Vietnam* (New York, 1978), 7.

65. Pike, *History of Vietnamese Communism*, 159n4; Fall, *The Two Viet-Nams*, 129.

66. Buttinger, *Vietnam*, 362–63; Lewy, *America in Vietnam*, 7.

party, putting the French working class in solid opposition. Finally, the last vestiges of resistance broke down when it was clear the Navarre plan was failing. On March 9, 1954, the French Assembly voted to negotiate.[67]

Indochina was the topic of discussion at Geneva from May 8 (the day after the fall of Dienbienphu) to July 21. Throughout the talks the Western allies were disunited, and the American delegation was itself at cross-purposes. Secretary of State Dulles was unhappy with the direction of the conference, refused to shake Chou En'lai's hand, and left the proceedings on June 30. Part of the American displeasure was due to the French attempts to gain Russian support for a compromise peace in Indochina in exchange for the French rejection of the European Defense Community. On the other side, while the Viet Minh were discomfited by these machinations and perhaps surprised by the Soviet suggestion of a two-year delay in elections, the Communist side was at least outwardly harmonious.[68]

On top of the discord among the British, French, and Americans, the French government fell in the middle of the conference. On May 6, two days before the Indochina talks began, the Laniel government barely turned back a no-confidence motion, making a successful outcome at Geneva crucial to its survival. Laniel's foreign minister Georges Bidault tried to use the threat of United States intervention as his trump card, but he foundered on his failure to secure an explicit American commitment. Impatient at Bidault's lack of progress, the National Assembly voted the Laniel government out of office on June 12.[69]

Pierre Mendes-France immediately formed a government and, choosing to rely more on French public opinion than on the Americans, announced that he would resign if there was no cease-fire by July 20. If he failed, he vowed his last act before resigning would be to send a large new contingent of French troops to Indochina. As an earnest to his intentions, he promptly dispatched some reinforcements to the war zone, inoculated two French divisions for tropical duty, and went to Geneva to conduct the negotiations personally. His shock tactics injected some unity into the Western side, and the Viet Minh suddenly became

67. Lewy, *America in Vietnam*, 7; Buttinger, *Vietnam*, 354–55.

68. Buttinger, *Vietnam*, 371; Fall, *The Two Viet-Nams*, 229, 232–33; Lewy, *America in Vietnam*, 7.

69. Philippe Devillers and Jean Lacouture, *End of a War: Indochina, 1954* (New York, 1969), 46, 198–99, 226–27, 230–31.

more forthcoming. They accepted the French position of a demarcation line at the seventeenth parallel rather than at the thirteenth and agreed to a two-year delay in the national elections. This matter of national re-unification elections became a centerpiece of controversy during the talks. The elections were provided for only in the final declaration, with just four of the nine parties solidly committed to them. The fledgling government of South Viet Nam specifically repudiated them.[70]

When the conference closed on July 21, 1954, the "accords" con-cluded consisted of six unilateral declarations, three cease-fire agree-ments, an unsigned final declaration, and the minutes of the last plen-ary session. The Americans refused to sign any of the agreements, but they officially took note of the accords and arrangements and promised not to disturb them. The political arrangements (elections, reunifica-tion, and the legal status of the demilitarized zone and the demarcation line) were handled in the final declaration, whose fate left these matters in limbo. The more detailed cease-fire agreements provided for a provi-sional division at the seventeenth parallel, a regroupment of French Union and Viet Minh forces south and north of this parallel within ten months, a civilian resettlement in either zone until May, 1955, a prohibition of new military arms and bases, and a supervision of the cease-fire by an international control commission of India, Canada, and Poland.[71]

Considering their situation, the French did well at Geneva, having secured an honorable exit with only the loss of North Viet Nam to the Communists. Geneva marked a partial completion of Ho Chi Minh's revolution. Inexorably, it would continue; the Communists carried with them the memory that at Geneva they had been outmaneuvered, and they vowed "never again."

The Transition

The period from the Geneva conference until 1960 marked a lull be-tween the two phases of the Viet Nam War (often called the Indochina

70. Devillers and Lacouture, *End of a War,* 252; Buttinger, *Vietnam,* 375; Fall, *The Two Viet-Nams,* 229; Lewy, *America in Vietnam,* 7–9.
71. Buttinger, *Vietnam,* 378–79.

War). On both sides of the seventeenth parallel, however, the time was eventful. If the intention at the Geneva conference was only to provide for a temporary division of Viet Nam, subsequent events quickly belied it. Close to a million refugees fled to the South, while 50,000 went north. Reunification talks were not held and the national elections were not conducted. While publicly the Hanoi regime complained about a fundamental violation of the accords, party documents reveal that the elections were never expected to take place. Meanwhile, both regimes received substantial international recognition—South Viet Nam from sixty governments—and two separate states emerged.[72]

That Ngo Dinh Diem was able to create a stable government at all in South Viet Nam was no mean accomplishment. His obstacles were many. His triumph emerged from intrigues, bribes, posturing, and fighting against his several opponents. One significant obstacle was Bao Dai. Although invited by Bao Dai to form a government on June 16, 1954, Diem arrived in Saigon to find that he had been granted no real authority. It soon became clear that he would not get this authority until Bao Dai (all the while in Paris) was removed from the political scene. After much infighting, he finally organized a general assembly that demanded Bao Dai's resignation as chief of state on April 30, 1955. On October 22, 1955, Diem held a referendum between himself and Bao Dai, and he delivered the monarchy its coup de grâce by garnering 98 percent of the vote.

Diem's first obstacle, though, was the Vietnamese army and its chief of staff Nguyen Van Hinh. Through judicious bribes the army leaders backed off, and under French pressure, Hinh was recalled to France and dismissed by Bao Dai on November 29. Diem, however, was no friend of the French. They yielded their power to him reluctantly and only in stages, making the transition awkward for the incoming Americans, who by and large supported Diem. Indeed, several French officers intrigued against him through the sects.

The gradual French cessions did allow Diem to consolidate his position. In February, 1955, the French stopped their subsidies to the sects and transferred authority for the Vietnamese army to Diem, putting

72. Pike, *History of Vietnamese Communism*, 160, n. 4; Jeffrey Race, *War Comes to Long An: Revolutionary Conflict in a Vietnamese Province* (Berkeley, Calif., 1972), 34.

him in a position to move against the sects. In late March, after he had bribed many sect leaders, Diem attacked the Binh Xuyen, who controlled the Saigon police, but the French intervened to stop the fighting. On April 28 he struck again and drove the Binh Xuyen from the city. The Cao Dai had been mostly bought over, but its imperial guard in Tay Ninh had to be disarmed in October. After some skirmishing, the Hoa Hao were defeated by April, 1956. Diem had the situation finally under control.

Diem never could have done it without American support, for all of his skills at political maneuver. American money paid for his bribes, Americans such as Colonel Edward Lansdale gave him political advice and support, and American pressure largely induced the French to make their concessions. Most important, President Eisenhower wrote Diem that all American aid would be funneled through him in January, 1955.[73]

Diem was determined to hold onto this support. To show his democratic side, he stage-managed five national elections during his tenure and, in his early years anyway, was lauded as a great democrat. A group of his American admirers formed a society called Friends of Vietnam. It included Senators Lyndon Johnson, John Kennedy, and Mike Mansfield, and Justice William O. Douglas. Diem's other side, however, was that of an autocratic Confucian. Although he cracked down on Communists, he also suppressed nearly every other form of opposition. He sought to centralize all power in himself and his family. He discontinued village elections, and all officials from village chief to province chief became his appointees. Yet his regime, like many fledgling governments in the developing world, lacked the penetration to collect taxes from its own people. This is why, in any evaluation of tax burdens in Viet Nam and elsewhere, actual collections are a far more significant measure than official tax rates. Instead, Diem relied on import taxes and the generous amounts of American aid, which from 1954 to 1959 totaled $1.8 billion. Kahin and Lewis noted that the unfortunate effect was that the aid "provided Diem with a degree of financial independence that isolated him from basic economic and political realities and

73. The above account of Diem's rise to power is based on Buttinger, *Vietnam*, 377–415.

reduced his need to appreciate or respond to his people's wants and expectations."[74]

For the Communists in the South these were lean years. A strict interpretation of the Geneva accords kept them quiet when Diem was most vulnerable. For example, they easily could have thrown in a 6,000-man force of "volunteers" to aid the Binh Xuyen, but did not. Instead, some 80,000 Viet Minh forces went north, leaving behind a small cadre of 5,000. At the time of the Geneva accords, Pike estimates the party had some 60,000 members and another 130,000 loyalists in the South; however, by the late 1950s, with Diem's anti-Communist campaign and Hanoi's call for a weeding out, the totals were reduced to 14,000 party members and a guerrilla force of 3,000 to 4,000. Even though Hanoi politburo member Le Duan made a tour of the South in 1957 and recommended inaugurating armed struggle, a decision was over two years in the coming.[75]

The main reason for the delay was that the Democratic Republic of Viet Nam in Hanoi had enough problems of its own. It, too, was heavily dependent on foreign aid. Unlike the South, whose army numbered 290,000, it maintained a large military force of 675,000. Grants and loans from Communist countries from 1955 to 1961 totaled more than $1 billion.[76]

Shortly after the Communists came to power in the North, they launched a major two-year land reform program under the direction of the party's secretary general Truong Chinh. The program was an epic disaster, and though estimate of casualties vary, it shook the regime to its foundations. In November, 1956, Catholic peasants in Nghe An Province broke out in an open rebellion. The services of an entire army division were required to put it down. During that same time, the regime had to cope with a revolt of urban intellectuals in a miniature version of the unrest in China during the late 1950s, when Mao briefly permitted a liberalization in his famous "one hundred flowers" speech. Particularly awkward was the fact that one of the hardest hit by the re-

74. *Ibid.*, 440, 442; Duncanson, *Government and Revolution in Viet Nam*, 285; Cooper, *The Lost Crusade*, 157; Kahin and Lewis, *The United States in Vietnam*, 80.
75. Race, *War Comes to Long An*, 36; Pike, *History of Vietnamese Communism*, 99.
76. Fall, *The Two Viet-Nams*, 175.

forms in North Viet Nam was General Giap's esteemed officer corps. The party was forced to acknowledge its errors, and Truong Chinh was dismissed from his post. The official party history acknowledges, "We made some serious mistakes in the process of carrying out land reform."[77]

On the eve of the American involvement in Viet Nam, some important conclusions about Vietnamese national legitimacy emerge from the evolution of Vietnamese history until 1960. The most fundamental point is that *all* of Viet Nam's history—even as far back as the period of Chinese domination—continued to be important to the Vietnamese as they tried to establish a "right" modern society. Although, in a land wracked by war, physical security was their immediate concern, the traditional features of their sense of well-being were not eliminated. Ultimate security to the Vietnamese still depended on the Mandate of Heaven. Despite the emergence of a modern society with modern standards of legitimacy, it was still incumbent on the power holders to preserve Vietnamese identity, maintain correct social relations, protect the fatherland from foreign intervention, and dispense justice through equitable redistributions of land.

In the development of more modern forms of this national legitimacy, the importance of the French colonial period, and the nationalistic reactions to it, cannot be overemphasized. The very success of the French intervention did much to discredit the old order represented by the Nguyen dynasty. It made the Vietnamese susceptible to the precepts of a new mandate; the values, ideas, economics, and institutions of the West flooded the Vietnamese elite, touching off a ferment from which the Vietnamese have still not settled down. Carrying the implications of their own ideas and institutions to logical, sovereign conclusions, the French would have shunted themselves aside from the new order they were trying to create. And the more the Vietnamese tasted of French culture, the clearer these implications became—and the less willing they were to settle for anything less. In the fusion of the principles and values of the new order with the traditional verities—a process that can serve as

77. Buttinger, *Vietnam*, 429, 451; Joint United States Public Affairs Office [hereinafter JUSPAO], "Forty Years of Party Activity," *Viet-Nam Documents and Research Notes* [hereinafter VNDRN], No. 76, p. 54.

a definition of modern nationalism—the Vietnamese experience was unique in all of Asia in that it was the Communists who eventually secured for themselves the role of champions of this new (and old) order.

With the exit of the French after the Geneva accords, the Americans began to look for ways to "save" Viet Nam. Since, with few exceptions, the ignorance of Americans about Viet Nam was as vast as their western prairies, they scrambled for analogies to guide them in this very unfamiliar terrain. Thus, as options were weighed, Viet Nam was seen as another Korea, Greece, Malaya, Philippines. Rather than looking at everything else in Viet Nam, the Americans should have looked at the terrain itself, and particularly at what happened to the French in this terrain. The French took all of Indochina with a force of only 3,000 men, but they could not hold onto it with 500,000 after World War II. Ironically, the Americans had already backed off from climbing too high on an escalation ladder at Dienbienphu. There was no reason to suppose that the ladder would be any less high the second time around. Put bluntly, one could not imagine a more unfavorable place for the United States to extend the dikes of its containment policy or a worse laboratory for its counterinsurgency theories.

Yet I do not subscribe to the view that the Americans had lost the struggle even before they began. History is never that inevitable. The Communists had their handicaps, too, and in their quest for national legitimacy they had managed to acquire a fair amount of karmic dust to tarnish their national virtue. It was really impossible to disguise the essential foreignness of the Communist ideology. Attempts to paint the Tay Sons as proto-Marxists and all the aristocratic national heroes as proletarian paragons simply could not stick. Their reliance on outsiders, both for ideological sustenance and for material support—even though, in all fairness, their competitors were more guilty of this than the Communists—raised questions about their identity as Vietnamese. Further, the insistence of the ICP on playing its internationalist role was more confusing than helpful to the party's drive for a national mandate.

In seeking to capture the traditional image of dispensers of justice, as expressed in their slogan "land to the tiller," the Communists had at some point to face the imperative of the Communist ideology of a collective agriculture, which runs counter to the individual desires of peasant proprietors. For all Communist parties, the unveiling of this new justice has been nearly ruinous. The disastrous land reform program carried out in North Viet Nam in 1956 was a clear example of this dilemma.

Finally, in two respects, the history of the Communists' rise to power at Dienbienphu had by 1960 created something of a riptide against them. First, even though the Communists were the national salvation heroes, they had nevertheless alienated large numbers of their countrymen along the way. The allegations about the Communist treatment of Phan Boi Chau and the Trotskyites raised questions, their deception of the Catholics in the Lien Viet front caused defections, and their brutal treatment of the sects in the Mekong Delta created enemies. In brief, by 1960 there was a real, if inchoate, base of anticommunism that could be built on. Second, the historical development of communism in Viet Nam was regionally imbalanced. Up until World War II the growth of the ICP was truly national in scope. But the premature and adventurist uprising in the Mekong Delta in 1940 was devastating to party fortunes in the South. This misadventure was compounded by the terroristic errors of the party there during the war against the French. The effect of this was to give some credence to subsequent American charges that the war was one of aggression from the North.

Although the Americans did face a tide of history flowing against them, they were not like an impotent Don Quixote tilting against windmills. They were, at least, young and strong, with some favorable winds blowing at their backs.

CHAPTER TWO

During the
American Involvement

Philip Geyelin termed Viet Nam the "orphan war," because it was the war no one wanted. Yet the Americans and the people of Viet Nam paid dearly for it. Guenter Lewy's careful analysis of war casualties puts total war dead at 1.3 million, including 282,000 allied soldiers killed. Estimates of Communist military deaths range from 444,000 to 666,000, and civilian deaths, both North and South, range from 365,000 to 587,000. Of the American troops 55,000 were killed in an effort costing roughly $150 billion.[1]

But America lost something more than money and men in its fifteen-year involvement in Viet Nam. Clichés describing that loss abound: a "collapse of national will," the "breakdown of a foreign-policy consensus," a "loss of innocence." The clichés, though, only hide the hurt; it may be some time before anyone can summon the intellectual power and moral courage to give it utterance.

In the Americans' quest to help establish a legitimate, popular political order as an alternative to that offered by their Communist adversaries, something eluded them. William Duiker concludes that in its fight to reverse a historical trend that culminated in 1941, "the most basic

1. Weldon A. Brown, *The Last Chopper: The Denouement of the American Role in Vietnam, 1963–1975* (Port Washington, N.Y., 1976), 6; Lewy, *America in Vietnam,* 453.

miscalculation made by the U.S. . . . . was its misreading of history." Alexander Woodside implies that Americans hardly read history at all, thereby failing to see that some of the secrets of the Communist revolutionaries' ability to convert themselves into leaders of the lower classes lay in their own history rather than in modern theories.[2]

As the Communists sought to complete their revolution in the South, the United States' resistance to it came to be seen as a test case of the American global resolve and foreign policy of containment. Yet the immediate audience and locale was in Viet Nam, and unfortunately, this resolve and policy had to be judged on its effectiveness there, in the terms of the struggle as it was seen there. For the Communists, the greater cause of the revolutionary tide of scientific socialism and its advance by applications of the strategy of people's war had to be proven in Viet Nam. How well they grappled with and transformed the demands of national legitimacy also had to be judged by the Vietnamese.

Beginnings, 1960–1963

By 1961 the period of relative calm was over. The Communists had consolidated their rule in the North, and they were ready to complete their revolution in the South. Correspondingly, the security situation in the South as well as Diem's political position began to deteriorate, prompting the United States to take steps committing itself directly to the survival of South Viet Nam.

In a secret decision of the Lao Dong party's Central Committee in January, 1959, ratified at the Third National Congress of the party in September, 1960, a formal commitment was made to launch armed struggle in the South.[3] In relatively short order, a time-tested structure for military and political struggle was in place. Southern Viet Minh forces, who had regrouped to the north, accelerated their military reinfiltration south in 1959 and 1960. In February, 1961, all southern insurgent forces were brought under the central control of the South Viet

2. Duiker, *The Rise of Nationalism*, 13; Woodside, *Community and Revolution in Modern Vietnam*, 236.
3. This commitment did not, however, include direct intervention by regular military units. Giap, evidently, did not feel that the army was ready. Such a decision was not made until December, 1963. See JUSPAO, *VNDRN*, No. 98, pp. 1–22.

Nam People's Liberation Armed Forces. Lewy reports that from 1959 to early 1964 at least 28,000 men had been reinfiltrated into the South. The political struggle began with the proclamation of a National Liberation front (NLF), announced on December 20, 1960. Like its predecessor, the Viet Minh, the NLF was in theory a coalition of political parties, functional organizations, and interest groups. Mirroring the Fatherland front in the North, the NLF created two puppet parties of its own—the Radical Socialist party in July, 1961, and the Democratic party in December, 1961. The vanguard of the NLF, however, was the People's Revolutionary party (PRP), whose existence was revealed in January, 1962. Avowedly Marxist, the PRP was simply a southern extension of the Lao Dong party in the North. A captured document contained this statement from Hanoi: "The P.R.P. has only the appearance of an independent existence; actually, our party is nothing but the Lao Dong Party of Viet-Nam, unified from North to South, under the direction of the Central Executive Committee of the Party, the chief of which is President Ho." Organizationally, the whole effort was orchestrated by, and brought under the control of the Central Office of South Viet Nam (COSVN), which was reactivated in early 1961. COSVN was an administrative headquarters organization (first employed from 1951 to 1954) that reported to the Hanoi Politburo. Its leadership was made up of Lao Dong party appointees, and its director was typically a politburo member. Some of the most notable directors were Le Duan, Le Duc Tho, Nguyen Chi Thanh, and Pham Hung. Although the Communists certainly had native roots and measurable support in the South, their propaganda attempts to depict the movement as autonomous and southern-directed were patently false. Nevertheless, Western critics of the American war effort succeeded in giving the myth a long life.[4]

It was not long before the activities of this apparatus began to have their effects. Hit-and-run attacks by guerrilla forces began to chew up units of the Army of the Republic of Viet Nam (ARVN) and put them on the defensive. In the first large engagement of the war, in December, 1962, at the Mekong Delta village of Ap Bac, a Viet Cong battalion stood its ground against a far superior ARVN force backed by helicopters and artillery before slipping off. Less dramatic, but equally impressive, by

4. Ibid., 23; Lewy, America in Vietnam, 40; Turner, Vietnamese Communism, 229–32; JUSPAO, VNDRN, Nos. 36–37, p. 11; JUSPAO, VNDRN, No. 40, pp. 1–6.

June, 1963, the Viet Cong were levying taxes in forty-two of South Viet Nam's forty-four provinces.[5]

The term *Viet Cong*, or Vietnamese Communist, is an epithet coined by Ngo Dinh Diem. It came to refer to those units and leaders who were strictly local southerners. However, as the lines became harder to draw (many Viet Cong units had a high proportion of North Vietnamese "fillers"), that distinction became blurred, and the acronym VC/NVA (meaning combined Viet Cong and North Vietnamese forces) came into use. Vietnamese used the term *Viet Cong* for any Communist, regardless of regional origin, much like the American southerners in the Civil War called all northerners Yankees, even though the term originally referred only to New Englanders.

Not all of Diem's problems during this period could be blamed on the Communists. Crackdowns on his opposition were indiscriminate. In April, 1960, eighteen old-time politicians called on the president in the Caravelle manifesto to guarantee democratic liberties to ensure public support for his government. Most of the men were jailed. A more serious threat to Diem came from the military, which attempted a coup in November, 1960. To prevent further cabals, Diem took more personal control of the military and transferred senior officers frequently, making loyalty the key value in assignment and promotion. Even so, his palace was bombed in February, 1962, in another abortive coup. Increasingly, his regime became a family affair, with his brother Ngo Dinh Nhu acquiring more and more power through his control of the police and the semisecret Can Lao party. American suggestions to remove Nhu and his flamboyant wife only strengthened their positions with Diem. At the regional level, his brothers, Ngo Dinh Can and the Catholic Bishop Ngo Dinh Thuc, had carved out a fief for themselves in Annam. The commander of Military Region 1 in Hue reported that he had to clear all his decisions with Can. All of this left Diem in an isolated position, especially from the Buddhists.[6]

His isolation from the populace was best exposed at the village level

5. Bernard B. Fall, "The Agonizing Reappraisal," *Current History*, XLVIII (February, 1965), 98.
6. Kahin and Lewis, *The United States in Vietnam*, 131; Lewy, *America in Vietnam*, 26; Tran Van Don, *Our Endless War: Inside Vietnam* (San Rafael, Calif., 1978), 56.

in the shambles of his Strategic Hamlet Program. Begun in 1959 as the Agroville Plan, it was an imitation of a similar scheme in Malaya. In the parlance of Maoist guerrilla war theory, its purpose was to deny the Viet Cong "fish" its "human sea" of support by regrouping the rural population into "agrovilles" (protected and fortified villages) linked by strategic highways. The plan was rechristened the Strategic Hamlet Program in February, 1962, and the agrovilles were called "new life hamlets" because of the infusion of social services that was supposed to follow the construction of the fortified villages. By the summer of 1962 the Saigon government claimed 3,225 hamlets had been set up, accommodating four million people. After the fall of Diem in 1963, it was evident that these gains were mainly on paper. Bernard Fall reports that only 1,500 were ever established. Since many peasants were torn away from their ancestral burial grounds in order to populate the hamlets, the program in general was bitterly resented.[7]

Already committed to a massive aid program, the Americans found themselves more and more directly involved as they tried to shore up the Diem regime. Upon assumption of office in January, 1961, President Kennedy was strongly urged by outgoing president Eisenhower to hold the line in Laos and South Viet Nam. The new president initiated a series of fact-finding missions in his first year of office to bring back recommendations. In May Vice-President Johnson returned from Saigon, cautiously backing President Diem. Professor Eugene Staley toured the country from May to July and recommended a strenuous antiguerrilla effort. However, the October trip of presidential adviser Walt Rostow and General Maxwell Taylor convinced them of the need for more direct American military involvement. On such advice Kennedy decided by spring to continue the engagement in Viet Nam. After the Rostow-Taylor trip, he raised the ante and sent in advisers, planes, and tanks. When the situation continued to deteriorate, in early 1962 the Administration began to provide full assistance short of direct involvement by American combat units. One piece of advice the young president failed to heed was a personal warning from French president Charles de Gaulle: "I predict that you will sink step by step into a bottomless military and political quagmire." By the end of each successive year the

7. Lewy, *America in Vietnam*, 25; Fall, "The Agonizing Reappraisal," 95.

contingent of American advisers grew larger: 1960—875; 1961—3,164; 1962—11,326; 1963—16,263; and 1964—23,210.[8]

The Coup Against Diem

Despite American efforts, Diem's isolation only increased. His nearly exclusive reliance on the Catholic population for support, particularly from recent northern refugees, only drove the wedge further between his regime and the Buddhist majority. The beginning of the end for Diem came on May 8, 1963, the anniversary of Buddha's birthday. Government troops fired on a procession of celebrants in Hue waving Buddhist flags in defiance of a government ban on the flying of all flags save the national one. Nine people were killed. In reaction a spasm of protest by the Buddhists continued unabated through the summer and gained strength through the self-immolations of seven Buddhist monks and the organizational skills of the militant bonze, Thich Tri Quang.

The Buddhist protests soon involved the two other participants in the somewhat unholy and incompatible triangular alliance that toppled Diem—the generals and the Americans. Spurred by the scent of victory in the chaos, a cabal of generals began to plot again. Diem's failure to respond to American suggestions to ameliorate the crisis prompted Kennedy to cut off further shipments of agricultural commodities to Saigon. While the Administration debated on a course of action regarding Diem and the plotters, the CIA kept in contact with the generals through Lieutenant Colonel Lucien Conein. In fact, one of the plotters asserts that Conein offered them material support several times.[9]

Diem and Nhu, despite the mounting odds, were not powerless. Nhu began some plotting of his own, repositioning senior officers, sowing doubts and rumors, and forming counter-coup cabals. As the drama of the coup unfolded, Nhu almost succeeded in staving it off. Keeping all his options open, he is even said to have been negotiating with agents of the Viet Cong (an allegation that the intemperate Madame Nhu cor-

8. Kahin and Lewis, *The United States in Vietnam,* 128–29; William P. Bundy, "Path to Viet Nam," 656–57; "DeGaulle's Warning to Kennedy: An 'Endless Entanglement' in Vietnam," New York *Times,* March 15, 1972, Sec. L, p. 47; Lewy, *America in Vietnam,* 24.
9. Tran Van Don, *Our Endless War,* 98.

roborated after the coup). But the Diem brothers were never quite able to pinpoint who the plotters were. Nhu's machinations, though, gave the plotting generals cold feet, and they told Conein that they would not proceed without a guarantee of noninterference from the Americans.[10]

The crisis came in late August in a brutal raid by Nhu's secret police on a pagoda of Thich Tri Quang's militant An Quang sect. On August 24, 1963, a highly controversial cable was dispatched to Saigon by Roger Hilsman, Averell Harriman, James Forrestal, and George Ball (all Diem opponents) without review by the president, Dean Rusk, or Robert McNamara. Vaguely worded, the cable in effect authorized Ambassador Henry Cabot Lodge to establish a liaison with the conspirators. Understandably, Lodge interpreted this as the guarantee of noninterference that gave the generals the green light from Washington for their coup. General Maxwell Taylor was highly critical of this maneuver, but it served the immediate purpose of the Administration, which was convinced the days of the Diem regime were over. On November 1, 1963, the conspirators struck, overthrowing Diem, and, intentionally or unintentionally, killing both Nhu and Diem. In any case, the affair was sordid. Lyndon Johnson later lamented to Henry Graff, "The worst mistake we ever made was getting rid of Diem."[11]

The breakdown of authority would seem to have provided a perfect opportunity for a move by the Viet Cong, yet, strangely, they were quiet. According to defectors, the Party would have called for a general uprising (*khoi nghia*) in the confusion, but it held back because its armed forces were still deemed to be too weak. The coup, however, prompted a decision to remedy this.[12]

Interregnum

The removal of the Diem regime did not produce the desired stable, legitimate political order committed to American-sponsored reforms. Instead, to the near despair of the American mission under the new

10. *Ibid.*, 53; Fall, "The Agonizing Reappraisal," 96.
11. Maxwell D. Taylor, *Swords and Plowshares* (New York, 1972), 292–93; Henry F. Graff, *The Tuesday Cabinet: Deliberation and Decision on Peace and War Under Lyndon B. Johnson* (Englewood Cliffs, N.J., 1970), 136.
12. Jeffrey Race, *War Comes to Long An*, 136.

ambassador, Maxwell Taylor, it ushered in a two-year interregnum of political chaos in which the war in the countryside was all but forgotten. Politics in these two years became an elaborate intrigue played on the stage of Saigon. Jockeying for power were military factions, civilian bureaucrats, and political parties like the Dai Viet, VNQDD, and Can Lao remnants, as well as Roman Catholic and Buddhist organizations. The Buddhists, particularly, emerged as a powerful pressure group, with their repeated demand for national elections. Attempting to preside over this boiling caldron was General Nguyen Khanh, who took over from the original coup leader, Duong Van Minh. He proved unequal to the task. Before the flashy Air Vice-Marshall Nguyen Cao Ky stepped in on February 10, 1965, and finally stabilized the situation, there had been nine changes of government.[13]

The prime American concern during this period was stability. However, while American support was crucial to power aspirants, direct attempts at king making or policy guidance were frequently either counterproductive or went unheeded. The lack of American support, for example, probably prevented the Buddhists from securing a regime to their liking. Ambassador Taylor held a great antipathy for Thich Tri Quang and the chaos he created. Many have argued that the United States could have created a strong nationalist alternative to the Communists by backing the Buddhists at this crucial juncture. The Buddhists, however, had serious political weaknesses and were ill equipped to compete with the Communists, which vindicated the embassy's disassociation from them. Nevertheless, the subsequent denial of any political role to the Buddhists was a mistake nearly as serious in the other direction. Direct American attempts, however, to prevent Khanh from overthrowing the civilian government of Pham Khac Suu and Tran Van Huong by threatening to cut off aid backfired when Khanh made the threat public. In general, because the American assistance and commitment had become so fundamental to the survival of South Viet Nam, ironically the United States had lost its room for maneuver. Nevertheless, George Kahin has secured documents which show that the United States did play a major role in finally forcing Khanh out of of-

13. Buttinger, *Vietnam*, 477–78.

fice. In any case, the pluses and minuses to the American score card in all these machinations obviously did not add up to much stability.[14]

Meanwhile, in the countryside, pacification efforts virtually ceased, and the continued need for land reform went unheeded. Consequently, the rural population felt even more divorced from national life and became utterly indifferent to all the bewildering urban events. The Communists took advantage of this period to build up their strength and to burrow more deeply into the villages. They were particularly successful in the Mekong Delta, moving into many areas where Saigon had exercised unbroken control since 1946. Even the *montagnards* had grown restive. Although resentment of the lowland Vietnamese dates back to the reign of Le Thanh Tong, more recently they had been upset by encroaching settlements of northern refugees and stirred up by Viet Cong promises of autonomous zones similar to the ones in North Viet Nam. A *montagnard* organization, FULRO (United National Front for the Struggle of Oppressed Races), demanded autonomy for the twelve northern provinces and staged two brief revolts in September, 1964, and August, 1965.[15] In short, the country was on the verge of collapse.

Decisions by the Two Sides

Contrary to the assertions of war critics, a captured top secret Communist document makes it clear that it was the North Vietnamese who made the first major move in the spiral of escalation that led to direct fighting between them and American troops. In December, 1963, after the fall of Diem and the assassination of President Kennedy, the Central Committee of the Lao Dong party made a secret decision to escalate the war in 1964. Building on a record of successful company-sized attacks in 1963, the Central Committee declared, "Our main force should launch more mobile attacks in strategic areas of operation." It stated in

14. Taylor, *Swords and Plowshares*, 319–20; Kahin and Lewis, *The United States in Vietnam*, 165; George McTurnan Kahin, "Political Polarization in South Vietnam: U.S. Policy and the Post Diem Period," *Pacific Affairs*, LII (Winter, 1979–80), 647–73.

15. Buttinger, *Vietnam*, 477–78; David Hunt, "Organizing for Revolution in Vietnam: Study of a Mekong Delta Province," *Radical America*, VIII (January–April, 1974), 38.

effect that the time was right to launch Mao's second phase. The operational vehicle for this new phase was the decision to move regular North Vietnamese army (NVA) units into the South. In April, 1964, elements of the 325th PAVN (People's Army of Viet Nam) Division prepared to move south. The first regiment skirted around the demilitarized zone (DMZ) in late September, the second regiment in October, and the third regiment in December. By March, 1965, when the first American combat units splashed ashore in Danang, in addition to groups of individuals infiltrated as "fillers," or replacements, for local Viet Cong units, 5,800 regular PAVN troops were in the South.[16] A 1965 State Department white paper asserted that 4,400 infiltrators had come south in regular units, but the necessity to preserve sensitive sources rendered the paper's evidence unconvincing. Predictably, the paper came under sharp attack from such war critics as I. F. Stone, Roger Hilsman, and Theodore Draper. Much of this sensitive information, however, has now become available and provides stronger confirmation of the original White House claims.

While American attention was riveted on the infiltration down the Ho Chi Minh Trail, the Viet Cong made a strenuous effort to raise troops for phase two of their rendering of the stages of the people's war through recruitment in the South. On July 20, 1964, the Viet Cong announced a nationwide mobilization. Of those men deemed eligible, one-third was drafted into military units, one-third was given noncombat duties, and one-third evaded. While this may hardly be considered a stellar performance, it far outshone ARVN recruitment efforts. Bernard Fall asserts that in 1965 the ARVN only increased its net strength by 60,000, having lost 93,000 to desertions and AWOL; but Communist forces, suffering 100,000 casualties, still increased to 200,000 men with the help of 40,000 northern replacements and 160,000 fresh recruits.[17]

The decision to launch phase two achieved concrete expression in the Battle of Binh Gia (a hamlet between Saigon and Vung Tau) from December 27, 1964, to January 1, 1965. During the fighting two Viet Cong regiments linked to form a division-sized unit that overran the hamlet and decimated two ARVN battalions. Somewhat less dramatic,

16. JUSPAO, *VNDRN*, No. 96, p. 38; Lewy, *America in Vietnam*, 38–40.
17. Race, *War Comes to Long An*, 136; Fall, *The Two Viet-Nams*, 361.

but equally ominous, during the interregnum in Saigon the Viet Cong had put into place across the country a political machine that paralleled the Saigon administrative structure and contained an administrative cadre of 8,000 to 10,000. A final favorable political shift in Saigon was all that was needed to reveal this apparatus.[18]

While Hanoi may have made the first moves, it is understandable that certain American steps, such as the annual increase in the number of American military advisers and material assistance, were interpreted as provocations. Furthermore, in early 1962 the proscription against field advisers taking part in combat was lifted. On another track, the Pentagon papers reveal that President Kennedy approved two harassing covert activities against North Viet Nam: OPLAN 34A and the DE SOTO patrols. OPLAN 34A was a program of seaborne raids along the North Vietnamese coast by South Vietnamese troops with American logistical support (which did not actually begin until February, 1964), and the DE SOTO patrols were conducted by the 7th Fleet to test North Vietnamese coastal radar.[19]

These programs led to the famous Gulf of Tonkin incident. On August 2, 1964, the destroyer USS *Maddox* was attacked by North Vietnamese PT boats thirty miles from the location of an OPLAN 34A strike that was conducted two days before. Two days later the torpedo boats struck again at the now reinforced American patrol. Congressional leaders were briefed as retaliatory air strikes over North Viet Nam were being flown. On August 7, 1964, America crossed its Rubicon River in Viet Nam with the passage of the Gulf of Tonkin resolution in both houses (Senate 88–2, House 416–0), authorizing the president to take military action in Southeast Asia. Subsequently, a controversy arose between war critics and defenders as to whether the attacks actually took place or, if they did, whether they were politically designed to gain public support for a more active American role. The Pentagon papers make clear that both attacks did take place, that they occurred in international waters, and that the North Vietnamese were well aware that they

18. William Childs Westmoreland, *A Soldier Reports* (Garden City, N.Y., 1976), 104; Kahin and Lewis, *The United States in Vietnam*, 161.
19. Neil Sheehan, *et al.*, *The Pentagon Papers as Published by the New York Times* (New York, 1971), 235.

were attacking American ships. During McNamara's testimony on the incident in 1968 before the Senate Foreign Relations Committee, Senator William F. Fulbright praised the secretary of defense for his forthrightness. Three years later Fulbright accused McNamara of being deceitful.[20]

Once across the Rubicon, the Americans had a policy, but the path of implementation was unclear. Most steps that had been taken appeared to be *ad hoc* reactions to perceived threats. William P. Bundy describes the official American policy proceeding from the Gulf of Tonkin as the fundamental protection of South Viet Nam's independence from external interference and the encouragement of the Saigon regime toward a constitutional government, internal reconciliation, and an emphasis on the nonmilitary aspects of the conflict. More immediately, the Americans sought to convince the North Vietnamese that they could not achieve their goals in the South by force, with the hope that the Hanoi leaders would then be willing to negotiate.[21]

The steps taken from October, 1964, to July, 1965, however, found the Americans in the thick of a land war in Asia once again. In October the White House launched a number of secret operations to interfere with movement down the Ho Chi Minh Trail, including air strikes code-named BARREL ROLL. Following several attacks on American installations, President Johnson sent an air strike against the North in February in retaliation for an attack on an American compound in Pleiku. Later that month Johnson began a sustained air campaign against the North called ROLLING THUNDER. On March 7 he sent 3,500 Marines to Danang to guard American installations. The decision to land the troops was difficult, and President Johnson described his dilemma to Henry Graff thus, "When I land troops they call me an interventionist, and if I do nothing I'll be impeached." But as more troops arrived, their mission continued to be confined to the defense of American installations. Finally, in June the American commander General William C. Westmoreland, in requesting 175,000 troops immediately and another 100,000 later, submitted a three-phased plan to defeat the Communists: phase one, halt the losing trend by the end of 1965; phase

20. Lewy, *America in Vietnam*, 32, 35–36; Eugene G. Windchey, *Tonkin Gulf* (Garden City, N.Y., 1971), 223.
21. Bundy, "Path to Viet Nam," 657–62.

two, in the first half of 1966 take the offensive in high-priority areas and reinstitute pacification once they were cleared; and phase three, if the Communists persisted, destroy them in their base areas within a year to a year and a half after the end of phase two.[22] In July Johnson essentially agreed to the plan, and the war was on.

War and Politics Until Tet, 1968

From July until the spasm of the Tet offensive, the war went through its period of fiercest struggle, with both sides hotly contesting at all levels. Well before the offensive, it was evident (at least in hindsight) that this broadly based intensity could not go on indefinitely.

Until the massive American intervention, the Communists were close to a takeover. By 1966 Viet Cong tax collections were bringing in several hundred million piastres annually. The Pentagon estimates that even with a massive increase in their forces, the Communists were still able to acquire 80 to 90 percent of their supplies locally. Hence, in early 1966, North Vietnamese shipments to the South amounted to a mere twelve tons per day. This performance, however, was difficult to sustain under the growing American onslaught. At this stage, escalation was easy for the Americans. As David Hunt observes: "On the one side, escalation was to some extent a matter of augmenting the mechanical war-making apparatus, and in this sense American capacity for intensifying the fighting was almost limitless. On the other side, escalation involved a growing political crisis, in which the NLF had to demand even more of peasants already driven almost beyond the limits of endurance by the experience of the struggle."[23]

Because of the hardships posed by the American escalation, the Viet Cong were forced to phase out their 1964 mobilization and sharply reduce their taxes. In one Mekong Delta province, for example, the reduction was from 1.8 million piastres to .8 million piastres a year.

22. Graff, *The Tuesday Cabinet*, 55; Westmoreland, *A Soldier Reports*, 140–42.
23. Duncanson, *Government and Revolution in Vietnam*, 414; Lacouture, *Vietnam: Between Two Truces*, 182; Roger Hilsman, *To Move a Nation: The Politics of Foreign Policy in the Administration of John F. Kennedy* (Garden City, N.Y., 1967), 447–40; Hunt, "Organizing for Revolution in Vietnam," 70.

Nevertheless, the Viet Cong continued to make a game effort at recruitment in the South. From early 1965 to August, 1966, total VC/NVA forces rose from 116,000 to 282,000. Half of this increase of 166,000 came from infiltration, and the other half came from recruitment. Even until August, 1966, 96 of their 177 battalions were southern. But, increasingly, the burden shifted to the North. This shift is reflected in the sharp jumps in infiltration from the North from 1964 to 1967. The yearly totals were: 1964—12,400; 1965—36,300; 1966—92,287; and 1967—101,263.[24]

Allied forces, meanwhile, had risen to a total of 1,018,000 by the end of 1966, giving them better than a three-to-one numerical superiority. With these imposing forces President Johnson meant to apply increasing pressure on Hanoi through bombing and ground offenses. In ever increasing graduated responses to Communist battlefield activities, he hoped to push Hanoi across its threshold of pain, after which it would desist and retire or come to terms with American negotiators. In the war theater this translated into interdiction by air and attrition on the ground. To secure an attrition rate greater than the Communists' replacement ability, General Westmoreland launched search-and-destroy sweeps in an effort to trap VC/NVA troops into big-unit battles. The first such major battle was in the Ia Drang valley of the Central Highlands in November, 1965, between an American brigade and two North Vietnamese regiments. Although their casualties were heavy, the NVA troops managed to slip away into Cambodia. Proceeding from this baptism of fire, American forces then embarked on phase two of their commander's game plan by launching continual search-and-destroy sweeps throughout 1966 and 1967, leaving ARVN forces with the task of defending centers of population. By the second half of 1967, Westmoreland moved into his third phase and began to strike Communist base areas and supply systems along the Laotian and Cambodian borders. Although Westmoreland and other Pentagon officials began talking optimistically of the "light at the end of the tunnel," the Communists were able to replace their losses and conserve their forces, despite heavy casualties, by offering battle only when they chose.[25]

24. Hunt, "Organizing for Revolution in Vietnam," 98–99; Kahin and Lewis, *The United States in Vietnam*, 187–88; Lewy, *America in Vietnam*, 66.

25. Lewy, *America in Vietnam*, 42–51, 56, 64–66.

The priority given to big-unit war produced an obsession with the body count of Communist dead. Westmoreland contended that given the political constraints placed upon his command, there was no alternative; however, this focus proved to be a serious distraction from the objective of pacification, which was supposed to receive a strong emphasis in official American policy and objectives. Instead, the pacification effort became a castoff bureaucratic orphan running through repeated reorganizations and twelve name changes. In 1968, for example, the United States spent only $850 million on pacification and aid, while lavishing $14 billion on bombing and offensive operations in the South. These operations, however, had a definite effect on pacification. The insecurity caused by the American bombing in the South (which was far greater than the more publicized campaigns against the North) raised questions about the legitimacy of a Viet Cong mandate by disproving their ability to protect populations under their control. This started a trend of urbanization to more secure government areas. One Viet Cong village in the Delta, for example, shrank from a population of 3,000 to 142.[26]

The air armada assembled by the Americans was by far the largest to fly over the skies of Southeast Asia. At its peak it consisted of over 6,000 aircraft of all types, including over 3,500 helicopters, 1,200 attack aircraft, and 80 gunships. The amount of ordnance dropped was greater than in World War II and Korea combined, and it wreaked tremendous havoc; yet it did not seriously interfere with the infiltration of either men or materials to the South, nor did it push the North Vietnamese over any threshold of pain. A fact not known until it was revealed by documents captured in the Cambodian "incursion" in 1970 was that nearly 80 percent of the supplies for the Viet Cong operating in the southern half of South Viet Nam came by sea via the Cambodian port of Sihanoukville. The Ho Chi Minh Trial, though, became crucial after the March, 1970, Lon Nol coup in Cambodia, which brought in a government more sympathetic to American interests and shut off the port to the Communists.[27]

26. Westmoreland, *A Soldier Reports*, 336; Lewy, *America in Vietnam*, 89; Hunt, "Organizing for Revolution in Vietnam," 54–57.
27. Raphael Littauer and Norman Uphoff (eds.), *The Air War in Indochina* (Rev. ed.; Boston, 1972), 172; Frank Snepp, *Decent Interval* (New York, 1977), 20.

Numbers Interlude

In the peculiar environment of a war where one could kill the enemy but not corner him, bomb him but not destroy him, it was difficult to gauge one's progress. Numbers, however, were "objective" and supposedly not culture bound. Americans seized upon them with a passion. Chester Cooper describes this well.

> Numbers! There was a number mill in every military and AID installation in Vietnam. Numbers flowed into Saigon and from there into Washington like the Mekong River during the flood season. Sometimes the numbers were plucked out of the air, sometimes the numbers were not accurate. Sometimes they were relevant but misinterpreted. The emphasis on quantification came early in the game. In 1962 McNamara was at the American Pacific Headquarters in Honolulu, and after a briefing by General Harkins he said, "Now General, show me a graph that will tell me whether we are losing or winning in Vietnam."[28]

Throughout the war three sets of numbers went into the charts that told McNamara, and the American public, how the United States was doing: reports of the Hamlet Evaluation System (HES), the body count of Communist dead, and the numerical strength of the VC/NVA. HES grouped South Viet Nam's twelve thousand hamlets and villages into six categories according to the degree of their "security," which was based on indicators of Viet Cong activities. What HES measured was control. It said very little about the underlying balance of social forces between the government and the Viet Cong; yet HES reports became synonymous with the term *pacification*. In the absence of any other measures, these reports were even used to show the degree of support and legitimacy of the government. Statements of qualification concerning these reports were quickly forgotten. When asked how much support the government had with the people, briefers usually responded like this: "We really have no way of knowing that, sir, but HES reports indicate . . ."

The body count and the numerical strength of Communist forces were the two bellwethers of performance for the military strategy of attrition. General Westmoreland saw his mandate as reaching a crossover

28. Cooper, *The Lost Crusade*, 422.

point at which his forces were killing the Communist forces faster than new enemy troops could be recruited. Judging the arrival at this point, however, was hampered by serious problems besetting both sets of figures. In regard to attrition rates, Communist casualties were no doubt overstated to some extent because of command pressure to produce high body counts, duplication, and failure to distinguish between civilian and military dead. In 1968, however, in an interview with Italian journalist Oriana Fallaci, Giap admitted to a loss of 500,000 men. The rather flippant context of his remark, however, casts some doubt on its accuracy. The Pentagon count at year's end was 435,000 enemy killed. A Department of Defense study concluded that the problems attendant upon body counting resulted in as much as a 30 percent error of inflation in the reported number of enemy casualties. Despite imprecision in the numbers, the range of reported casualty figures bears out the contention that Communist losses were indeed heavy.[29]

As for the size of the enemy, far too much faith was placed in intelligence estimates of VC/NVA strength. In an iconoclastic exposé in Harper's magazine, Sam Adams, a CIA analyst assigned to keep track of the Communist order of battle, asserted that the official estimate of these forces on the eve of the Tet offensive was 300,000, whereas the true figure was closer to 600,000. General Westmoreland retorts in his memoirs that Adams included part-time guerrillas and even mere sympathizers in his estimate but that Military Assistance Command, Vietnam, based its number on units comparable to those on the allied side.[30]

Still, such a wide variance is disturbing. As a Defense Intelligence Agency analyst in Saigon in 1973, I felt that the official estimates could have easily been off by 100,000 then. In July, 1973, I helped organize a two-day order-of-battle conference between the Defense Attaché Office and the ARVN Intelligence Headquarters to try to iron out the discrepancy between American reports that placed PAVN troop strength in the South at 145,000, and Government of Viet Nam reports of 300,000. Actually, by the end of the conference there was very little difference in total numbers, but ARVN analysts were calling many more units North Vietnamese than we were. Like Adams, I also found that many units

29. Lewy, *America in Vietnam*, 78–82, 450.
30. Sam Adams, "Vietnam Cover-up: Playing with Numbers," *Harpers*, CCL (May, 1975), 42–45; Westmoreland, *A Soldier Reports*, 416.

carried the same totals for years (meaning that they had not been checked for new reports). However, on the GVN rosters I also found several strange Communist units that I felt did not merit counting among military forces. Some of them were very likely dummy outfits, and others were composed of part-time coolies.

There was a lack of clarity on the numbers for the allied side as well. American sources counted among their numbers only those forces in the territory of South Viet Nam. With some justification, however, Communist sources contended that the true maximum American force level in the Viet Nam War was not 545,000 but 800,000, because American forces in Thailand as well as the sailors and aviators of the Seventh Fleet were also directly involved in the fighting. Further, in 1967 the United States had in its employ 180,000 Vietnamese nationals that were never counted in allied force totals. If part-time guerrillas were counted for the Communists, then these Vietnamese workers should have been counted for the Americans too.[31]

The point to stress here, then, is that claims of absolute validity for any of these figures cannot be accepted; instead, the figures should be used as relative indicators whose variations over time may help to explain the impact of various events and policies. Part of the numbers problem, too, was one of comparing apples and oranges. The force structures of the two sides were so different in organization and function that mere comparisons of total numbers revealed little. For example, allied forces were tied to a massive American logistics system and a political function of static, territorial defense. Thus, of a total allied force of 1,593,000 in August, 1968, only 223,000 (14 percent) were in main force combat units, and because of static defense requirements, of this figure only 88,000 troops were ready to maneuver against a VC/NVA main combat force of 70,000, a situation not dissimilar to that confronting the French at the time of the Navarre plan. Unlike the French, however, the airborne mobility and overwhelming firepower available to American forces still gave the allied side a tremendous force ratio to their advantage. Thus, the real measure of meaning was the quality behind these numbers. This also meant that in comparing total numbers of rural administrative personnel, for example, it was far more impor-

31. John T. Bennet, "Political Implications of Economic Change," *Asian Survey*, VII (August, 1967), 584.

tant to recognize the fact that the NLF sent its most enthusiastic cadres to contested hamlets, while the GVN kept its most competent officials in the cities.[32]

In brief, what was missing in all the numbers and charts was a set of facts or indicators to show how the two sides were meeting the fundamental challenges of national and revolutionary legitimacy. Throughout the war, then, the Americans seemed to be flying blind through clouds of indigestable numbers.

War and Politics Until Tet, 1968 (Continued)

Whatever the numbers, as the fighting raged, Premier Nguyen Cao Ky attempted to impose some political stability on the national level and to attain legitimacy for his regime. Although he stayed in command, he could not contain the rivalry between General Nguyen Van Thieu, chief of the National Leadership Committee, and General Nguyen Chanh Thi, commander of I Corps. In March, 1966, this struggle spilled out into the open. Aligning himself with the Struggle Force of Tri Quang's militant Buddhists, Thi acquired a volatile popular base. Demonstrations in Hue and Danang became so violent that Ky declared Danang to be an enemy-held city. For awhile it appeared that Ky's government would either lose control of I Corps (nearly all public officials had resigned over the repression of the Buddhists) or succumb to a reaction from the Right. But anarchy was averted by June when Thi was forced to resign and Tri Quang, sensing he had lost control of his own movement, agreed to calm his mobs. This time, unlike their quiescence during the Diem coup, the Communists exploited the chaos and managed to seize control of the Struggle Force contingent in Hue.[33]

The price for peace was Ky's and Thieu's commitment to hold elections for a Constituent Assembly. Despite a Buddhist boycott, because several of their other demands were not met, the promised elections

32. Lewy, *America in Vietnam*, 175–76; Hunt, "Organizing for Revolution in Vietnam," 17.

33. Robert Shaplen, *The Road from War: Vietnam, 1965–1971* (Rev. ed.; New York, 1971), 29; Allan E. Goodman, *The Lost Peace: America's Search for a Negotiated Settlement of the Vietnam War* (Stanford, Calif., 1978), 37; JUSPAO, *VNDRN*, No. 102-I, p. 8.

took place on September 10, 1966, and Robert Shaplen, a well-regarded observer of the Vietnamese scene, reported that they were the fairest elections ever conducted in Viet Nam. From April to June, 1967, village council elections were held throughout the country, and a national election campaign was underway for the president, vice-president, senate, and national assembly provided for under the constitution of the new government. In a tearful and tense meeting of forty-eight generals in June, 1967, the military agreed to run a single slate of Thieu for president and Ky for vice-president to stand against ten civilian tickets. These elections, held on September 3, 1967, were less fair. For example, even though the Buddhists had decided to reenter the political process, their slate was arbitrarily disqualified. In winning 35 percent of the vote against runner-up Truong Dinh Dzu's 18 percent, Thieu and Ky, despite losing in all the major cities, drew support from the military, civil service, Catholics, and other minorities, and scored well in the Central Highlands and Mekong Delta. Because Viet Cong-held areas were declared ineligible, however, the actual size of Thieu and Ky's mandate was only 20 percent of the voting-age population. Nevertheless, the election did accord a mark of legitimacy to the government, both in the South, and, more important, in the United States.[34]

Yet this legitimacy was tarnished by the overwhelming South Vietnamese dependence on the Americans. Their entire economy was kept afloat by American aid, commodity exports, and GVN taxes on imports. No truly independent country could continue with a trade deficit equal to three-fourths of its total currency in circulation, as South Viet Nam did in 1965. In the field, American GI's undertook most of the offensive operations, while Thieu continued the South Vietnamese practice of selectively implementing existing conscription laws. While ARVN troops did fight, they deserted in large numbers. This pointed to an asymmetry of will between the Communist and the government side that was perhaps as unbalanced as the material superiority available to the Saigon forces. The problem of willpower also extended to Washington. As Richard Nixon observed, after a trip to Viet Nam in 1967: "The Communists . . . had a total commitment to victory. We had, at most, a partial commitment to avoid defeat. If this situation continued, in the end

34. Shaplen, *The Road From War*, 83, 156; Buttinger, *Vietnam*, 480.

they would win." The situation did continue. Primarily because of the growing disagreement over the Viet Nam War, antiwar demonstrations and intellectual dissent became an integral feature of the American political landscape.[35]

Despite their total commitment, the Communists were not able to go it alone. Although the Viet Cong were initially able to continue on a trickle of supplies from the North, the weapons given to new recruits all came from the Socialist bloc (Russia, China, and eastern Europe). By March, 1966, a speech at the People's Revolutionary Party Congress acknowledged that the Democratic Republic of Viet Nam had begun to underwrite half of the NLF's expenses. The DRV, in turn, increasingly relied upon Soviet and Chinese assistance to continue the war. The Communist powers were able to underwrite the Viet Cong war effort at a relatively low cost. At the height of the American involvement, it cost the United States Treasury $30 billion a year, while the peak of Russian support was only $1 billion a year. Nevertheless, despite the seemingly relative insignificance of the Russian support, Nixon, as a presidential candidate in 1968, noted that this aid was vital to Hanoi's war machine. Eighty-five percent of its oil and 100 percent of its sophisticated weapons came from the Soviets. Chinese aid provided most of the light arms and other logistical equipment. In addition, China sent 50,000 engineer troops to help keep the DRV transportation system functioning. Moreover, recent information suggests that the amount of Chinese aid has been understated. As part of the polemics preceding the outbreak of the Sino-Vietnamese War in February, 1979, China accused the Vietnamese of ingratitude for the $10 billion in aid it provided during the war against the Americans. The Vietnamese never issued a denial of this figure.[36]

The marked differences in approach between the Soviet and the Chinese assistance programs frequently required a delicate political balancing act in Hanoi. Soviet assistance became important after Prime Minister Alexei Kosygin's visit to Hanoi in July, 1966. The increase in

35. Fall, *The Two Viet-Nams*, 302–303; Richard Milhous Nixon, *RN: The Memoirs of Richard Nixon* (New York, 1978), 282–83.

36. Duncanson, *Government and Revolution in Vietnam*, 414; Goodman, *The Lost Peace*, 79; Kahin and Lewis, *The United States in Vietnam*, 190; James P. Sterba, "'Friendship Pass' No Longer Links Peking to Hanoi," New York *Times*, February 5, 1979, Sec. 1, p. A3.

aid was resented by Peking as an interference, especially because the Soviets, with their more sophisticated equipment, were amenable to Hanoi's preference for urban offensives. Such a strategy would only increase Hanoi's reliance on the Russians. Hence the Chinese, most pointedly in Lin Piao's speech "Long Live the Victory of People's War" in September, 1965, urged the Vietnamese to take a more cautious, protracted war strategy and to rely on their own local forces. Further, the Chinese exhorted the Vietnamese to shun negotiations.[37] On both counts, Hanoi spurned its Chinese benefactor.

The Tet Offensive

Much like the siege of Dienbienphu in the French war, the Communist Tet offensive, which lasted from January 31 until mid-June, 1968, was the landmark event of the American war. Unlike Dienbienphu, which produced a clear winner and loser, everyone—Americans, South Vietnamese, Viet Cong, and North Vietnamese—lost in Tet. It changed the nature of the war fundamentally. Although still fiercely contested, the struggle was no longer so well-rounded or theoretically straightforward. Mao's classic stages and Westmoreland's neat phases had to be abandoned.

The prelude to Tet came at Khe Sanh, the westernmost string of defensive camps south of the DMZ, which sat astride a major supply corridor. Holding this camp was to be the last of Westmoreland's phase 3 operations, and by November, 1967, the struggle over Khe Sanh was shaping into a major battle. Soon, twenty thousand PAVN troops were besieging six thousand Marine defenders. The ghost of Dienbienphu became terrifyingly real to the American leadership, despite repeated assurances by field commanders that Khe Sanh could not be taken. Westmoreland asserts that a B-52 bomber strike on a PAVN forward headquarters was instrumental in thwarting an all-out Communist attack on the base during Tet. In maintaining, then, that Khe Sanh was a major target, he heatedly denies that the siege was part of a larger

37. O'Ballance, "Sino-Soviet Influence," 70–76; King C. Chen, "Hanoi vs. Peking: Policies and Relations—A Survey," *Asian Survey*, XII (September, 1972), 815.

Communist plan to lure American units into remote areas prior to the Tet offensive. Yet American concern for Khe Sanh caused Westmoreland to send the 1st Marine Division from Hue to reinforce units along the DMZ and to send two brigades of the 1st Cavalry to the Khe Sanh battle area from the Central Highlands. It was probably no accident, then, that the only city held by the Communists for any length of time in the offensive was Hue.[38]

While the offensive was not a total surprise to the American command, its intensity and breadth had a shocking impact that no one could disguise. The first Communist attacks struck Nha Trang as well as five cities in the northern part of the country on the evening of January 30. The premature blow provided precious hours of warning. The full attack came the next evening. In one week thirty-four province capitals, sixty-four district towns, and all of the seven autonomous cities had come under attack. Most dramatically, the United States Embassy grounds were penetrated for a few chaotic hours.

The American and South Vietnamese counterattack was destructive and bloody. By February 9 Viet Cong units in Saigon had been dispersed, and on February 24 the Hue citadel was finally retaken from stubborn North Vietnamese defenders. Once the attackers had been driven back into the jungles, Operation PEGASUS, which was put into effect by April 1, successfully relieved the garrison at Khe Sanh. A second wave of attacks struck in May with Saigon again briefly penetrated, but by June the Tet offensive was over.

Part of the shock was over the enormous number of casualties and amount of physical destruction. Official Military Assistance Command, Vietnam, figures for the number of casualties in the first wave ending on March 31 were: Americans, 3,895; ARVN, 4,954; civilians, 14,300; and VC/NVA, 58,373. By mid-May the number of Communist dead had reached 92,000. Once again, these figures provide a relative guide. But, even if the figures are off by 30 percent, Communist casualties were indeed heavy. Equipment losses were also serious. In the first hours of the offensive, one thousand allied planes were destroyed or damaged on the ground, which was a force twice the size of the entire French air

38. Westmoreland, *A Soldier Reports*, 317, 335–49; Lewy, *America in Vietnam*, 308.

force in Indochina earlier. In the course of being retaken, many cities suffered heavy destruction, particularly Saigon and Hue. One million people were left homeless by the fighting.[39]

In Hue, during their brief occupation, the Communists turned brutal. Despite attempts by war critics like Frances FitzGerald to minimize it, captured documents confirm reports that the Communist Security Service systematically executed between three and five thousand citizens (mostly professionals and bureaucrats). Thus began the real fear for the South Vietnamese of a Communist bloodbath. Three weeks later in a separate action, a jittery platoon of the U.S. Americal Division gunned down 175 to 200 innocent villagers in the hamlet of My Lai (actually Song My) south of Quang Ngai.[40]

Far more important than the shock of the casualties and destruction was the profound impact on American perceptions of the war at all levels. A Gallup poll in February, 1968, showed a sharp reversal in the optimism revealed in an earlier poll in November, 1967. Certainly the dramatic impact of the television coverage of the carnage, set against the official statements of optimism, had its effects. The fact, however, that all of the televised footage was of American- or ARVN- initiated actions made the coverage decidedly one-dimensional. As Lewy wryly observes, "The VC were notoriously uncooperative in allowing Western cameramen to shoot pictures of the disembowling of village chiefs."[41]

It was perhaps no accident that the offensive occurred in an American election year. The effects were quickly felt. In the March 12 New Hampshire primary, Senator Eugene McCarthy, running on an antiwar campaign, received 42 percent of the vote. This response encouraged Senator Robert Kennedy to announce his candidacy, also based on an antiwar platform, on March 16.

39. Don Oberdorfer, *Tet!* (New York, 1971), dedication page; Shaplen, *The Road from War*, 219; Lewy, *America in Vietnam*, 78–82, 108, 450; Buttinger, *Vietnam*, 312.
40. Frances FitzGerald, *Fire in the Lake: The Vietnamese and the Americans in Vietnam* (New York, 1972), 234–35; Oberdorfer, *Tet!*, 205–234; Turner, *Vietnamese Communism*, 251; U.S. Department of the Army, *Report of the Department of the Army Review of the Preliminary Investigations into the My Lai Incident, 14 March 1970* (Washington, D.C., 1970), I, 2–3.
41. Lewy, *America in Vietnam*, 433. Peter Braestrup, of the Washington *Post*, provides a lengthy analysis of the distortionary effects of the American press coverage of the Tet offensive, in *Big Story: How the American Press and Television Reported and Interpreted the Crisis of Tet 1968 in Vietnam and Washington* (2 vols.; Boulder, Colo., 1977).

Although the Communists had suffered a military defeat in the offensive, the magnitude of their onslaught caused a major reassessment of American strategy. A Pentagon request for 206,000 reinforcements, which Westmoreland denies was a specific plea of his, occasioned an overall policy review chaired by Secretary of Defense designate Clark Clifford. A reluctant conclusion of Clifford's study group was that the strategy of graduated response and attrition was just not working. By the end of 1968, for example, the VC/NVA had lost 291,000 casualties but were able to bring in 300,000 replacements through infiltration and recruitment. A National Security Council study in early 1969 showed that even at half the 1968 casualty rate, it would take thirteen years to exhaust the manpower pool in the North. Thus, despite the massive American effort, only a stalemate had been achieved. Regarding Johnson's strategy, Admiral Ulysses S. Grant Sharp pronounced a profane benediction: "It was the most asinine way to fight a war that could possibly be imagined."[42]

In any case, honoring the Pentagon's request would have necessitated a significant call-up of the Reserves and National Guard, a grave political cost for an ambiguous military benefit. The end of Johnson's escalation ladder revealed his own threshold of pain rather than that of his enemies. On March 31 he announced an end to the bombing of North Viet Nam (south of the twentieth parallel), a willingness to negotiate, a modest troop increase, and his withdrawal from the presidential race.

As for the government and forces of South Viet Nam, their main achievement was that they survived. Despite an uneven performance, ARVN units did not disintegrate or defect, nor did the people rise up against the government. In fact, Thieu was able to rouse the shaken urban populace somewhat. He announced a mobilization and eventually nearly doubled ARVN troops from 670,000 to 1,100,000. Tet did give the GVN the image of a winner, and peasants began to flock to government areas. However, as Lewy points out, these were calculations of the minds, not yet of the hearts. Thus, with any major Communist resurgence, these calculations could be reversed. This meant that the rather optimistic statistics of the Hamlet Evaluation Surveys should

42. Westmoreland, *A Soldier Reports*, 350–62; Lewy, *America in Vietnam*, 84, 130; Ulysses S. Grant Sharp, *Strategy for Defeat: Vietnam in Retrospect* (San Rafael, Calif., 1978), 233.

have been read with more caution. They reflected government control, but not active, popular support. As an American province adviser, for a province listed as 80 percent "secure," commented, "The GVN is surrounded by fair-weather friends."[43]

Turning to the Communist side, not only was the Tet offensive a military disaster, it was also a political setback. Militarily, Tet was a watershed in the local Viet Cong–North Vietnamese relationship. Prior to the offensive, 45 percent of the Communist troops were Viet Cong recruits, but by April, 1968, 70 percent of the combat forces were North Vietnamese. Thus, continuation of the fighting rested solidly on the North. Politically, the Tet offensive may have been an act of desperation for the Viet Cong. Robert L. Sansom notes that whatever the attractiveness of Viet Cong policies, from 1965 to 1967 security became the dominant concern of the peasantry, and when they fled to government areas, the guerrillas lost a revenue and recruitment base. For example, in 1965 the Viet Cong claimed control of 75 percent of the population of Phu Yen Province in coastal Annam, but a secret party document admitted that by the summer of 1967 its control had slipped to a mere 6 percent. Hence, the impulse in the offensive, Sansom argues, was to convince the villagers to return by demonstrating that no place was safe under the GVN.[44]

The hoped-for outcome was that the military shock would induce entire ARVN units to defect, which would inspire another general uprising, or *khoi nghia*, on an even grander scale than the August revolution. But the groundwork had been poorly laid. The party acknowledged that the military proselyting effort was a failure. Also, the Communists evidently had their reporting problems as well. Jeffrey Race comments that "because of excessively optimistic reporting from the village level, higher echelons in the Party had erroneously believed that a general uprising could be successful." Consequently, on April 10, 1968, the Viet Nam Alliance of National, Democratic and Peace Forces, conceived to accommodate this popular groundswell in the NLF framework, was stillborn. Rather than a broadening of support, one decisive result of the Tet of-

43. Oberdorfer, *Tet!*, 330; Lewy, *America in Vietnam*, 193.
44. JUSPAO, *VNDRN*, Nos. 36–37, pp. 1, 13; *VNDRN*, No. 23, p. 3; Robert L. Sansom, *The Economics of Insurgency in the Mekong Delta of Vietnam* (Cambridge, Mass., 1970), 241.

fensive, according to Allan Goodman, was the alienation of a large segment of the Buddhists from the Viet Cong.[45]

To judge the extent of the Communist defeat would require an accurate assessment of their intentions. While a definitive answer is not possible, the contention that their basic objective was merely to shock the Americans into disengaging from the war was only their minimal goal. Their hope was for much more. In Van Tien Dung's account of the 1975 victory, and particularly of his capture of Hue, one cannot help but feel his earlier frustration: "I could not control my emotions. Hue had been liberated forever, not just come under our desperate control for twenty-five days and nights as had been the case at Tet Mau Thanh in 1968."[46]

In 1968, their forces momentarily shattered, Hanoi responded to Johnson's gestures and adopted the strategy of fighting while negotiating. Nevertheless, the orientation of the American leadership, if not the American public, had shifted away from further escalation.

From Tet to the Cambodian "Incursion"

The period just after the Tet offensive was a low point for the Communists. They had expected a quick victory, and it was difficult to convince the troops to resume the drudgery of protracted guerrilla war. As part of their negotiating strategy, the Communists proclaimed the Provisional Revolutionary Government on June 6, 1969, made up of representatives of the NLF and Viet Nam Alliance of National, Democratic and Peace Forces, to "perfect a system of revolutionary administration," that is, to set up a rival government to Thieu's. But neither the negotiating nor the fighting went particularly well; the negotiating in Paris was nothing more than public posturing, and a COSVN report all but acknowledged that a 1969 autumn offensive was a complete failure. This was particularly disappointing because Ho's death in September, 1969, occurred right in the middle of the offensive, and a battlefield victory would cer-

45. JUSPAO, *VNDRN*, No. 18, p. 4; Race, *War Comes to Long An*, 270; Allan E. Goodman, "South Vietnam: Neither War nor Peace," *Asian Survey*, X (February, 1970), 197–33.
46. Van Tien Dung, *Our Great Spring Victory: An Account of the Liberation of South Vietnam*, trans. John Spragens, Jr. (New York, 1977), 104.

tainly have helped to ease the blow of this loss. Gamely, COSVN Resolution 14, issued after the offensive, called for continued guerrilla war and a program of political agitation in the cities to develop support from an almost nonexistent urban base.[47]

But exhortations to continue could not arrest a decline in strength and activity. According to the Military Assistance Command, Vietnam, VC/NVA combat strength declined steadily from 1968 to 1971. Year-end totals for the four years were 250,000; 237,000; 214,000; and 198,000, respectively. More dramatic, the number of battalion-sized attacks dropped off sharply in the three years from 1968 through 1970, with respective totals of 126, 34, and 13. This perhaps only reflected a decision in Hanoi after the Tet offensive to allocate more resources to the "great rear base" in the North than to the war effort in the South.[48]

Meanwhile, Nixon came to the White House in January, 1969, with a "secret plan" to end the war. Actually, his plan consisted of twin measures that had been visible parts of the Viet Nam debate for years, but he gave them new twists. The first measure was to continue the public negotiations started by Johnson, but Nixon also made it a first priority to open parallel secret talks. The other was to continue the program of Vietnamization but more rapidly and with greater fanfare than it had received under Johnson. Coupled with this, he began phased withdrawals of American troops, who reached a peak number of 543,000 in April, 1969, in order to cut down on American casualties. By the end of his first term, Nixon had pulled out all but 25,000 of the American GI's, dramatically reducing the number of casualties. Frances FitzGerald concedes that Nixon's strategy earned him a degree of popular support. Within the government, his policies largely silenced the intramural struggle over advice that had been rampant in the Johnson years. Except for the immediate-withdrawal supporters, advocates of all the alternative policies could see at least some elements of their recommendations being followed.[49]

On all fronts, 1969 and 1970 were probably Thieu's best years. Ameri-

47. JUSPAO, VNDRN, Nos. 30–32, pp. 1–2, *An Outline History of the Viet Nam Workers' Party*, 137; VNDRN, No. 82. pp. 5–11; VNDRN, No. 81, p. 2.

48. Lewy, *America in Vietnam*, 191; David W. P. Elliott, "North Vietnam Since Ho," *Problems of Communism*, XXIX (July–August, 1975), 35–52.

49. FitzGerald, *Fire in the Lake*, 539; Goodman, *The Lost Peace*, 87.

can support was solid. Vietnamization appeared to be going well. ARVN units carried out three times as many large operations as in 1966 and 1967, and suffered only double the casualties. The expansion of such local forces as the Regional Forces/Popular Forces (dubbed by the Americans as "Rough Puffs") and village People's Self-Defense Forces by providing them with modern M-16 rifles in quantity was making a difference in the countryside. At the regional level, the government improved its position in the Central Highlands and Mekong Delta. In the delta this was largely because of the psychological impact of the March, 1970, land-to-the-tiller land reform legislation, long a priority item with the Agency for International Development. Financially underwritten by the United States, in its essential features the program provided for a free grant of land to the tiller and a cessation of rent payments. While it would have been far more effective if promulgated a decade or more earlier, for the first time the Saigon government had a land policy that compared favorably with that of the Viet Cong. Also contributing to an improved government position in the villages were a series of administrative circulars that decentralized many bureaucratic procedures. Village councils, for example, were granted the power to spend 100,000 piastres by themselves. With due allowance for the mushiness of HES statistics, these measures certainly played some role in the improved percentages of people living in secure hamlets from 47 percent in 1968 to 71 percent in 1969 to 75 percent in 1970 and 84 percent in 1971.[50]

The Cambodian Incursion

A long-standing irritant to the American command was the Communist use of border areas across the Cambodian frontier as supply bases to outfit troops and offer them recuperation from the battlefield. "Privileged sanctuaries," they were called. Furthermore, after the Tet offensive COSVN headquarters had moved from north of Tay Ninh into the Cambodian jungle just across the Vietnamese border. To prevent an attack on the withdrawing American troops, the Joint Chiefs of Staff

50. Lewy, *America in Viet Nam*, 167, 192; Race, *War Comes to Long An*, 272–73; FitzGerald, *Fire in the Lake*, 540.

sought approval for a sweep into Cambodia. A popular image of American troop withdrawals at the time was that of a western sheriff retreating with both guns blazing from the pandemonium in a saloon.

The first guns to blaze, as revealed by William Shawcross, were in a secret campaign of B-52 bombing strikes on Cambodian base areas. Begun in March 18, 1969, the campaign was code named Operation MENU. All told, 3,600 B-52 strikes were flown against these base areas in the next fourteen months. Whether the Cambodian king, Norodom Sihanouk, authorized or acquiesced in these raids remains a matter of bitter controversy between Shawcross and Henry Kissinger. The rightist coup d'état by Marshal Lon Nol against King Sihanouk on March 18, 1970, provided the opportunity for the second round of guns to open up. On April 30 Nixon announced that American and Cambodian troops had launched an incursion into Cambodia to destroy Communist headquarters and supply buildups in order to forestall another offensive. He promised that the American contingent would be out in sixty days. More than this, Daniel Ellsberg asserts that Nixon wanted to signal Hanoi that the Johnson policies of measured restraint were over and that the new administration was prepared to use whatever force it had at its disposal to maintain the American position.[51]

Although the elusive COSVN headquarters was not captured, thousands of tons of North Vietnamese equipment and supplies were destroyed and a gold mine of intelligence documents was seized. The Pentagon estimated that a planned offensive was set back by a year. Liberation Radio broadcasts acknowledged that the incursion caused logistical difficulties and morale problems. But the reverberations of this twenty-five-mile incursion had more far-reaching effects than the disruption of supplies and communications. ARVN troops did not return to Viet Nam on the June 30 American deadline. Two divisions remained to fight poorly equipped Cambodian Communist guerrillas as well as North Vietnamese troops, greatly enhancing ARVN morale. In fact, until the Easter offensive in 1972, most of the large-scale fighting shifted to Cambodia. Chased from their border sanctuaries, Vietnamese Communist forces retreated further into Cambodia, developed a supply system along the Mekong River, and began to directly support the

51. William Shawcross, *Sideshow: Kissinger, Nixon, and the Destruction of Cambodia* (New York, 1979), 28, 398; FitzGerald, *Fire in the Lake*, 555.

Cambodian Communist guerrilla insurgency against the Lon Nol regime. The war had become enlarged to an Indochina war. It is wrong, however, to assume that the expansion of the war into Cambodia was triggered solely by the American incursion. COSVN documents captured in the attacks clearly show that the Communists were themselves planning, prior to the incursion, to expand the war into Cambodia.[52]

The most serious repercussions of the entry into Cambodia, though, were felt in the United States. Student demonstrations and protests erupted all over the country. When six students were killed (four at Kent State University and two at Jackson State University in Mississippi), Nixon confronted a major domestic crisis. Senate doves passed a symbolic but ominous amendment calling for the prohibition of American troops and air support in Cambodia after July 1. Within the administration, Secretary of Defense Melvin Laird and Secretary of State William Rogers as well as other staff members opposed the way the incursion was carried out.[53] Thus, while the incursion into Cambodia may have bought time on the ground in Viet Nam for an orderly withdrawal of American troops, at home it fanned the old flames of opposition and burned away whatever margins of time Nixon's twin policies had bought for him earlier.

Failures of War and Politics

Following the Cambodian incursion, a further signal to Hanoi in February, 1971, did not turn out too well. After the Communists lost access to the Cambodian port of Kampong Som (Sihanoukville), the Ho Chi Minh Trail became even more vital to them. Realizing this, the American command laid plans for Vietnamese troops to cross the trail into Laos to deliver a decisive blow to the Communist supply system and to provide dramatic proof of the progress in Vietnamization. The operation was even given a Vietnamese name, Lam Son 719. Elements of two of ARVN's best divisions (the 1st Division and the Paratroop Division) set out along Route 9 for the Laotian town of Tchepone. They met with disaster. Of the sixteen thousand men in the invading force, 50 percent

52. JUSPAO, *VNDRN*, No. 94, pp. 5–6; *VNDRN*, No. 88, pp. 1–2.
53. Shawcross, *Sideshow*, 139–43.

became casualties. Fifty American helicopters were shot down in two weeks of trying to bring out troops and supplies. It took only three months for the Ho Chi Minh Trail to get back to normal. Whatever boosts ARVN morale had received in Cambodia were largely nullified by the blows received in Laos.[54]

While not a total failure—many units did maintain some integrity in their withdrawal—Vietnamization was revealed as a machine with many of its parts still defective. Although Lam Son 719 may be taken as evidence of ARVN willingness to undertake operations and absorb casualties, high desertion rates indicated that the overall morale problem was getting worse. The gravity of this problem is often underscored by a comparison of ARVN desertions with VC/NVA defections from 1967 to 1971. For each year the lower number is that of the Communist defections: in 1967—77,714 versus 16,672; 1968—116,064 versus 12,560; 1969—107,942 versus 28,405; 1970—126,753 versus 17,145; 1971—140,177 versus 10,914.[55]

This has been a typical way to measure the problem of ARVN morale. Again, these figures need to be kept in some perspective. From 1967 to 1971 the size of the South Vietnamese forces roughly doubled, so the rising numbers of desertions are not out of line with this expansion. Further, there is the "apples and oranges" problem of comparing desertions with defections. It is far easier to desert and fade into the social milieu than it is to desert and then take the additional step of going over to the other side. Frustrating true comparisons are the lack of statistics on South Vietnamese defections and Communist desertions. As a rough measure of comparative legitimacy, however, it is interesting that ARVN desertion rates, even at the end in 1974 and 1975, never approached a fraction of that of the Afghan army after the arrival of their "invited" Soviet comrades in 1979. Thus, although there *was* a commonly acknowledged morale problem among some sections of the South Vietnamese armed forces during this period, unlike the case of the Afghans, force levels were at least preserved.

Nevertheless, South Viet Nam had become so politically fragmented that it was like a broken dish glued together, for the time being, by American aid. In senatorial elections held in August, 1970, an An

54. FitzGerald, *Fire in the Lake*, 553–55; Lewy, *America in Vietnam*, 167.
55. Lewy, *America in Vietnam*, 174.

Quang Buddhist slate beat a slate favored by Thieu 1,148,000 votes to
1,107,000 votes, with two other slates receiving 883,000 and 779,000
votes. Despite these impressive vote totals, only 1 percent of the adult
population of South Viet Nam belonged to any political group. By the
time of the October, 1971, presidential election (or, more correctly, referendum), these groups had splintered even further. The Buddhists
were broken into five blocs, the Hoa Hao into seven, the Catholics into
two, the VNQDD into three, and the Cao Dai into four. It is no wonder,
then, that Thieu was able to outmaneuver his opponents and achieve a
one-man race. In fact, Donald Kirk argues, the withdrawal of Nguyen
Cao Ky and Duong Van Minh from the race was because of their own
political weaknesses in Viet Nam, and the election itself was a demonstration of Thieu's power. Whatever its interpretation in South Viet Nam,
the one-man race seriously tarnished Thieu's legitimacy for Americans,
even among war supporters. If Thieu could have counted on strong
support within Viet Nam, perhaps he could have shrugged his shoulders; but as the head of a VNQDD faction observed after the election,
"All the system is based on American aid."[56]

The Easter Invasion

Sometime in late 1970 or early 1971 the Hanoi politburo decided that
an advantageous time to launch another offensive would be in 1972.
American combat troops would be mostly withdrawn, and the VC/NVA
could strike a decisive blow at Vietnamization that might jeopardize
Nixon's reelection campaign. In the fall of 1971, Le Duan made an extended trip to Moscow, where arrangements were made to provide the
necessary heavy weaponry. Chinese premier Chou En'lai is said to have
told Kissinger that he advised the North Vietnamese against such a
move but that, when they were adamant, he agreed to help.[57]

The Republic of Viet Nam Armed Forces (RVNAF) were very imposing by 1972, having completely taken over the ground combat role from

56. Donald Kirk, "The Thieu Presidential Campaign: Background and Consequences of the Single-Candidacy Phenomenon," *Asian Survey*, XII (July, 1972), 611,
616, 624; Goodman, "South Vietnam: Neither War Nor Peace," 113; Woodside, *Community and Revolution in Modern Vietnam*, 288.
57. Lewy, *America in Vietnam*, 196; Goodman, *The Lost Peace*, 124.

the 100,000 American troops remaining in the country. The army was organized into 120 infantry battalions in 11 divisions supported by 50 artillery battalions and 19 battalion-sized armor units. However, due to the static defense requirements of the RVNAF as well as the emphasis on logistics inherited from the Americans, the actual ratio between maneuverable combat units at the time of the Easter invasion favored the VC/NVA by .8:1. As long as the firepower was lavish and air support plentiful, this was no cause for alarm. In March, 1972, this support was ample. At the height of the invasion, the United States had mustered 618 strike aircraft, including 138 B-52s, and a naval force of 2 cruisers and 5 destroyers to pound coastal positions.[58]

Once again, the timing of the invasion caught the Military Assistance Command, Vietnam, by surprise. When massed North Vietnamese forces along the DMZ failed to attack during Nixon's China tour in February, analysts breathed a sigh of relief. But on Easter Sunday, March 30, three North Vietnamese divisions struck across the DMZ. This time the Communists mounted a conventional Korean-style invasion supported by 200 T-54 tanks and 130-millimeter, long-range artillery pieces. A second attack by three more VC/NVA divisions, again supported by tanks and artillery, was aimed at Saigon via Binh Long Province. The Communists' use of heavy tanks and long-range artillery within South Viet Nam was unprecedented in the long years of the Indochina War. It was especially shocking to discover them so close to Saigon. Although Military Assistance Command, Vietnam, analysts had received reports of heavy southward truck movement in Cambodia, no tanks were mentioned. In a ploy reminiscent of Dienbienphu, the Communists had crated the tanks and trucked them separately down to Cambodian base areas, where they were reassembled. In the Saigon salient the district town of Loc Ninh fell in short order. An Loc, the next town down the road, was under siege by April 13, but the defenders held and the attack faltered. On April 23 the third Communist blow fell on the Central Highlands and on the adjacent coastal province of Binh Dinh. After a three-week pause, in the northern sector of the country the attack south of the DMZ toward Hue was resumed. Quang Tri City fell on May 1, and the entire province three days later.

58. Lewy, *America in Vietnam*, 167, 175–76, 200; Frizzel, Donaldson D., and Ray L. Bowers (eds.), *Air Power and the 1972 Spring Invasion*, USAF Southeast Asia Monograph Series, Vol. II, Monograph 3 (Washington, D.C., 1976), 14.

Despite the shock of an onslaught of fourteen divisions and twenty-six independent regiments (nearly the entire armed force of North Viet Nam), this was as far as the Communists got. On April 6 President Nixon unleashed LINEBACKER I on North Viet Nam. This was a far more effective aerial campaign than ROLLING THUNDER due to the relatively unrestricted target lists and to the new technology of "smart" bombs. Nixon delivered a bigger shock, however, by ordering the mining and blockading of Haiphong and other North Vietnamese ports on May 8. In the South, ships and planes (notably B-52s) pounded enemy positions and troop concentrations. By the end of May, the sieges of An Loc and Kontum were lifted, and by July all district towns were recaptured in coastal Binh Dinh. On June 28 Thieu announced a counteroffensive to retake Quang Tri. After a bitter frontline campaign reminiscent of World War II battles, ARVN paratroopers and marines wrested the Quang Tri citadel from elements of four hardened PAVN divisions on September 15. The invasion was over.[59]

This time, except for the area around Saigon, virtually no local Viet Cong units participated. Also, unlike Tet, it was almost purely a military enterprise with very little attendant political agitation. Although the invasion produced 970,000 refugees, the setback to pacification was not as severe as with Tet. In March, 1968, 4,093 hamlets temporarily fell under Viet Cong control compared to only 963 in July, 1972. The Communists ended up gaining Loc Ninh, most of Quang Tri Province except for the capital, and most of the unpopulated border regions at a cost of nearly 100,000 killed.[60]

The performance of ARVN units during the invasion was varied. The elite units—the rangers, marines, and paratroopers—fought tenaciously. In addition, the 23rd Division in Kontum and elements of the 5th Division at An Loc performed creditably. The generalship of Ngo Quang Truong, the commander of Military Region 1 (embracing Hue), was a national inspiration. However, the 22nd Division in Kontum and the 3rd Division at the DMZ disgraced themselves, as did the relieving force at An Loc, which only managed to advance five hundred yards after two months of supporting B-52 strikes. Although ARVN troops did all the fighting on the ground, American fire support by air and sea was

59. The preceding account of the Easter Invasion is based on Lewy, *America in Vietnam*, 196–98.
60. *Ibid.*, 198.

so overwhelming that the invasion was not a decisive test of Vie
ization. American planes flew 75 percent of all sorties. Air pow
decisive at Kontum and An Loc, having inflicted half of the Comr
casualties and tank losses. Moreover, LINEBACKER I and the
ade blunted the invasion by reducing Communist resupply
appreciably.[61]

The performance of the North Vietnamese was hardly flawless.
eral Giap made two strategic mistakes that were magnified by the
cal errors of his field commanders. First, he attacked on three fron
staggered time intervals, thereby dissipating his forces. Second, arter
reaching the Cua Viet River in the North, the North Vietnamese paused
for three weeks, giving the ARVN time to rush in reinforcements. Field
commanders showed a tactical inability to coordinate their tanks and
artillery with their infantry movements. Also, all too often they threw
away an initial numerical superiority by concentrating their forces in
bloody, repeated, and futile shock assaults. These assaults may well
have been an example of applying the analogy of the experience of their
Chinese comrades in Korea too closely.[62]

There is very little doubt that the failure of the Easter invasion made
the Paris Peace Agreement possible. Stymied in the guerrilla war earlier, Hanoi was convinced by the huge costs of the conventional invasion that it could not militarily defeat the combination of Nguyen Van
Thieu and a Vietnamese military machine backed up by American
firepower.

The Paris Peace Agreement

It certainly took the Democratic Republic of Viet Nam some time to
reach this conclusion. The agreement earlier to sit down with Lyndon
Johnson on April 1, 1968, was part of its bellicose policy of fighting
while negotiating. Three principles undergirded this strategy. First, according to the tradition of determination to fight and win, as at Dienbienphu, key points were to be scored on the battlefield. Second, the
DRV was committed to protracted struggle in both spheres. At the conference table it would hold out for as many American concessions as

61. *Ibid.*, 198–200.
62. *Ibid.*, 199; JUSPAO, *VNDRN*, No. 106–III, p. v.

possible while at the same time gradually driving a wedge between the Government of Viet Nam and the United States. Third, basic DRV politburo decisions had to be insulated from the pressures of Soviet and Chinese allies.[63]

About the only accomplishment at the Paris peace talks in the closing days of the Johnson administration was an agreement on the size and shape of the table and the composition of the two delegations. Despite American and South Vietnamese reluctance to accord any status to the Provisional Revolutionary Government of the South, it was finally accepted as a participant in the talks. Nixon came to the White House in January, 1969, convinced that real progress could only be made in secret negotiations.

While the public talks went on interminably, Nixon's national security adviser, Henry Kissinger, picked his own staff and his own strategy for the secret talks. His objectives were to bring about a cease-fire to extricate the United States from Viet Nam and to secure the release of American prisoners of war as well as to guarantee the political independence of South Viet Nam from Hanoi. His approach used the carrot of gradual concessions and the stick of threatening the destruction of North Viet Nam. The first signal of destruction was Operation MENU. On August 4, 1969, the first secret session was held in a meeting arranged by the Frenchman Jean Sainteny (the same man who tried to negotiate Franco–Viet Minh differences in December, 1946) between Kissinger and Xuan Thuy, head of the DRV peace talks delegation. Soon Kissinger began meeting with DRV politburo member Le Duc Tho. Until October, 1972, they held six series of talks that fell into the pattern of a marathon of discussions, an abrupt termination, a long hiatus, and a sudden resumption. The pattern was closely tied to developments in South Viet Nam. For example, following the debacle of Lam Son 719 the talks resumed in the spring of 1971 and discussions for the first time centered on concrete substantive proposals, but the talks broke off abruptly in August when the United States refused to pressure Thieu out of the presidential elections. Throughout these talks, the chief stumbling block, from an American viewpoint, was the DRV insistence that Thieu must resign before an agreement could be signed.[64]

The big break came on September 26, 1972, eleven days after the

63. Goodman, *The Lost Peace*, 11–12.
64. *Ibid.*, 91–122.

recapture of Quang Tri, when Le Duc Tho dropped his demand for Thieu's resignation. On October 8 Kissinger received a draft agreement from Le Duc Tho containing the further Hanoi concession that the proposed National Council of Reconciliation and Concord was to be defined as an administrative structure, not as a coalition government. Kissinger was euphoric, but snags developed. When Thieu was finally briefed on the terms of the draft, he could not be budged from an insistence on a total withdrawal of North Vietnamese troops. In turn, Hanoi became irritated because of previous American assurances that there would be no problem in gaining Saigon's acceptance. Nevertheless, in perhaps the most celebrated gaffe of his career, Kissinger went on television October 26 to announce that "peace is at hand."[65]

From then until December 18, there followed an intensive effort to get the negotiations back on track. It is also likely, however, that the United States was in no hurry to sign an agreement until Operation ENHANCE PLUS was completed. In six weeks in November and December the Pentagon delivered nearly $2 billion in heavy military equipment, including seventy tanks, hundreds of armored personnel carriers, artillery pieces, and six hundred helicopters and jet fighters (enough to make the Viet Nam Air Force the fourth largest air force in the world). This obviously made it difficult for Thieu to continue to balk at the agreement. It also provided Saigon with some insurance in the event of a congressional curtailment of aid in 1974 and 1975. Secret letters from Nixon to Thieu on November 14 and January 5 containing guarantees of swift American retaliation in the event Hanoi violated the agreement were enough to obtain Thieu's compliance.[66]

By mid-December, however, the negotiations had reached a stalemate. On December 11 the North Vietnamese began taking back earlier concessions. Once again, they chose to link the release of American prisoners with that of civilian detainees in the South. Three days later the negotiators were deadlocked on previously resolved substantive questions like the status of the Provisional Revolutionary Government, its zones of control, and the nature of the National Council of Reconcilia-

65. D. Gareth Porter, *A Peace Denied: The United States, Vietnam and the Paris Agreement* (Bloomington, Ind., 1975), 121–22, 126, 132.

66. Goodman, *The Lost Peace*, 146; Porter, *A Peace Denied*, 144; Van Tien Dung, *Our Great Spring Victory*, 8; Lewy, *America in Vietnam*, 202–203.

tion and Concord. On December 15 Nixon threatened to bomb North
Viet Nam within seventy-two hours if the deadlock were not broken.[67]

He was true to his word. From December 18 to 30, Nixon unleashed
the "Christmas bombing" on Hanoi and Haiphong. Known also as
LINEBACKER II, it was designed to paralyze the North Vietnamese economy and bring the agreement to a conclusion. In twelve days of bombing, 2,000 sorties were flown, 720 by B-52 bombers hitting targets in
the heart of both cities. The North Vietnamese fired nearly all their
surface-to-air missiles and brought down twenty-six planes, including
fifteen B-52s. In the last few days of the attacks, however, the North
Vietnamese were utterly defenseless. The damage was unprecedented.
Vast stocks of military supplies and four power plants were destroyed,
the entire country's railroad system was crippled, and ten airfields were
rendered inoperable. Despite the bitter public outcry over the bombing,
civilian casualties were quite low. Estimates ranged from 1,300 to 4,000
people killed.[68]

Since the bombing, a bitter controversy has swirled around its efficacy in securing the Paris Peace Agreement. In his analysis of the negotiations, Gareth Porter views the Christmas bombing as a great American failure revealing Nixon's exhaustion and forcing him ultimately to
return to Hanoi's October draft proposals. This is hotly disputed by others. Sir Robert Thompson avers that Hanoi was brought to its knees by
the bombing and would have agreed to any terms. Alan Dawson has the
intriguing opinion that had the bombing continued, Hanoi would have
accepted a demand for surrender. More soberly, Allan Goodman simply
concludes that the bombing was instrumental in achieving the final
agreement.[69]

Ironically, Porter's analysis only confirms Goodman's point. Porter
acknowledges a substantive stalemate in mid-December, and his narrative of the resumed negotiations on January 8 depicts two sides
finally making the many necessary compromises for an agreement.

67. Porter, *A Peace Denied*, 154–56.
68. Robert N. Ginsburgh, "Strategy and Air Power: The Lessons of Southeast
Asia," *Strategic Review*, II (Summer, 1973), 23; Goodman, *The Lost Peace*, 161. For
different opinions regarding the number of casualties, see Sharp, *Strategy for Defeat*,
254; Porter, *A Peace Denied*, 160.
69. Porter, *A Peace Denied*, 136–37, 156–65; Sharp, *Strategy for Defeat*, 255;
Alan Dawson, *55 Days: The Fall of South Viet Nam* (Englewood Cliffs, N.J., 1977),
123; Goodman, *The Lost Peace*, 160–64.

As the intensity of the last-minute bargaining in the SALT II agreement demonstrates, it is at the end of a negotiation that feelings become most heated and agreements can be easily derailed by seemingly inconsequential details. Without the Christmas bombing, the only agreement signed would have been completely on Hanoi's terms, as embodied in its December demands. The final compromise came from the bombing.[70]

The agreement was signed in Paris on January 28, 1973. Its essential provisions were: an immediate cease-fire, release of all prisoners as well as a complete withdrawal of the remaining American troops within sixty days, the establishment of a National Council of Reconciliation and Concord to set up elections for a new government in the South, a commitment to reunification, the establishment of an International Commission of Control and Supervision, one-for-one replacement of military equipment and supplies, and a promise from the United States to assist in the reconstruction of North Viet Nam. In a significant omission, the 145,000 North Vietnamese troops in the South (300,000 according to Saigon sources) were allowed to remain. Yet the Communist were not much of a threat by the time of the agreement. The Viet Cong had been decimated and the "great Socialist rear" in the North was in shambles. The party admits that in 1973, gross national income was less than in 1965, and labor productivity was one-third lower. Even *Nhan Dan*, the official Hanoi newspaper, conceded that in the South the Government of Viet Nam was "comparatively more stable and better organized from the central to the village and hamlet levels than the army and government which existed at the beginning of the Diem period."[71]

On the verge of collapse in 1965, when the United States intervened with its own combat troops, South Viet Nam found the tide in 1973 decidedly in its favor for the next stage, the struggle for the political loyalty of its people. A question, however, hung heavily in the air: Was Thieu, who had always relied on a military approach tied to American aid, ready for battle on this new political ground?

70. Porter, *A Peace Denied*, 167–73.
71. *An Outline History of the Viet Nam Workers' Party*, 174; JUSPAO, *VNDRN*, No. 113, p. iii.

Liberation

Descending from a position of considerable strength to total defeat in slightly more than two years, the obvious answer is no. But the story of Saigon's fall—or liberation—is a saga interwoven with several strands.

To begin, the Paris Peace Agreement had been concluded with a great deal of hypocrisy and forced marriages of convenience. The Americans, though concerned that Saigon be given a "decent interval," basically wanted out; the South Vietnamese had been rather unwillingly forced into the agreement; and the Communists, who needed a respite, wanted to grant the Americans their wish to get out so that the struggle could be resumed without their interference. From the beginning, the pact was violated. The fighting never stopped. In fact, the Communists appeared to seize upon the termination of American bombing as a golden opportunity to run their own version of ENHANCE PLUS. The Ho Chi Minh Trail was moved eastward inside the Vietnamese border and literally converted into a highway. According to Douglas Pike, in 1973 North Vietnamese troops in the South increased to 170,000, the number of tanks grew from 100 to 600, large artillery pieces tripled in number, and 12 airfields were built in Communist-controlled territory, 10 of them defended by surface-to-air missiles.[72]

Such increases hardly fell under the agreement of one-for-one replacement. On March 15 Nixon warned the Democratic Republic of Viet Nam against further violations, a warning he repeated March 29 on the occasion of the final American troop withdrawal. Lewy reports that by mid-April Nixon had reached the decision to unleash the B-52 bombers again, when he learned that John Dean had talked to Watergate prosecutors and linked the break-in directly to the president. The project was cancelled.[73]

Thus, the first card to fall from Thieu's apparently strong deck was his support from Nixon. Despite his letters of support to Thieu, Nixon could no longer deliver. By June, Nixon's vulnerability on Viet Nam had reached Congress. On June 30, Congress voted to cut off funds for all American military operations in Indochina after August 15, effectively

72. Pike, *History of Vietnamese Communism*, 164.
73. Lewy, *America in Vietnam*, 203–204.

ending the ongoing bombing in Cambodia. A second blow fell on November 7, 1973, in the War Powers Resolution, which required congressional approval for overseas troop deployments in excess of thirty days.

More than Watergate was involved in the congressional rancor toward Thieu. Beyond their animus toward Nixon and everything associated with him, many congressmen did not like what Thieu was doing. No doubt echoing the sentiments of these congressmen, Richard Falk dismissed Hanoi's violations of the agreement through its troop and supply buildups as negated by Saigon's failure to cooperate in carrying out the political provisions of the peace agreement. Furthermore, Thieu continued to display a penchant for a military approach rather than a political one. In the first eighteen months after the cease-fire, he claimed to have brought an additional one thousand hamlets under Government of Viet Nam control. While even the Communists conceded GVN gains, those gains had the effect of tying too many troops down in static defense as well as giving congressmen the image of Thieu as an aggressor. His attempts, politically, to expand his New Democracy party to the "rice roots" were phlegmatic. He displayed considerable energy, though, in political repression: breaking up Buddhist and student protests, outlawing opposition parties, imposing censorship, and harassing the Catholic Anti-Corruption League.[74] It was reminiscent of the last days of the Diem regime.

The effect of all this was a cut in aid to South Viet Nam. For fiscal year 1973 Congress voted $2.2 billion in aid. In 1974 this was cut to $900 million and in 1975 to $700 million. Communist aid to North Viet Nam remained relatively constant at $300 million in 1973 and $400 million in 1974, although China's claim of having provided $10 billion in aid to North Viet Nam over the course of the war suggests that these figures might be understated.

The withdrawal of American troops and the quadrupling of oil prices in October, 1973, dealt further blows to the South Vietnamese economy. From 1971 to 1974 prices on all items rose 330 percent. In 1974 alone basic commodity prices rose 100 percent, while an infantryman's salary only rose 25 percent. The inflationary economy and aid cutbacks had a predictable effect on ARVN morale, which by 1974 *was* a serious prob-

74. Richard A. Falk, "Vietnam: The Final Deceptions," *Nation*, May 17, 1975, p. 583; Goodman, *The Lost Peace*, 169.

lem. A Defense Attaché Office study showed that an ARVN soldier's pay was only one-third of that required to support an average family. Of Thieu's total armed force of over one million men, 100,000 were "flower soldiers," who paid their commanders to let them take civilian jobs. In Military Region 4 alone, 24,000 were "ghost soldiers" (who paid others to serve for them). In 1971 the armed forces lost 140,000 men to desertion. In 1974 they lost 240,000.[75]

Meanwhile in the field, the entire American-devised system of firepower superiority and maneuverability had broken down under the aid cutbacks, supply bottlenecks, and Vietnamese inability to keep sophisticated equipment functioning. At any one time, more than half the helicopters and planes were grounded with maintenance problems. South Vietnamese jet fighters were often forced to drop their ordnance at heights above ten thousand feet. From this altitude the bombing was so scattershot that it was virtually useless as support to ground troops. Tanks no longer had the gasoline for field operations that they once had. With respect to ammunition, in 1972 the ARVN expended 66,500 tons of it per month. From July, 1974, to March, 1975, the average was down to 18,000 tons a month. Frank Snepp, however, reveals that a Pentagon logistics team conducted a survey in late 1974 to ascertain ARVN ammunition supplies. The team uncovered many untapped stocks and concluded that there was enough ammunition to last until the end of 1975 at an 18,000-ton monthly rate of use, and an adequate supply until August at the 1972 rate. Nevertheless, it would have served Thieu well if he had husbanded his military resources by expending greater energies in the political sphere.[76]

Thieu, however, was not alone in spurning a political approach; Hanoi, too, embarked on a decidedly military course. Van Tien Dung, commander of Communist forces in the South, admits that a huge buildup was begun in October, 1973. By the fall of 1974, total Communist troop strength stood at 285,000. Despite ARVN's numerical superiority, nearly half its numbers were committed to static defense, while only 10 percent of the North Vietnamese troops were similarly tied

75. Falk, "Vietnam: The Final Deceptions," 583; Lewy, *America in Vietnam*, 209–10; Snepp, *Decent Interval*, 116; Woodside, *Community and Revolution in Modern Vietnam*, 302–303.

76. Lewy, *America in Vietnam*, 208; Snepp, *Decent Interval*, 145–46.

down. Of greater significance was the fact that Communist firepower had drawn even with that of the South Vietnamese. In March, 1974, Hanoi decided to take the initiative in the South, and, beginning in the summer, it made gains across the country as ARVN reactions became increasingly passive. The results in the field were encouraging, and in October the army's General Staff presented the politburo and Central Military Committee a plan for an all-out offensive to be started in the Central Highlands. The one factor causing hesitation was a possible American reaction. When the probe and capture of Phuoc Long Province in December elicited no American response, the politburo decided, in its meetings from December 18 to January 8, on a two-year strategic plan. Large, widespread attacks in 1975 would pave the way for another general offensive and uprising in 1976.[77]

At the same time on January 7, the Ford administration sent to Congress a supplemental request for $300 million in military aid to Saigon. Before Congress acted, the Communists struck on March 10 at Ban Me Thuot, the unofficial capital city of the *montagnards* in the Central Highlands. Enjoying a decisive local superiority in numbers, artillery, and armor, they had chosen their target well. The next day Ban Me Thuot fell and the United States House of Representatives rejected the administration's supplemental request. Three days later Thieu convened a fateful meeting of his generals at Nha Trang in which he ordered the recapture of Ban Me Thuot and a withdrawal from Pleiku and Kontum, two other provincial capitals in the Central Highlands. Ban Me Thuot was not recaptured and the withdrawals from the two Central Highland capitals on March 18 turned into a rout that proved irreversible. Thieu compounded this blunder by ordering the withdrawal of the 1st Airborne Division from Hue to Saigon, over the strenuous objections of General Truong, the military region commander. Bereft of this division, the local balance shifted decisively to the Communists. On March 28 Hue fell, and two days later Danang collapsed under the weight of hordes of panic-stricken soldiers and civilians.[78]

Determined not to give Saigon any chance to regroup its forces as they had in 1972, members of the politburo met again on March 25 and

77. Van Tien Dung, *Our Great Spring Victory*, 13, 16–20; Lewy, *America in Vietnam*, 210–11.
78. Lewy, *America in Vietnam*, 211, 13.

resolved to liberate Saigon within two months. On April 8 politburo member Le Duc Tho went south to convey the decision to COSVN and established a forward headquarters to effect the final liberation. Fifty-eight thousand fresh North Vietnamese troops poured into South Viet Nam in the final battles. It is noteworthy that indigenous Viet Cong participation, both in the battles and in the decision making, was virtually nonexistent. At the same time, from March 30 to April 7, the Pentagon's chairman of the Joint Chiefs of Staff, General Fred Weyand (a hero of the Tet offensive and General Creighton W. Abrams' successor as head of the Military Assistance Command, Vietnam), was in Saigon to develop a plan for the Government of Viet Nam's survival. He returned to Washington with a request for $722 million to reoutfit four divisions needed to hold a line at the border of Military Region 3, just 75 miles northeast of Saigon. The request provoked such an intense debate on Capitol Hill that no action was taken.[79]

Meanwhile events marched on in Viet Nam to their by now inevitable conclusion. By April 3 North Vietnamese forces had crossed the border of Military Region 3. Between the invading forces and Saigon lay the 25,000 men of the ARVN 18th Division at Xuan Loc. For eleven days they put up a very stubborn defense, but on April 21 the town fell. Thieu resigned and fled the country the same day. A former civilian premier, Tran Van Huong, was given the reins of government by the National Assembly. He faced an encircling army of 120,000 men with a dispirited garrison of 30,000. He could only lament the lack of American aid, saying that it had made the difference in 1968 and 1972, and could once more in 1975. It was not to be. He resigned, and achieving the goal he had sought for so long, Duong Van Minh became president on April 28. Two days later he surrendered the Government of Viet Nam to the Communists.

In these last two days the American ambassador, Graham Martin, finally yielded to the inevitable and agreed to the final evacuation of Americans and some of their employees in Operation FREQUENT WIND. Seven thousand people were lifted out in just over 24 hours. All told, 130,000 escaped in the last month before the Communist takeover. Mil-

79. Van Tien Dung, *Our Great Spring Victory*, 120, 152; Lewy, *America in Vietnam*, 213; Tiziano Terzani, *Giai Phong! The Fall and Liberation of Saigon*, trans. John Shepley (New York, 1975), 103; Snepp, *Decent Interval*, 306–307, 430.

itary booty left behind by the departing Americans and the decimated ARVN was enough to field an entire army. The value of the equipment was put at $5 billion and included 550 tanks, 1,300 artillery pieces, 73 jet fighters, and 1.6 million M-16 rifles.[80]

After a thirty-five-year struggle for power, the Communists, in a modern version of the march south, had finally taken possession of their country after fighting the French, the Americans, and their fellow countrymen. The final prize, Saigon, was renamed Ho Chi Minh City in honor of the architect of this triumph. Yet this was not the triumph of a balanced political and military revolution like the August Revolution or the subsequent Resistance War against the French. Such an attempt had perished in the rubble of the Tet offensive. Saigon fell to the conquering invasion of a conventional army.

At the heart of the war in Viet Nam lay the quest for legitimacy between two competing social orders. On both sides, Communist and nationalist, the combatants had no doubt of their national identity as Vietnamese. What was disputed was the very nature of authority for the nation, a classic crisis of legitimacy. The origins of this dispute date back at least to the French defeat, but can be dated earlier to the rise of the Communist party, or even to the impact of the French and the early resistance to them. However, as Jerry Silverman contends, at the time of the French defeat a tension existed between two points of view within the Vietnamese elite. Traditionalists viewed the Viet Minh victory as a signal to return to traditional values and structures, but the modernists saw it as an opportunity for Viet Nam to embark on a program of rapid development and modernization. The dilemma confronting the traditionalists was that the traditional hierarchical relationship of patron and client, all the way down to the landholder and his landless laborers, had been too badly shattered to be revived. The patron at all levels was simply not strong enough to do what he was supposed to do—provide security.[81]

Subsequent governments of South Viet Nam could not decide which of these two approaches to follow. The result was a sense of drift similar

80. Snepp, *Decent Interval*, 563, 567.
81. Jerry Mark Silverman, "Local Government and National Integration in South Viet Nam," *Pacific Affairs*, XLVII (Fall, 1974), 307–308.

to that besetting Tu Duc's court in the face of the threat from the French. There was no such drift in the Indochinese Communist party. It turned its back on the traditional order in recruiting its leaders, knowing full well that the path to modernity involved "critical changes in legitimacy from transcendental to immanent sources."[82] Thus, the Communists unveiled Marxism as a new secular and ideological icon to replace the traditional Confucian virtues and social order. Yet the prime constituency for the revolution was the peasantry, which for all the blows rained on the authority of the royal court, still adhered to traditional concepts. This required that the Communist revolution be translated into Vietnamese terms by the age-old formula of the Mandate of Heaven.

The first premise or term was for an orderly, legitimate succession embodied in the words *hoang de* (emperor). Care, therefore, was taken to have Bao Dai formally and publicly abdicate in the August revolution as well as to have Communist rule ratified through the decision-by-consensus tradition of Vietnamese villagers during the 1946 national elections. This tradition does not encourage open competition between parties for votes because of the risk of losing face. Instead, the competition is customarily concluded behind the scenes before the public consensus ratifies the position of the victor. Nearly unanimous votes, then, are entirely in keeping with this tradition. In addition to the 1946 elections, other modern examples of elections by consensus are the Diem–Bao Dai referendum and the 1971 presidential elections. Among the Vietnamese elite, this practice may be acceptable to the traditionalist, but not to the non-Marxist modernist.

In the Confucian court legitimacy was governed by hierarchical social principles; in the Communist politburo it was governed by adherence to international Communist orthodoxy. The split between the Chinese and the Russians was troublesome to the Vietnamese because (perhaps with their Confucian tradition) it shattered the unity of this orthodoxy; and throughout the war they always took great pains to pay tribute to both revolutions.

A recognized part of the Confucian order was the right of revolution when an emperor had lost the Mandate of Heaven. To gain the mandate

82. Leonard Binder, "Crises of Political Development," in Binder, *et al.*, *Crises and Sequences of Political Development*, (Princeton, 1971), 53.

for themselves, the revolutionaries had to show all the signs of their special mission, and the foremost sign was the ease and fluidity of success. As John McAlister and Paul Mus put it, "The revolution must succeed in everything as if miraculously."[83] With only five thousand armed men, the August revolution appeared to fit this description well. Further, it was not difficult to describe in similar terms the final defeat of the French, the survival of the American bombing campaign, and the ability to continue fighting in the face of a half-million GI's.

The idea of the king as protector (*vua*) was the second term and premise for a Vietnamese Mandate of Heaven. Part of the obligation of protection was to Vietnamize the external source of legitimacy. The August revolution itself is always offered by Vietnamese Communists as a unique Vietnamese contribution to the Socialist revolutionary lexicon. Even on a more theoretical plane, during the American involvement, Le Duan, the party secretary, spoke of the Vietnamese revolution as distinctively embodying three revolutions—in production relations, in culture and ideology, and in technology—with a clear implication that this was a Vietnamese refinement of general Marxist revolutionary theory.[84]

Whatever the cultural mediation, the king was supposed to be close to the people and their concerns. Hence, while *hoang de* was a borrowed Chinese word, *vua* was specially Vietnamese. A prime concern was always the fear of domination by powerful foreign states. Thus, the Viet Minh secured "national salvation" for the people from the French, and the Viet Cong were protecting this hard-won national independence from the American "imperialists." While the Communists had to rely heavily on foreign help themselves, they successfully avoided the image of hapless dependence that adhered to every Saigon regime. For one thing, Ho Chi Minh was a genuine national hero who, despite his Marxism, remained a true Vietnamese figure. He was affectionately addressed as "Uncle," never as "Comrade." Yet the king still had to guarantee physical protection. In this, at least during the American war, the Communists were less successful. The creation of an elaborate organizational network of political links and associations was only partially successful as a substitute.

83. John T. McAlister and Paul Mus, *The Vietnamese and Their Revolution* (New York, 1970), 65.
84. The analysis of these two terms comes from Alexander B. Woodside, *Vietnam and the Chinese Model*, 10; JUSPAO, *VNDRN*, Supplement to No. 77, pp. 17–19.

A regime's writ of legitimacy is always sealed by its dispensation of justice, however the word is culturally defined. In Viet Nam justice was operationalized through land reform. Thus, it is no accident that the golden age occurred in the reign of Le Thanh Tong, whose land reforms were the most extensive. The Communists have, with a varying degree of emphasis, pursued a land-to-the-tiller policy, though always with the proviso that their grants of land were contingent on support to the party. It was not until the March, 1970, land reform bill that Saigon developed an effective program of its own that met the claims of this traditional standard of justice.[85]

In the struggle for legitimacy, the Communists were not invulnerable. Although they were careful to follow traditional formulas in their path to power, the order they sought to establish was a modern, Socialist one inimical to traditional leadership groups. This obviously guaranteed some opposition. Paradoxically, as avowed modernists, the Communists were not as successful in winning over nonbelievers who also wanted to modernize Viet Nam. Urban intellectuals, for all their cynicism toward the Saigon regime, never flocked to the NLF banner.[86]

Saigon, for its part, did take some steps in establishing a writ of legitimacy. The Constituent Assembly elections of 1966 and the presidential elections of 1967 did appeal to modernists by at least going further than Hanoi in establishing legitimate constitutional government. Many legislators in the National Assembly did see themselves as modern ombudsmen and developed links with the constituents. Although the 1971 presidential election was a setback, it was no worse than any election in Hanoi.[87]

The crux of the South Vietnamese government's difficulty in establishing its legitimacy, however, was the common dilemma facing the fledgling governments of all developing states—its very weakness. It was caught in a vicious cycle in which the regime lacked the political support and participation of the citizenry in its system—support necessary to encourage bureaucratic services dynamic enough to, in turn,

85. Race, *War Comes to Long An*, 174.
86. Woodside, *Community and Revolution in Modern Vietnam*, 291.
87. Milton I. Sacks, "Restructuring Government in South Vietnam," *Asian Survey*, VII (August, 1967), 526; Allan E. Goodman, "Conflict and Accommodation Within Legislative Elite in South Vietnam," *Pacific Affairs*, XLIV (Summer, 1971), 211–28.

encourage the participation of its citizens. For example, Saigon, teeming with a myriad of needs and social problems among its three million people, had a city budget equivalent to that of Lynchburg, Virginia. What services the GVN was able to perform were mainly owing to American aid. The clear reflection of this dilemma is that in 1970 only 1 percent of the adult South Vietnamese populace belonged to any political group on the government side. At the same time, Pike admits that Communist party membership in the South may have been as high as 350,000 to 500,000.[88]

What is perhaps most striking about this orphan war that no one wanted is, in a struggle for national legitimacy in Viet Nam, how much of the burden was carried by the United States. The creation of a non-Communist portion of Viet Nam at the Geneva accords in 1954 was a tribute to French diplomacy. Its preservation for nearly twenty-one years was the gradually shouldered burden of the United States. Diem's rise to power would not have been possible without the Americans, nor would the maintenance of all the subsequent Saigon regimes. That Nguyen Van Thieu could not survive without the Americans was made starkly clear in the two painful years after the 1973 peace agreement. In playing Atlas, the United States was struggling to stand with its burden against the flow of a Communist historical tide. Yet during this period of artificial propping, some strides were made to reverse this tide. A measure of political stability was achieved, a major land reform program was enacted, fair elections were held, and Communist military forces were kept at bay. In fact, the effort made so much of an impact that, even as the American Atlas grew tired and finally shrugged off the burden, the Communists, in achieving their victory, were forced to abandon the high road of their lofty revolutionary ideals and strategy of people's war, and settle for the far less ideologically salutary victory of a simple military seizure of power. Any victory is savory at first, but that of the Communists has left the bitter aftertaste of unresolved questions of national and revolutionary legitimacy.

88. Goodman, "South Vietnam: Neither War nor Peace," 113; Pike, *History of Vietnamese Communism, 1925–1976,* 147; FitzGerald, *Fire in the Lake,* 621.

PART II

Revolutionary Legitimacy

CHAPTER THREE

The Odyssey of
Communism to Asia
and Viet Nam

For the second audience, the global one, the war in Viet Nam represented a struggle between two opposing world views or paradigms, the liberalism of the Western democracies and the Marxism of the Communist states. Essentially, according to George Sabine, the liberal political thought of the West developed as an elaboration of two fundamental social or moral ideas: "that politics is distinctively an art of reaching non-coercive adjustments between antagonistic interests, and that democratic procedures are the only effective ways for making such adjustments."[1] This faith in democratic procedures is intended not only for national governments but also as an underpinning for the international order. The League of Nations, the United Nations, World Court, the World Bank, and other international institutions organized under Western initiative stand as concrete expressions of this faith.

The faith of the Communists is of a different order. It stems from the fundamental Marxist tenet that the motive force of history lies in the antagonism between social classes and that these antagonisms can only be resolved through revolution. Hence, basic social change both within countries and in the international system as a whole can come

1. George H. Sabine, *A History of Political Theory* (3rd ed.; New York, 1961), 755.

about only through social violence. Communism, though totally secular in its outlook, can be compared to an organized and institutionalized religion. It has answers for all of life's questions, though it provides a path for human realization in the here and now rather than in the hereafter. Similar to any developed religious organization, communism has its sects, the Eurocommunists, the Soviet Russians, and the Chinese Maoists and post-Maoists being the most prominent political manifestations today. Whatever their differences, the goal of all Communists is the transformation of human society starting from the initial base of the seizure of political power. Pursuant to this goal, it provides a complete package of political action: an ideology to expose the "objective reality" that needs to be changed as well as an identification of the principal target for elimination, and an organized, disciplined political party to map and carry out the correct strategy for seizing power.

The world's first Communist state emerged in Russia in 1917, and the Communists were eager to spread the success of their October revolution to western Europe. But in the interwar period the threat never materialized, as Communist take-over attempts in the rest of Europe proved amateurish. The Russians became preoccupied with internal problems, and the looming menace of fascism quickly overshadowed the danger of communism. With the defeat of fascism in World War II, however, and the emergence of a score of Communist states in its aftermath, the threat, or perceived threat, of communism became a central feature in the foreign policies of the Western democracies. The political conflict that developed was called the "cold war" and followed along two tracks. One was a series of direct confrontations and disputes between the Soviet Union and the Western powers, and the other was a competition for the "hearts and minds" of the emerging, underdeveloped countries of the Third World. As Robert Tucker points out, contrary to the expectations of Marx and Engels, communism succeeded in a setting of economic underdevelopment rather than of ripe capitalism, and it thus became a competing model for, and revolution of, modernization.[2]

In this second track, one of the most potent Communist strategies for the seizure of political power was the people's war of national liberation that Mao Tse-tung practiced and preached in China in the Communist

2. Robert C. Tucker, *The Marxian Revolutionary Idea* (New York, 1969), 137–38.

party's victory in 1949 over the Kuomintang (Nationalist) party. The Vietnamese followed essentially the same strategy in their Resistance War against the French from 1946 to 1954 and in their war against the Americans from 1960 to 1975. Thus, the Vietnamese Communists, and others who support them, have heralded their victory in 1975 over the South Vietnamese government and the Americans as a triumph of people's war and a vindication and commendation of this strategy to other countries toiling under the oppression of American neocolonialism. Throughout the war Vietnamese Communist leaders were sensitive to and proud of their movement's place in history, which, in their view, represented an important contribution to the worldwide advance of socialism. The military leader Vo Nguyen Giap said during the war that their struggle was "on the frontline of the national liberation movement." The Communist party secretary Le Duan seconded this by describing the war as the "spearhead of the world revolutionary tide." Finally, Tran Van Dinh, in his introduction to a selection of Le Duan's writings, intoned, "The Vietnamese Revolution . . . can stand by itself as one of the most important contributions to human liberation in both theory and practice."[3]

Despite these ringing certitudes, the crucial question remains: was the Vietnamese victory in 1975 what the Vietnamese claimed it was, a triumph of a Marxist, people's war of national liberation? Underlying this question is the issue of the legitimacy of the Communist take-over of the South. Legitimacy invests a seizure of power with authority accepted by the society, and although it is usually the legitimacy of the incumbent regime that is most closely scrutinized, a revolutionary movement's legitimacy is also important, and it depends on a coherent, consistent, and functioning ideology. In short, laying aside the question of legitimacy in terms of a country's political culture, to be legitimate on its own terms, a revolutionary movement must be true to its own ideology. Thus, how it seizes power is as much a part of its legitimacy as the goal of the revolution itself.

The definition of people's war, then, is crucial to assessing whether or not the Vietnamese triumph in 1975 was revolutionarily legitimate in

3. Russell Stetler (ed.), *The Military Art of People's War: Selected Writings of General Vo Nguyen Giap* (New York, 1970), 255–56; JUSPAO, *VNDRN*, No. 9, p. 15; Tran Van Dinh (ed.), *This Nation and Socialism Are One: Selected Writings of Le Duan* (Chicago, 1976), xviii.

Viet Nam and generally relevant for further applications of the Communist doctrine of people's war. If so, then it ranks as an important example of the efficacy of people's war and can serve as a lesson for revolutionary comrades elsewhere. If not, then the significance of the doctrine of people's war to Viet Nam is merely as a mask disguising a raw bid for power, devoid of revolutionary legitimacy.

In setting forth definitions of Communist concepts or doctrines, two points need to be stressed. First, any term whose definition stems from an interrelationship of theory and practice must be flexible. Communism and its strategy of people's war are living, dynamic, and continually evolving both in response to changing situations and to the changing thinking of Communist leaders and theoreticians. In fact, flexibility has been a key to communism's survival and success as a viable ideology, and such Communist leaders as Marx, Lenin, Mao Tse-tung, and Ho Chi Minh have all placed great stress on it. As a result, changes in communism over the years have been major. Indeed, some have been so great that questions have been raised as to whether some doctrinal applications can still be considered Communist. For example, can a revolution that purports to be a Marxist revolution of the proletariat but in fact depends almost exclusively on the exploitation of rural and peasant unrest be allowed under the rubric of communism, or should it be called something else? The answer to this question is best left to the theorists, but it illustrates the point that despite the need to be flexible in defining Communist concepts and doctrines, there are definitional breaking points with these terms. Beyond them, the definitions become involved in so many contradictions that they become meaningless.

An excellent case in point is the Communist use of the term *democracy*. According to the Western notion, democracy is a system of government whereby ordinary citizens affect the making of policy through such means as free and competitive elections. Lenin, however, variously called it equality, the abolition of class domination, and the accurate calculation of the middle position between running ahead of the people and lagging behind. Yet in his principle of democratic centralism, Lenin does not allow the opinion of individual citizens to affect the making of policy. Thus, either the Communist meaning of democracy contradicts the Western term or Lenin's principle must be dropped from inclusion in the definition. As Sabine simply states, any form of government that does not grant its citizens a role in affecting national policy "has no claim to call itself democratic."[4]

Hence, for concepts and doctrines to have any meaning, and legitimacy to have any standard of measurement, a certain amount of definitional faithfulness is required. With the recognition that definitions of Communist concepts and doctrines must be flexible but fulfill certain minimal requirements, the central question may be rephrased as follows: was the Vietnamese Communist triumph of 1975 what the Communist leaders claimed it was, according to the terms and definitional requirements they themselves set forth?

People's war as a revolutionary strategy for seizing political power arose from a mutation of Communist ideology. It could not be propounded from an "orthodox" European Marxist base. It had to spring from a countrified Marxism, rather than from a revolution built on an urban proletariat. In a colonial or "semi-colonial" environment a revolution could be ripened by its strategists' tapping traditional rural and nascent nationalist sentiments. Tracing this doctrinal mutation provides the context from which the development and definition of the strategy of people's war can be explained—and judged.

When this mutation arrived in Viet Nam, it took root in one of the world's most remarkable Communist parties. The Indochinese Communist party was remarkable not only for its dedicated and generally harmonious leadership, but also, flowing from this, for its theoretical sophistication and the resilient adaptations of its theory in the long march to power. The rich history of the ICP forms an important background to answering the question of the revolutionary legitimacy of the Communist victory.

Mutation of Marxism to Asia

In the development of communism, it was Karl Marx and Friedrich Engels who set it in motion as a philosophy and political doctrine of revolution. It was Vladimir Lenin, however, who enunciated a concrete

4. Sabine, *A History of Political Theory*, 817, 865; Robert C. Tucker (ed.), *The Lenin Anthology* (New York, 1975), 14, 381–82.

Communist political strategy and acted on it to create the world's first Communist state. Lenin also provided a basis for extending the Communist revolution to the colonial countries of Asia. From this, Mao Tsetung articulated a formula (people's war) for actualizing the Communist revolution in Asian peasant societies. The Vietnamese took in all of this and adapted it to their setting, in a sense Vietnamizing communism.

In the *Communist Manifesto* (1848), which E. H. Carr described as the quintessence of Marxism, Marx distilled his philosophy of history to one operative principle: "The history of all hitherto existing society is the history of class struggles"—one class of producers against another. Their struggles are over political power, which Marx defines as "merely the organized power of one class for oppressing another." This dialectic of struggle between oppressed and oppressor social classes is an immutable, scientific law of history. The historical epoch of Marx's day was that of the bourgeoisie, who had just acted out their own revolution. In Marx's view the bourgeois revolution consisted in severing all feudal, patriarchal, and sentimental ties between men, leaving no other bond than naked self-interest and callous "cash payment." This had the distinctive effect of simplifying social antagonisms into those between two hostile classes, the bourgeoisie and the proletariat, and set the stage for the "inevitable" and final destruction of the bourgeoisie at the hands of the proletariat.[5]

Regarding the peasantry as a whole, Marx was ambivalent. On one hand, he held rural life in contempt, considering rural and underdeveloped countries as barbarian and urban countries as civilized. In the *Manifesto* he went so far as to thank the bourgeoisie for rescuing "a considerable part of the population from the idiocy of rural life." On the other hand, he was not blind to the revolutionary potential in rural life. Marx held that although the peasantry is politically inert, under proper direction, it can affect the struggle between the bourgeoisie and the proletariat. He proposed as early as 1850 an alliance between the working class and the peasantry, though the role of the peasantry was to be distinctly subordinate.[6]

This proposal of a worker-peasant alliance fit in with Marx's revolutionary strategy for a backward economy. In this strategy Marx recog-

5. Edward Hallett Carr, *Studies in Revolution* (London, 1950), 17; Karl Marx and Friedrich Engels, *The Communist Manifesto* (1848; rpr. New York, 1964), 57–62, 95.
6. Marx and Engels, *The Communist Manifesto*, 65.

nized that a distinction needed to be made between the appropriate revolutionary paths for ripened industrial economies like those of France
and England and for a relatively backward economy (like, Marx believed, Germany's!). Only in the former did he feel a proletarian revolution could succeed on its own. In backward economies, the Socialist
party must first cooperate with the middle-class revolutionists and then
turn against them once the bourgeois revolution succeeded and launch
the proletarian revolution. Since, in a backward economy, the majority
of the toiling masses were peasants, they were the critical factor, and
their discontent needed to be channeled into supporting the proletarian
minority.

Thus Marx provided the world with a philosophy that enshrined social conflict and set in motion a political doctrine of revolution. But
Marx wanted to be more than a philosopher. "The philosophers have
only *interpreted* the world . . . the point is to *change* it," he wrote.[7] Try
as he did, though, his own attempts at changing the world were not
terribly gratifying.

It was Vladimir Lenin who gave Marxism a functioning revolutionary strategy, both for Russia and the East. In fact, his contributions
were so extensive that his name was added to Marx's as a cotitle for
communism. As Tucker quips, Marxism-Leninism is "Marxism according to Lenin."[8] In making communism globally adoptable, Lenin combined a rigid orthodoxy in doctrine with great flexibility in practice.
This was certainly in keeping with the tradition of Marx, and Lenin's
elevation to coequal stature with Marx reflects the fact that Lenin's revolutionary strategy still serves as a bible of revolutionary instruction for
Communists.

As a practical strategist Lenin gave special emphasis to the crucial
factor of timing in a revolution. In "An Infantile Disorder" (1920), he
stated that a revolution should be launched only when a society reaches
a "revolutionary situation," which he defined as a time "when the
'lower classes' do not want the old way, and the 'upper classes' cannot
carry on in the old way."[9] This definition has been used as a signal for
revolution ever since.

7. Robert C. Tucker (ed.), *The Marx-Engels Reader* (New York, 1972), xxviii.
8. Tucker, *Lenin Anthology*, 461.
9. Vladimir Ilyich Lenin, *"Left-Wing" Communism: An Infantile Disorder* (New
York, 1934), 65.

Marx and Engels were ambivalent on whether Communists should form themselves into a party, and what this party should do if it were formed. Lenin gave the Communist party both its *raison d'être* and its mission. He organized his party around two principles: the party as the vanguard of the proletariat, and democratic centralism as its organizational system.

In his principle of the party as the revolutionary vanguard, Lenin broke with Marx's view that "the emancipation of the working class is the work of the working class itself." In his famous tract "What Is to be Done?" Lenin said that the difficulty with letting the proletariat develop the revolution by itself was that its efforts could produce only trade-union consciousness. The consciousness of socialism "has to be brought to them from without" by bourgeois intellectuals who, because they stand outside of the employer-worker relation, have superior knowledge of all classes and strata. In effect, Lenin's "revolution from without" revealed a lack of faith in Marx's historical determinism in that for the proletarian revolution to be fulfilled, history had to be helped along by these far-seeing bourgeois intellectuals, the core of the revolutionary leadership.[10]

This elite retains its power by the principle of democratic centralism, the distinctive feature of the Leninist party. Lenin devised it to meet the twin needs of outflanking the tsarist police by preserving the protective secrecy of the revolutionary core while at the same time trying to maximize the scope of the party's influence on the masses. Thus democratic centralism linked a secret, illegal leadership with a legal mass following based on a clear distinction between leadership cadres and the rank and file. It operated by a two-way flow of authorization, suggestions, and sometimes new leadership from below, and immediate policy and tactical direction from above. The interplay of this system gave rank-and-file members the *democratic* right to discuss policies prior to official party pronouncements; but once decisions were announced, *centralism* demanded that every party or government organ obey anybody superior to it in the chain of command. These two principles continue to shape Communist parties and governments today.[11]

10. Sabine, *A History of Political Theory*, 813–14; Tucker (ed.), *Lenin Anthology*, 24, 50.
11. Jeff Lustig, "On Organization: The Question of the Leninist Party," *Politics and Society*, VII, No. 1, 37–38; Tucker (ed.), *Lenin Anthology*, 69–78; Sabine, *A History of Political Theory*, 862.

Lenin's great achievement was to activate his theory that the Communist revolution must be carried out by a united front and that it must be preceded by a bourgeois democratic revolution. He also stressed that the proletarian revolution could only succeed in combination with a peasant war, but that the countryside must play the role of the subordinate "rear" and the cities that of the "front." The Russian Revolution was just that, a combination of strikes and demonstrations by the Moscow and Petrograd Soviets and land seizures and upheavals in the countryside, with the rural activities playing a necessary but decidedly secondary part. In short, Lenin did what he said he was going to do.[12]

Beyond making the Communist revolution come alive in Russia, Lenin provided the basis for its spread to Asia by his recognition of the importance of the peasantry and his famous contention that because imperialism was the highest stage and weakest link of capitalism, revolutions could begin in the colonies and eventually destroy the mother countries.

Regarding the peasantry, in his "Two Tactics of Social-Democracy in the Democratic Revolution" (1905), Lenin called for a temporary worker-peasant alliance to establish a "democratic dictatorship of the proletariat and peasantry."[13] Even though Lenin viewed the peasantry as the junior partner in the temporary alliance, his idea opened the door for Asian revolutionaries to build a Communist movement on a "temporary" peasant base. Few of them, however, did this initially. They had to discover the peasantry as the foundation for a strategy of people's war on their own.

While Lenin's essay, "Imperialism, the Highest Stage of Capitalism" (1916), was written mainly to explain why the European proletariat was showing no inclination to revolution, it had the effect, theoretically at least, of opening up the floodgates of revolution in Asia. Lenin's explanation was that the European proletariat was quiescent because it was sharing in the benefits of imperialism. By transferring the exploitation of capitalism to the colonies, however, the European capitalists were creating the conditions for revolution overseas. Hence, Lenin sought to make common cause with oppressed peoples in the colonies. In another break with Marx, he made this possible by redefining the proletariat to include the "oppressed nations" and "the working people of

12. Tucker, *The Marxian Revolutionary Idea*, 146–48.
13. Tucker (ed.), *Lenin Anthology*, 120, 135.

the colonial and semi-colonial countries," even though he realized this was not the proletariat created by the capitalist system. As Lenin conceded: "From the point of the *Communist Manifesto*, this is wrong. But the *Communist Manifesto* was written under completely different conditions; and from the point of view of the present political situation, this is correct."[14]

The vehicle Lenin created to spread the revolution was the Communist International (Comintern). He convened the first gathering in 1919, but it was in 1920 that rules for membership and a program were drafted. The goal of the Comintern was a World Soviet Republic, but in the meantime members were to follow the model and direction of the Russian party. In short, the Comintern was a forum for the extension of Soviet foreign policy.[15]

For the second Comintern Congress, Lenin prepared and delivered the speech, "Theses on the National and Colonial Question," which served as Comintern's political platform. While neither Marx nor Lenin ever wrote on Viet Nam, Lenin's "Theses" was the Communist writing most applicable to the situation in Viet Nam, and it was largely responsible for Ho Chi Minh's conversion to communism. Among other things, Lenin exhorted the Comintern to support all revolutionary groups in subject countries, even non-Communist groups; the formation of small Communist groups who could cooperate with non-Communist groups, but not lose their identity; the promotion of peasant movements against landlords; and, in return for the support of these groups, their profession of ultimate loyalty to the international working class. By including peasant movements in his list of approved revolutionary stratagems, as long as other toiling classes were brought in, Lenin, in effect, permitted the establishment of Communist parties in colonial and semicolonial countries, based on the peasantry. Two of Lenin's theses in particular were astute in easing the way for Asian Communists. One was that backward nations in a precapitalist stage of development do not have to go through the capitalist stage of development. This would allow the Communists to foment revolution immediately. The other acknowledged the deep roots of nationalistic feelings. Lenin advised Communists to exercise sensitivity in dealing with these feelings. In transla-

14. Sabine, *A History of Political Theory*, 837–41.
15. *Ibid.*, 858.

tion, this gave the Communists the freedom to appeal to and exploit nationalistic sentiments.[16]

Lenin carried communism a long way from the pens of Marx and Engels. He created a revolution and provided tools for others to spread his handiwork. In Asia, Communist parties and movements were not long in coming. Ho Chi Minh, in summing up the lessons he learned from Lenin, reveals them to be fundamental: the primacy of a Communist party, the worker-peasant alliance, the united front strategy, the need for revolutionary violence, and the linkage of nationalism with proletarian internationalism.[17]

Once Lenin had opened the floodgates for Marxist revolutions in Asia, Mao Tse-tung, taking basic Leninist concepts, provided the blueprint for the Sinification of Marxism and thereby made it relevant to other Asian countries. In Mao's rationale, the streak of flexibility, the hallmark of a successful Communist revolutionary, was clearly visible. He seized on the Marxist notion of general and particular truths and explained that Marxism was the general truth and Leninism the particular and relative truth and that one particular truth can be superseded by another without nullifying the general truth. What Mao was saying was that Leninism's general, Marxist character was relevant to China, but its particular, Russian character was not. Thus Mao sought to fashion a new particular form of communism suitable to the Chinese environment. Never a modest man, Mao felt this theoretical synthesis would represent a higher formulation of revolutionary theory than the works of Lenin himself. On the international plane, Mao's synthesis elevated the struggle against imperialism in the colonial periphery to a level of historical significance in its own right and not simply as a blow to be struck at the weakest link in the European imperialist system.[18]

Mao's continual one-upmanship did not endear him to the Kremlin. As a charter member at the Chinese Communist party's founding in 1921, though, he *was* excited by the struggle between the proletarians

16. Pike, *History of Vietnamese Communism,* 58; Vladimir Ilyich Lenin, *Selected Works in Three Volumes* (New York, 1967), III, 450; Second Congress of the Communist International, *National and Colonial Questions* (London, 1920), 6–7, 10–12.

17. "Learn from President Ho's Book, 'Forever Follow the Great Lenin's Road,'" *Hoc Tap,* IV (April, 1970), 76–81.

18. Raymond F. Wylie, "Mao Tse-tung, Ch'en Po-Ta and the 'Sinification of Marxism,' 1936–1938," *China Quarterly,* LXXIX (September, 1979), 454–56; Johnson, *Autopsy on People's War,* 13–14.

and the capitalists. In his early writings, however, Mao revealed a fundamental and overriding Chinese nationalism that propelled him into being an enthusiastic supporter of the Communist party–Kuomintang party alliance. But in 1927 the White Terror in Shanghai provided a sobering and maturing experience for the Chinese Communist party (CCP) in general and Mao in particular. At that time the CCP was following a Comintern-dictated strategy for urban struggle, when Chiang Kai-shek, the Kuomintang leader, turned on the Communists in Shanghai, slaughtered thousands, and drove them from the city. Unlike in Russia, simple urban insurrections were not enough for a revolution in China. Mao, for one, was never again willing to subordinate the interests of the CCP to the global demands of the Comintern.[19]

Despite the debacle at Shanghai, the Comintern persisted in pushing an urban strategy on the bleeding and disoriented remnants of the CCP. In 1925, Mao had conducted a rather thorough investigation of peasant conditions in his native Hunan Province. In his findings, published in 1927 as the *Hunan Report*, Mao made the timely proclamation of the revolutionary power of the peasantry. With the destruction of the Communist urban base, the party was faced with two stark choices: continued Leninist orthodoxy and defeat, or tactical mutation. While the party quarreled, Mao chose mutation, and in Kiangsi Province he built around the peasantry an organization that still called itself the party of the proletariat and played the role of Lenin's vanguard.[20]

Mao's shift to the peasantry, however, went beyond a mere tactical mutation; it amounted to a shift in the very social basis of communism. All Marxists, including Marx, Lenin, and Stalin, regarded the peasantry as an extremely important revolutionary force, but none before Mao thought it capable of independent action or as playing anything but an auxiliary role. With respect to Asia, however, they were prepared to make certain allowances. They accepted the argument that the peasantry must of necessity constitute the chief force of the Asian revolution, but Mao's further notion that the party itself could issue from the peasantry was inadmissible. Mao's spelling out the relative roles of the pro-

19. Stuart R. Schram, *The Political Thought of Mao Tse-tung* (Rev. ed.; New York, 1969), 25; Chalmers A. Johnson, "The Third Generation of Guerrilla Warfare," *Asian Survey*, VIII (June, 1968), 436; Johnson, *Autopsy on People's War*, 14–16.
20. Schram, *The Political Thought of Mao Tse-tung*, 33–35.

letariat versus the peasantry was almost too much. In the *Hunan Report* he attributed 70 percent of China's revolutionary accomplishments to the peasantry and only 30 percent to the proletariat. In fact, in the 1951 edition of Mao's *Selected Works*, this passage was deleted. In his dramatic shift to the peasantry Mao converted the Russian slogan, "All power to the soviets!" to "All power to the peasant associations!"[21]

Going even farther, Mao was not content to lay his revolution on the shoulders of the peasantry alone. When he confronted the Japanese and articulated the strategy of people's war, he sought the support of nearly the entire Chinese public. Mao managed this by expressing a very flexible definition of the term *people* as simply those classes and strata that favor the revolution, as opposed to those that do not. This definition, Mao argued, can vary in different countries and within countries in different periods of time. Stuart Schram contends that this broad-based definition of the people was a manifestation of Mao's need to legitimize the revolution and party rule in the eyes of the overwhelming mass of the population. Hence the term *people* became a twentieth-century equivalent of Rousseau's *general will*. It also allowed the notion of Confucian harmony to creep into a Marxist framework. These views on the people were at the base of Mao's united front strategy for a people's war.[22]

Mao Tse-tung took the rural and nationalist base of communism in Asia, granted as a tolerant dispensation by Lenin, and made it into a firm foundation for revolution. In the process he gave it something of a Confucian morality. Although Moscow never really accepted this mutation, Mao provided Asian Marxism with a vehicle for self-reliance by making the nation, rather than the social class, an appropriate context for the development of revolutionary consciousness. Such license may have been unpalatable to orthodox European Marxists, but it created the underpinnings for a new and powerful strategy of revolution, particularly in a colonial environment like French Indochina.

21. Winberg Chai (ed.), *Essential Works of Chinese Communism* (Rev. ed.; New York, 1972), 32, 34; Schram, *The Political Thought of Mao Tse-tung*, 31–32.
22. John Bryan Starr, "Conceptual Foundations of Mao Tse-tung's Theory of Continuous Revolution," *Asian Survey*, XI (June, 1971), 620; Schram, *The Political Thought of Mao Tse-tung*, 39–47; Chai, *Essential Works of Chinese Communism*, 151–69.

The Development of Vietnamese Communism

COMINTERN PHASE (1920–1941)

While the Chinese in many ways served as pathbreakers for the Vietnamese, the context in which Marxism developed in Viet Nam, both in theory and practice, was somewhat different. Although the Vietnamese have always borrowed from the Chinese, any such borrowing, to be regarded as legitimate, had to be authenticated or supplemented by Vietnamese practices and innovations. Vietnamese revolutionary doctrine, and the development of people's war in Viet Nam, can best be defined against the background of the four general phases of the Indochinese Communist party's history: the Comintern or urban phase; the Maoist or rural phase; a transitional phase in the 1960s, when the Maoist model of revolution was combined with such Vietnamese experiences as the August revolution and the victory at Dienbienphu; and the mature or modern phase, in which the Vietnamese have sought to chart their own course through Le Duan's "three revolutions."[23]

During the period of the Comintern phase the Vietnamese Communists followed the insurrectionist strategy of Lenin and adhered to the various shifts in the Comintern line. It was originally Lenin's famous "Theses on the Nationalist and Colonialist Question" (1920) that had propelled Ho eagerly to communism and to joining the French Communist party as a charter member. Yet he was deeply disappointed with the party's failure to respond to Lenin's theses with the same degree of enthusiasm. At the fifth Comintern Congress held in July, 1924, Ho, who by now had become a leading Asian Communist in Europe, publicly rebuked his French comrades for their passivity. Following Ho's speech, the Congress urged the French party to pay more attention to colonial questions. Ho also endorsed the thesis of the Indian Communist M. N. Roy that revolution must first start in the colonies, not in the metropole, since the only way the revolutionary situation could develop in the West was for the imperialist countries to lose their colonies. The

23. For the framework of all phases except the transitional I am indebted to William J. Duiker, "Vietnamese Revolutionary Doctrine" (Paper presented at the Vietnam Studies Group Conference on Vietnamese Marxism in Comparative Perspective, Washington, D.C., October 28, 1978).

real achievement for Ho in this Congress, however, was the dispensation allowing Vietnamese Communists to found a nationalist movement on their own initiative without cooperating with bourgeois nationalist movements, since in the case of Viet Nam, Ho had argued, there were none to begin with.[24]

The sixth Comintern Congress ordered a shift away from the close cooperation with bourgeois nationalist movements urged at the 1924 meeting. It was held in 1928 under the heavy shadow of the White Terror in Shanghai a year earlier. The delegates were told that the Asian bourgeoisie and middle class had proven themselves to be undependable allies. While Communists should not openly break with them or the peasants, the immediate task at hand was to build up a fundamental proletarian base. The Vietnamese at the conference dutifully fell into line. It is important to remember that Ho Chi Minh was acting in the name of Comintern when the ICP was established under his leadership in 1930. The Comintern immediately became involved in Vietnamese matters that same year when, after the outbreak of the Nghe-Tin Soviets and the decimation of the party by the French, it criticized the ICP for its peasant base and excessive nationalism. Further, the rebuilding of the ICP from 1931 to 1935 was conducted by young Vietnamese cadres, most notably Tran Van Giau, trained at the Toilers of the East School in Moscow.[25]

The seventh Comintern Congress, held in 1935, forced a difficult turn on Asian Communists. It called for a new popular front strategy to unite all progressive forces in the world against the menace of fascism. Asian Communists were accordingly instructed to promote broad popular fronts of all antifascist elements. At the first plenum of the ICP's Central Committee, held in 1936, Ho succeeded, despite some grumbling, in getting this policy accepted. The execution was made easier by the accession to power in France of Leon Blum's Popular front (led by the Socialists with Communist party support) in 1936. Blum sanctioned political activities in Indochina, allowing the ICP to operate legally.[26]

The Communists and other groups responded with enthusiasm, and

24. William J. Duiker, *The Comintern and Vietnamese Communism*, Papers in International Studies Southeast Asia Series No. 37 (Athens, Ohio, 1975), 4–6.
25. *Ibid.*, 11–12, 26–28.
26. *Ibid.*, 32–33.

under the general strategy of the "democratic front" the ICP made great strides. In fact, the growth made the colonial authorities nervous, and in September, 1939, political activities of the front were abruptly banned. The French were thereby able to suppress urban activities, and the ICP found itself at the same crossroads the Chinese came to in 1927: to continue to follow the Comintern line to certain oblivion or to survive through tactical mutation. Similar to the Chinese, the Vietnamese chose survival and discovered the countryside.[27]

Yet the Comintern played an invaluable role in the party's development, despite the fact that its advice was often ill conceived, as it tried to make Viet Nam fit into global terms sometimes in utter disregard of local realities. As William J. Duiker points out, it nevertheless provided the ICP with a structure of discipline, organization, and guidance that gave it a big advantage over its nationalist adversaries.[28] Also, during its period of loyalty to the Comintern, the party acquired an urban strategy, which it never totally abandoned. In following this urban strategy, particularly during the official colonial toleration that came with the Popular front interlude in France, the party gained experience in legal and what it called "semilegal" activities. To these two the ICP soon added the "illegal" activity of people's war.

MAOIST OR RURAL PHASE (1941–1955)

At the eighth plenum of the party's Central Committee, convened by Ho in 1941, the Maoist model of protracted, people's war was adopted as the Vietnamese guide to independence and liberation. The model consisted of the three-staged protracted war, a united front political program, a party-controlled army, and a war strategy of the country surrounding the cities. The work that foreshadowed the ICP's shift to the countryside was Truong Chinh and Vo Nguyen Giap's *The Peasant Question (1937–1938)*, which concluded that the peasantry was the major force in the Vietnamese population and that its support of the party should be encouraged, not shunned. It marked the first detailed study of peasant conditions by leading members of the ICP and provided a base for the subsequent rural policies of the party. In the article

27. Woodside, *Community and Revolution in Modern Vietnam*, 215.
28. Duiker, *The Comintern and Vietnamese Communism*, 40–42.

Truong Chinh and Giap concluded that "the key to the Indochinese peasant problem is to give the peasant land to till."[29]

In terms of policy for the ICP, they judged that although land reform was essential as a complete solution to the peasant question, total land reform would only divide the revolutionary forces by driving the landlords into the enemy camp. Such a solution would have to wait until after the revolution. In the end, Giap and Truong Chinh echoed Mao and Ho before them in their belief that any large-scale movement in any colonial and semicolonial country must have peasant participation to succeed. In their closing proclamation, they exclaimed that "whenever they [the peasants] have become conscious, are organized and have leadership, *they are an invincible force.*"[30]

Despite the fact that their tract was written for a national audience, only the ICP heard their message. With the French suppression of political activities in the cities, the ICP developed a knack for rural organization and, following the Maoist strategy of people's war, led the peasants to independence and victory over the French. Although this rural phase is aptly called Maoist, it was also a supremely nationalistic phase, with the Vietnamese declaring as their goal independence from both the Japanese and the French. They also added distinctive Vietnamese touches to the imported Chinese model of people's war. Two of the most important of these touches were the August revolution of 1945, orchestrated by Truong Chinh at the beginning of the war with the French, and Giap's dramatic victory at Dienbienphu in 1954, at the end.

TRANSITIONAL PHASE (1955–1969)

After achieving independence in 1954 at the price of two divided states, the Vietnamese Communists underwent an awkward transitional phase in which they tried to combine their own experience with that of both the Russians and Chinese. They embarked on an economic program of heavy industrialization on the Soviet model and followed the Chinese lead in land reform, although in this endeavor they met with disaster. Further, an attempt to emulate Mao's "one hundred flowers" campaign

29. Truong Chinh and Vo Nguyen Giap, *The Peasant Question (1937–1938)*, trans. and intro. by Christine Pelzer White, Data Paper, No. 94: Southeast Asia Program (Ithaca, N.Y., 1974), viii–ix, 12.
30. *Ibid.*, 20–22.

of liberalizing restrictions on the press and intellectuals met with a similar torrent of strident and embarrassing criticism.

In the struggle in the South, upon Le Duan's recommendation for armed struggle in 1957, the party sought to integrate the strategy of people's war with what it regarded as the unique Vietnamese traditions of the August revolution and Dienbienphu. Both the August revolution and Dienbienphu offered the ICP the opportunity to further develop its ideology around Vietnamese events rather than foreign ones, thereby enhancing the legitimacy of its Marxism by applying it to a Vietnamese context. With the failure of the Tet offensive, which was to have been a triumph of this integrated tradition, the Vietnamese were ready, or forced by circumstances, to move into what Duiker calls their mature phase.

MATURE PHASE (1969–)

This phase began with the acknowledgment by both Giap and his chief of staff Van Tien Dung that they could no longer mechanically follow the formulas of the past but would now have to be flexible in manipulating the revolutionary situation in their favor. Le Duan best expressed and summed up this new course for the Vietnamese revolution by describing it as an integration of three processes: the revolution in the relations of production between the owners of capital and the workers, the technological revolution, and the cultural and ideological revolution. The goal of the first revolution is to transform private capitalist industry and trade, as well as the small, individual economy of peasant producers, into a socialist relation of production in either of its two forms of ownership: by the entire people, that is, the state, or by collective ownership exemplified by collective farms. It is hoped that the laboring people will then realize that they are collectively the real masters of the social economy. This, however, is only a first step. In advancing toward socialism and bypassing the stage of capitalist development (with Lenin's permission), the key to establishing a socialist mode of production is the technological revolution, the essence of socialist industrialization. Le Duan's third revolution gives credit to what he calls the subjective point of view, the impact of creating the "socialist man." The first two revolutions, he contends, establish the social premises for consolidating the dictatorship of the proletariat as well as furthering the ideological and cultural revolution resulting in the emergence of so-cialist men. This will come about when laboring people understand their role as collective masters of society, of nature, and of themselves, a realization that will unleash undreamed-of human productivity. The motives called upon to release this energy will be a combination of ma-terial incentive, political education, and moral stimulation. Thus, these three revolutions together will provide Marx's "locomotive" for Viet-namese prosperity.[31]

The significance of Le Duan's three revolutions lies largely in their tacit rejection of any need for a split over the issue of "reds" versus "ex-perts," since both are needed to ensure socialism and prosperity. Hence the Vietnamese are eschewing any battle between the party and the bu-reaucracy similar to that occurring in China's Great Proletarian Cul-tural Revolution. Also, from a military point of view, the three revolu-tions allow the Vietnamese an escape from Mao's almost mystical "men over weapons" doctrine, which helped to underscore his emphasis on a people's war strategy. Le Duan allowed the Vietnamese to retain the strategy of people's war while preserving a respect for the importance of weapons per se. Theoretically and materially, he laid the foundation for a far more formidable military establishment. Indeed in an article in *Hoc Tap* (*Studies*) that appeared in April, 1972, at the height of the Easter invasion, Giap called for a modernization of the North Viet-namese army as part of the "highly developed form of people's war."[32]

In its broadest context, though, this mature phase represents a new look at the whole process of communizing and modernizing Vietnam-ese society. In coming up with the formulary of three revolutions, the Vietnamese were admitting that something about the old formulas (in-cluding people's war) was inadequate. Further progress, then, depended on distancing the Vietnamese revolution to some degree from them.

ORTHODOXY AND LEADERSHIP

From this brief account of the development of Vietnamese doctrines and strategies, two distinctive hallmarks of Vietnamese communism

31. Duiker, "Vietnamese Revolutionary Doctrine"; JUSPAO, *VNDRN*, No. 9, pp. 15–117.
32. JUSPAO, *VNDRN*, Nos. 106–III, pp. 13–14.

deserve mention: first, at least in comparison to China, its diligent attempts to conform to Leninist orthodoxy and, second, the collective, stable, and pragmatic nature of its leadership.

In Viet Nam, where his birthday is observed with near-religious reverence, Lenin has become something of a god, and Ho Chi Minh his revolutionary disciple and national saint. No year goes by without the occasion being marked in Hanoi's official publications. These anniversary issues always quote Ho's allegiance to Lenin's teachings and repeat that these teachings continue to be the basic principles of Communist parties the world over and that their correct implementation is still the standard for measuring genuine Marxist-Leninists. Thus it is not surprising that the Vietnamese take great pains to link their revolution with the Bolshevik revolution. In a typical congratulatory message to Moscow on the occasion of the fiftieth anniversary of the Russian Revolution, Le Duan, the party secretary proclaimed: "For the Vietnamese people, the victories of the October Revolution, of the resistance against Fascism, of the August Revolution, and of the Chinese revolution, and of the resistance against the French colonists and the American imperialists at present, are great events in one and the same historical chain."[33]

In this connection, it is curious that the top leadership has generally failed to adequately acknowledge its debt to the Chinese revolution. Such Vietnamese Communist luminaries as Vo Nguyen Giap, the defense minister, and Le Duan, the party secretary, have rarely given credit to Chinese contributions except in very general terms. Even Truong Chinh (actually Dan Xuan Khu) has been more sparing in his praise of China than his assumed name would suggest. (Truong Chinh is a *nomme de guerre* meaning "Long March.") It is really only Ho Chi Minh who has acknowledged his personal debt to China as well as making the obvious concession that "the influence of the Russian October Revolution and the Marxist-Leninist theory came to Viet Nam mostly through China."[34]

In any case, their obeisance to Lenin has kept the Vietnamese from going as far as the Chinese in several areas of revolutionary development. They have readily accepted the two-staged revolution that

33. JUSPAO, *VNDRN*, No. 9, p. 1.
34. Ho Chi Minh, *Selected Writings*, 262–65.

Marxist-Leninist orthodoxy demanded of them, although ever since the founding of the ICP in 1930, they have been grateful to Lenin for exempting Asia from the capitalist stage of development. The Vietnamese have also had little trouble accepting the party as the revolutionary vanguard. One writer (among many) for *Hoc Tap*, echoing Lenin, said that "the party is the vanguard unit, the staff element, and the political leader of the proletarian class."[35]

Accepting these teachings was not difficult for either the Vietnamese leaders, or even for Mao. Of some interest, however, is the fact that the Vietnamese have adopted Lenin's worker-peasant alliance more literally than the Chinese. This has led to an obstinate refusal to abandon the struggle in the cities, despite the overwhelming rural reality of Asia. The Leninist primacy of the proletariat, upon which the Vietnamese have also insisted to the point of enshrining it in their Constitution, has, in the face of the Vietnamese reality, caused difficulties for the Vietnamese Communist party. One writer for *Hoc Tap* explains the problem thus:

> Our party developed in a colonial and semi-feudal country, a backward agricultural country with a small working class, a country where most of the party members and cadres came from the petit bourgeois class. They came to the party usually because of patriotism. They have a high revolutionary spirit and an ardent patriotism but, initially, many still have little understanding of the working class, do not clearly understand the role and historic world duty of the working class, and do not have a self-awareness based on the working class position and viewpoint. Under these conditions, it is not a simple and easy matter to define and maintain the working class character of the party.[36]

In developing their revolutionary ideas and in accounting for such problems as their lack of a proletarian base, the Vietnamese have not had a towering theoretical leader like Lenin or Mao. While Ho was a gifted revolutionary politician, in general he did not turn his attention to major theoretical writing. Rather, the virtue of the Vietnamese leadership has been that of a flexible, stable, and long-enduring collective remarkable for its harmony. The same four men—Pham Van Dong, Le

35. Le Duc Binh, "The Party Theory of Lenin and the Development of Our Party," *Hoc Tap*, IV (April, 1970), 63–75, 81.
36. *Ibid.*, 71.

Duan, Truong Chinh, and Vo Nguyen Giap—who served as Ho's chief
lieutenants since World War II, still, fifteen years after his death,
guide the destiny of Viet Nam. This has been due, in part at least, to a
fundamental agreement on issues. Yet a collective of such duration
cannot help but contain some differences. Perhaps reflecting the regime's sense of security, in no other Communist country has there been
such a public airing of differences with such little political cost to the
participants.[37]

One reason for this harmony, even with differences, has lain in the
remarkable flexibility and adaptability of the Communist party and its
leadership to changing conditions, despite its concern for orthodoxy.
With the notable exception of Truong Chinh, none of the Vietnamese
leaders has staked his career on a public position, and so lost his political maneuverability. Instead, as Le Duan has said, "There has never
been and will never be a unique formula, one that is suited to all circumstances and all times, for making a revolution." The greatest impetus for this flexibility came from Ho himself. In justifying the March,
1946, accords with the French, he echoed Winston Churchill's "doing
business with the devil" defense of the wartime alliance with the Soviets, by saying, "Lenin said that one should make a compromise even
with bandits if it was advantageous to the revolution." In concurring, Vo
Nguyen Giap likened these accords to the Treaty of Brest-Litovsk which
Lenin concluded with the Germans in World War I and in which he
ceded large areas of the Ukraine to preserve the Russian revolution.[38]

More specifically, the basis for this harmony lies within the men
themselves. Foremost, of course, was Ho Chi Minh. After years of tutelage under the Comintern in Moscow during the 1920s, Ho was dispatched to China in 1930 to bring the quarreling Vietnamese Marxists
under one roof. From the time of the founding of the Indochinese Com-

37. President Pham Van Dong was Ho Chi Minh's closest collaborator throughout
the revolution. Pham owes his position to this relationship and, like Ho, to his abilities as a conciliator, not to his theoretical writings. In February, 1982, Giap was re-
tired from his politburo post after relinquishing his military responsibilities a year
earlier. Despite speculation about pressure, there is no firm evidence to indicate that
his retirement was not voluntary. See "Party Congress in Hanoi," *Indochina Chronology*, I (January–March, 1982), 7.

38. Le Duan, *The Vietnamese Revolution: Fundamental Problems, Essential
Tasks* (Hanoi, 1970), 41–42; Ho Chi Minh, *Selected Writings*, 112; Stetler (ed.), *The
Military Art of People's War*, 29.

munist party in 1930 until his death in 1969, he was the undisputed leader of Vietnamese communism. It was his leadership that guided the Communists to victory over the French and preserved the party's unity during its important shifts. Although he tended to leave the theorizing to others, he wrote a major piece on guerrilla warfare for the Comintern in 1928 that preceded Mao's published thoughts on the subject by ten years. He also made extensive comments on the international situation and offered an important exposition on revolutionary morality.[39]

Ho almost slavishly quoted from Lenin. Indeed he described his conversion to Leninism in Damascus Road terms. In "The Path Which Led Me to Leninism" (1960), Ho exclaimed: "In those Theses [of Lenin on the National and Colonial Question], there were political terms that were difficult to understand. But by reading them again and again finally I was able to grasp the essential part. What emotion, enthusiasm, enlightenment, and confidence they communicated to me! I wept for joy. Sitting by myself in my room, I would shout as if I were addressing large crowds: Dear martyr compatriots! This is what we need, this is our path to liberation!"[40]

Despite his ardent Leninism, Ho retained an essential duality of motive. His appeals to his fellow countrymen were always based on nationalism. Yet, at the same time, he continually took great care to tie the Vietnamese situation to the conditions of colonialism and neocolonialism, and to the great international proletarian revolution. His effect on Viet Nam has been so profound that, in many ways, Ho Chi Minh still rules Viet Nam.

Vo Nguyen Giap, as minister of defense and commander of the Viet Nam People's army, has been head of the military machine since he assembled the first mountain band of thirty-four guerrillas in 1940. Although initially tutored by Ho in guerrilla tactics, he was a quick study. The triumph at Dienbienphu in 1954 ranks as his greatest personal achievement. In the late 1950s and early 1960s, Giap was forced into a debate over military strategy that somewhat weakened his authority until the death of his rival Nguyen Chi Thanh in 1967. Thanh's death

---

39. Ho Chi Minh, "The Party's Military Work Among the Peasants: Revolutionary Guerrilla Methods," in A. Neuberg [pseud.] (ed.), *Armed Insurrection* (1928; rpr. London, 1970), 255–72; Id., *Selected Writings*, 195–208.
40. Ho Chi Minh, *Selected Writings*, 251.

did not completely restore Giap's eminence. The Tet offensive put the Communists into a further theoretical drift over military strategy, and later, in the 1972 Easter invasion, Giap is believed to have suffered some criticism. Even the glorious victory campaign of 1975 was more the work of Van Tien Dung, the chief of staff of the North Vietnamese army, than of Giap, and Dung was given the honor of writing the official account.[41]

Giap, nevertheless, has been responsible for most of the party's military formulations, though it has by no means been his exclusive province. He is at his best as a historian relating the contemporary Vietnamese revolution to various episodes in Vietnamese history. One significant factor underlying the stability of the Vietnamese leadership is that Giap, as a military man, in all his official writings has stressed the importance of the party's absolute leadership over the army.

Dang Xuan Khu, better known as Truong Chinh, has been accused of being the most pro-Chinese of the Vietnamese. In fact, the ultimate loyalty of all the Vietnamese leadership is to their own revolution. Along with Giap, he was the coleader of the party during World War II, delegated by Ho to handle party matters within Viet Nam. Truong Chinh's moment of glory was his masterminding of the revered August revolution. In 1951 he became secretary general of the Lao Dong party (Viet Nam Workers' Party). His nadir came in 1956, when, after pushing hard for land reform, he oversaw an effort that turned into a national disaster. He publicly confessed to his errors and lost the post of secretary general. The eclipse, however, proved temporary. In 1958 he was made a vice premier and in 1960 was named chairman of the Standing Committee of the National Assembly. All along he has retained his powerful seat on the politburo.[42]

Obviously a colorful figure, Truong Chinh has been something of a mixed blessing to his colleagues. On the positive side, he has been the chief theoretician of the party, especially on political mobilization and on squaring revolutionary developments in Viet Nam with Marxist-Leninist orthodoxy. He has consistently shown the greatest depth in

41. McAlister, *Viet Nam*, 152; Stetler, *The Military Art of People's War*, 47–50; JUSPAO, *VNDRN*, Nos. 106–II, p. iii.

42. McAlister, *Viet Nam*, 152; Truong Chinh, *Primer for Revolt: The Communist Takeover in Viet Nam*, intro. and Notes by Bernard B. Fall (New York, 1963), xvii, xix–xx.

rooting his theoretical expositions firmly in the writings of Marx, Lenin, and Mao. Truong Chinh has also played an important role in formulating military theory. In fact, his *Resistance Will Win* (1947) set forth the basic Vietnamese statement of people's war, of which Giap's *People's War, People's Army* (1962) was a mere reiteration.[43]

The other side is that Truong Chinh has been the least flexible member of the politburo and the most vitriolic in his criticisms. In his *August Revolution* (1946) he listed a series of shortcomings that added up to a criticism of Ho's negotiated settlement with the French in 1946. After his land reform debacle, he quarreled with Le Duan in the mid-1960s over the latter's pragmatism on agricultural collectivization. In September, 1968, he delivered a bristling criticism of the Tet offensive before the Hanoi regime had time to finish licking its wounds. Thus, although his theoretical brilliance has been indispensable, his persistent public criticisms have gradually diminished his influence. In 1960 Truong Chinh lost his job as secretary general and by the late sixties his position as chief party theoretician, both to Le Duan.[44]

The political fortunes of Le Duan, a native southerner from Quang Tri, have been intimately tied to the war in the South. He served as the Viet Minh leader in Cochinchina from the late 1940s until 1951. In 1957 he made a secret tour of the South and made the key recommendation that armed struggle be renewed. Since becoming secretary general, his main concern has been the balancing of the demands of the revolution in the South with "socialist construction" in the North.[45]

In his writings, Le Duan comes across as an avid pupil of Lenin. References to Lenin lace through his works. As a modernizer he has made a point of tying economic development to Marxist-Leninist theory. Thus his theoretical preoccupation has been with the socialist transformation after the revolution, and the proper mix of policies with which to maximize agricultural production and industrialization. As such he is far more pragmatic than Truong Chinh, with whom he has had his disagreements. Le Duan has also paid close attention to the party cadres (the agents of political and economic development) and their revo-

43. Truong Chinh, *Primer for Revolt*, vii–ix.
44. *Ibid.*, 35–42; JUSPAO, *VNDRN*, No. 51, pp. 1–20.
45. William S. Turley, "Civil-Military Relations in North Viet Nam," *Asian Survey*, IX (December, 1969), 895.

lutionary consciousness. With his focus on economic development, Le Duan's writings on military strategy reflect an impatient desire to have energies once again channeled into nonmartial pursuits. Particularly in the late 1960s and early 1970s, he displayed a desire for a quick end to the war, albeit on Communist terms.[46]

Theoretically, Le Duan has shown himself to be an innovative thinker. He is probably responsible for several distinctive Vietnamese twists to Communist revolutionary thought. The most important of these is the doctrine of the three revolutions. Further, his doctrine of the three strategic areas (hills and forests, plains, and cities) did much to turn the Viet Nam war into one in which the Viet Cong were everywhere, and his idea of revolutionary leaps (sudden shock assaults on enemy strongholds, designed to hasten the pace of the protracted war and even catapult the revolutionary forces into a position to seize power) provided support for at least some of the daring of the Tet offensive, the Easter invasion, and the final campaign of liberation in 1975.

Through the writings of these Communist leaders and the phases their movement has gone through, it should be clear that all major Communist doctrines have undergone significant changes and adaptations as they have traversed continents and moved through time, and through the thoughts of different individuals. The changes have brought some of these doctrines to definitional breaking points, where serious questions have developed as to whether the original theoretical formulations and precepts have been so gravely violated that it is no longer legitimate to use the terms. The development of the strategy of people's war is an integral part of this pattern of change.

46. This emphasis is especially pronounced in Le Duan's *On the Socialist Revolution in Viet Nam* (3 vols.; Hanoi, 1965–67).

CHAPTER FOUR
_____

The Fate of
People's War

The General or Chinese Definition of People's War

MAO TSE-TUNG'S EARLY VIEWS

Others before Mao Tse-tung had considered various features of a people's war, but he detailed it as an operational blueprint for a revolutionary seizure of political power. More than a blueprint, it is hardly an exaggeration to say that his strategy of people's war has grown into an entire political philosophy.

Historically, people's war had very humble and even desperate origins. Mao developed it in Yenan in the late 1930s as a solution to a contemporary strategic impasse. The occasion was the collapse of the Comintern-inspired united front with the Kuomintang during Chiang Kai-shek's White Terror of 1927, and the weakness of Communist forces after the Long March in 1935, compared to both the Kuomintang and the invading Japanese army in 1937. As Chalmers Johnson relates it, Mao had two problems to solve in developing his strategy: first, building up a red army and, second, devising tactics for an objectively weaker force to stay in the field and ultimately defeat an objectively stronger force. As Mao saw it, the key to the solution was to obtain a decisive intelligence advantage in order to reap the benefits of guerrilla tactics:

devastating lightning ambushes, sudden and overwhelming assaults on lightly defended positions, and the ability to avoid unfavorable engagements. Mao turned this key through his revision of Lenin's doctrine of the united front, which Mao redubbed "the mass line." Lenin saw the united front as a tactic to both legalize and legitimize the party's activities and to put it in a position to stage a coup d'état. Mao, however, saw it as a source for his army's manpower as well as an intelligence-collecting network for the longer march to power through a broadly based revolution. To gain these dividends, it was incumbent upon the party to win the support and loyalty of the masses through the championing of salient issues.[1]

From this revision, Mao enunciated a military doctrine that Ralph Powell distills down to four requisites for victory by people's war. First, a people's war must be led by a Leninist party, that is, by a disciplined party of revolutionaries who act as the vanguard. Second, it must be built on mass support and a united front. In this case, mass support was meant to come primarily from poor peasants, and the united front was the party's vehicle to attract other classes and groups. Third, it must be waged by a party army, that is, an army organized by, and loyal to, the party. Fourth, the revolution must have secure rural base areas as strategic havens or reserves both to support the fighting and to develop showcase models of the political system to come.[2]

Mao, then, sought to realize these four requisites through developing the mass line, self-reliance, and the three-phased protracted war. Regarding the mass line, Mao insisted that it could be developed solely through the support of issues evoking genuine popular feeling. Only painstaking, on-the-spot investigations could reveal those issues, which would then be interpreted in Communist ideological terms. However, according to Mao, to discover issues deductively from a preset ideological stance was to commit the sin of dogmatism.[3]

On external support, Mao's attitudes were ambivalent and even hypocritical. In stressing basic self-reliance, he was chiefly concerned that too much outside assistance would tempt the revolutionaries to take

1. Johnson, "The Third Generation of Guerrilla Warfare," 435–37.
2. Ralph L. Powell, "Maoist Military Doctrine," *Asian Survey*, VIII (April, 1968), 249.
3. Johnson, "The Third Generation of Guerrilla Warfare," 438.

shortcuts, leaving their revolutionary base insufficiently prepared. Chalmers Johnson suggests, however, that Mao preached self-reliance mainly because he had to do without foreign assistance. In *On Protracted War*, Mao showed no compunction against accepting outside help and depicted protracted war as a means of continuing the struggle until decisive international help arrived. In fact, he admitted that his third stage of the counter-offensive was possible only with international assistance.[4]

The feature of Mao's strategy of people's war for which he is most famous is the three-staged protracted war. As he described it: "The first stage covers the period of the enemy's strategic offensive and our strategic defensive. The second stage will be the period of the enemy's strategic consolidation and our preparation for the counter-offensive. The third stage will be the period of our strategic counter-offensive and the enemy's strategic retreat." What made Mao's protracted war a people's war was that the strength to wage it came from the mobilization of the masses. What made the people's war also a war of national liberation was that the chief motive appeal in gathering mass support was to a patriotic struggle for national salvation against the Japanese. Politically, the notion of a protracted war of three stages was a big morale booster because it gave the Chinese people in 1938 a credible strategy for eventually overcoming the seemingly invincible Japanese.[5]

Mao's more detailed descriptions of the three stages revealed that the divisions between them were blurred. In fact, each stage consisted of a tactical mix of the other stages which changed not only from one stage to another but also within each stage. Thus the first stage, the strategic defensive, was fought primarily along the lines of mobile warfare. It started, though, with positional warfare in its initial retreat after political struggles and establishment crackdown, and it ended with the emergence of extensively developed guerrilla war. In the second stage, which Mao termed the strategic stalemate, guerrilla war became primary, with mobile war serving an important supplementary role. But this was the transitional period in which mobile war was to play an increasingly prominent role and positional warfare was even to appear in

4. *Ibid.*, 438; Mao Tse-tung, *On Protracted War* (1938; rpr. Peking, 1967), 20, 39.
5. Mao Tse-tung, *On Protracted War*, 34; Johnson, "The Third Generation of Guerrilla Warfare," 439.

some areas. Mobile warfare was Mao's tactical favorite. He described it as the form in which large regular armies waged quick-decision campaigns over wide areas of operation, vying for superiority along a fluid battle front. The third stage, that of the strategic counteroffensive, was to move from mobile warfare to regular, positional warfare. In this stage, guerrilla warfare would supplement mobile and positional war with strategic support but would lose the dominance it may have enjoyed even through the second stage. Mao conceded that in the case of China positional warfare would never become primary because the enemy's superiority in conventional terms could never be overcome. Instead, victory would come through a combination of mobile war and guerrilla war in the third stage.[6]

Three essential points stand out in Mao's early writings about people's war and its stages. First, it is a highly interrelated strategy among both the three stages and the three forms of warfare (guerrilla, mobile, and regular war). In emphasizing regular warfare, Mao wrote, "Unless we understand this . . . that regular war will decide the final outcome . . . we shall be unable to defeat Japan." He quickly added that guerrilla warfare was nevertheless indispensable because without it a people's war could never get to stage two.[7]

Second, guerrilla warfare is not static but continually raises itself to the higher forms of mobile and regular warfare. Thus, Mao wrote, "the strategic role of guerrilla warfare is two-fold, to support regular war and to transform itself into regular warfare."[8] Hence, the formation and maintenance of regular units in a people's war do not come from outside but are developed internally from the guerrilla units recruited from the masses. In this regard, both the Chinese and Vietnamese main-

6. Mao Tse-tung, *On Protracted War*, 35–43, 83, 87–88. Mao's description of the three stages was largely fulfilled in the history of the Chinese revolution. Thus, in the first stage, the start from positional warfare no doubt referred to the fact that the Kuomintang's first blows in the civil war fell on a Communist force with entrenched urban political positions (or, alternatively, to Japan's first assault and the scattering of both Kuomintang and Communist party armies). The mobility in this stage referred to the party's retreat, regroupments, and breakouts from the encirclement campaigns, as well as the employment of small-scale, hit-and-run attacks, whereas the mobility of the second stage came true in the large-scale battles against the Japanese in World War II (for example, the "one hundred regiments campaign") and the Kuomintang in 1947 and 1948.
7. Chai (ed.), *Essential Works of Chinese Communism*, 129–30.
8. *Ibid.*, 132; Mao Tse-tung, *On Protracted War*, 85–86.

tained three levels of armed forces: village guerrillas, district militia, and main force units. In Viet Nam, though decidedly an unpopular practice, both the Viet Minh and the Viet Cong filled the ranks of their main forces with guerrillas sent up from below (both as individuals and as units), especially after they had suffered heavy casualties. The Viet Cong also fleshed out their large unit ranks with fillers from the North. This latter practice was, according to this precept, cheating.

Third, the value of the three stages of protracted war lies not in the importance of the stages themselves, but in their provision of a framework of analysis for assessing one's situation and the correct mix of revolutionary tactics with which to confront it. Thus, for example, in developing the concentrated form of attack that he called "the few against the many," Mao was careful to apply it only to the local battlefield, not the national. Regarding the larger battlefield, Mao warned, "We must not plunge into decisive battles until the time is ripe and unless we have the necessary strength." This impetuosity he described as "Left opportunism," which was the failure to assess the situation according to the framework of a protracted war. He faulted Li Li San for this in 1930, P'eng Teh-huai for his disastrous "one hundred regiments offensive" against the Japanese in 1940 and 1941, and finally the Vietnamese for their costly "general offensives and general uprisings" in the late 1960s.[9]

MAO AND LIN PIAO'S LATER VIEWS ON PEOPLE'S WAR

Some twenty-seven years after Mao's original writings on people's war and sixteen years after the Communist liberation of Peking according to its principles, the Chinese, in September, 1965, published an inflammatory speech by Lin Piao, the defense minister heralded as Mao's heir apparent, entitled *Long Live the Victory of People's War!* At the same time, *Red Flag*, the Chinese military journal, reprinted Mao's 1938 article, *Problems of Strategy in Guerrilla War Against Japan*. The editor noted that Mao's theory of people's war was especially relevant to those peoples fighting against American imperialism. While no country was

9. Mao Tse-tung, *Problems of Strategy in China's Revolutionary War* (1936; rpr. Peking, 1967), 35, 87; Chai, *Essential Works of Chinese Communism,* 53.

specifically mentioned, it required little imagination to guess that Viet Nam must have been uppermost in his mind.

In any case, it was correctly perceived in the West as a major Chinese policy statement, although the interpretations of this statement certainly varied. The immediate official explanation in the United States was that the Chinese were calling the rural, underdeveloped Third World countries to arms against the urban, developed Western nations. David Mozingo and T. W. Robinson, however, argued that Lin Piao's speech carried the message that China would not directly intervene on Hanoi's behalf largely because the Vietnamese should be waging their fight according to the principle of self-reliance. Agreeing with Mozingo and Robinson, Douglas Pike asserted that Lin Piao was also taking the Vietnamese to task for bungling their application of people's war.[10]

Indeed, it appears that Lin Piao's fundamental concern was to preserve the purity of the principles of people's war in Viet Nam so that it could be repeated elsewhere. Although American war critics may have rejected the domino theory, Lin Piao certainly did not. Rather than conjuring up the image of falling dominoes, he saw Viet Nam as producing a chain reaction.

> Viet Nam is the most convincing current example of a victim of aggression defeating U.S. imperialism by a people's war. The U.S. has made South Vietnam a testing ground for the suppression of people's war. It has carried on this experiment for many years, and everybody can now see that the U.S. aggressors are unable to find a way of coping with people's war. On the other hand, the Vietnamese people have brought the power of people's war into full play in their struggle against the U.S. aggressors. The U.S. aggressors are in danger of being swamped in Viet Nam. They are deeply worried that their defeat in Vietnam will lead to a chain reaction. They are expanding the war in an attempt to save themselves from defeat. But the more they expand the war, the greater will be the chain reaction. The more they escalate the war, the heavier will be their fall and the more disastrous their defeat. The people in other parts of the world will see still more clearly that U.S. imperialism can be defeated, and that what the Vietnamese people can do, they can do too.[11]

10. Johnson, *Autopsy on People's War*, 30; David P. Mozingo and T. W. Robinson, *Lin Piao on "People's War": China Takes a Second Look at Vietnam* (Santa Monica, Calif., 1965), 3; Douglas Pike, *Vietnam War: View From the Other Side* (Saigon, 1967), 8–10.
11. Lin Piao, *Long Live the Victory of People's War!* (Peking, 1965), 57–58.

With the war in Viet Nam occupying the global center stage (something flattering to all Vietnamese), Lin Piao was also reminding revolutionaries that the Chinese first developed the art of people's war and that their experience was still of universal relevance. He asserted that the United States was trying to repeat on a worldwide scale what the Japanese had tried in China and that the Chinese resistance war was able to defeat the Japanese because it was a genuine people's war. To make sure that his speech was not mistaken for an idle history lesson, near the close of it he stated: "Comrade Mao Tse-tung's theory of people's war has been proved by the long practice of the Chinese revolution to be in accord with the objective laws of such wars and to be invincible. It has not only been valid for China, it is a great contribution to the revolutionary struggles of the oppressed nations and peoples throughout the world."[12]

Lin Piao exuded confidence that people's war was destined to be successful wherever it was tried, but only if certain basic requirements were honored. "In order to win a people's war, it is imperative to build the broadest possible united front and formulate a series of policies which will ensure the fullest mobilization of the masses as well as the unity of all the forces that can be united." Mozingo and Robinson contend that this statement was intended as a barb to the Vietnamese both for their undue reliance on terror and for the narrow political base of the National Liberation Front.[13]

Concerning the principles of people's war itself, even though Lin Piao referred to Mao's classic three stages only in passing, thereby, in effect, downgrading their importance, the fundamental tenet of building and maintaining a people's war on the foundation of a mass supported guerrilla warfare remained unchanged: "Guerrilla warfare is the only way to mobilize and apply the whole strength of the people against the enemy, the only way to expand our forces in the course of the war, deplete and weaken the enemy, gradually change the balance of forces between the enemy and ourselves, switch from guerrilla to mobile warfare, and finally defeat the enemy."[14]

Finally, although he did concede that some assistance from other socialist states was acceptable, his words on self-reliance contain the core

12. *Ibid.*, 2, 43.
13. *Ibid.*, 13; Mozingo and Robinson, *Lin Piao on "People's War,"* 5–6, 10.
14. Lin Piao, *Long Live the Victory of People's War!*, 32.

of what was probably a Chinese refusal to a Vietnamese request for additional assistance.

> In order to make a revolution and to fight a people's war and be victorious, it is imperative to adhere to the policy of self-reliance, rely on the strength of the masses in one's own country and prepare to carry on the fight independently even when all material aid from outside is cut off. If one does not operate by one's own efforts, does not independently ponder and solve the problems of the revolution in one's own country and does not rely on the strength of the masses, but leans wholly on foreign aid—even though this be aid from socialist countries which persist in revolution—no victory can be won, or be consolidated even if it is won.[15]

While Lin Piao was forcefully clear on this point, it may have been as much a ploy of political expediency as it was a statement of doctrinal scruple. One cannot help but be struck by the similarity of Lin Piao's rationale to that of the Nixon Doctrine, expounded in Guam four years later. Thus, well before Nixon retrenched the American doctrine of containment to the provision of material support to countries facing Communist aggression (instead of promising direct American intervention), Lin Piao sounded the same theme to Communist revolutionaries embarking on people's wars. As in the case of the Americans, the Chinese had their domestic reasons for this policy. Hindsight reveals that by this time Mao had already decided to launch the Great Proletarian Cultural Revolution, and Lin Piao's speech helped clear the decks so that the campaign could be unfurled with no distracting foreign adventures.

Mozingo and Robinson sum up Lin Piao's speech as providing seven rules for a people's war, some of them slightly amended: 1) the strategy of the united front, 2) the leading role of the Communist party, 3) the formation and defense of revolutionary base areas, 4) an army arising from the masses, with the peasantry solidly behind both the army and the party, 5) the continued primacy of guerrilla warfare strategy (that is, protracted war), even though the three stages are no longer important, 6) self-reliance, though with the proviso that, 7) supplemental assistance from other socialist countries is permissible.[16]

Subsequently, the attention of the Chinese shifted to other matters, and little more was said about people's war. Nevertheless, people's war

---

15. *Ibid.*, 41–42.
16. Mozingo and Robinson, *Lin Piao on "People's War,"* 5.

remains as an invaluable Chinese legacy to the cause of Socialist revolution. However they may have mangled it in practice, the flexible Vietnamese Communist leaders were among the first to appreciate the utility of Mao's theory of people's war.

The Vietnamese Definition of People's War

In developing their military theory, the Vietnamese lacked a towering figure like Mao Tse-tung. Nevertheless, as William Turley points out, the principles of people's war and the lessons of the Resistance War that lasted from 1945 to 1954 have their own aura of sanctity in Viet Nam.[17] The road the Vietnamese have followed has not been without its twists and turns. From the Comintern's insurrectionist line, the ICP adopted Mao's people's war after being forced into the countryside. Despite attempts to follow the Maoist text during the Resistance War, the August revolution and the siege of Dienbienphu were departures from the formula. Following the war the Vietnamese attempted to amalgamate these experiences with people's war. The intervention of the Americans in the 1960s posed new challenges and prompted a search for an appropriate military strategy within the theoretical confines of people's war. After the Tet offensive in 1968, there were some major attempts at reformulating people's war, but after a few years these efforts lapsed into a silence that essentially continues today.

PEOPLE'S WAR AGAINST THE FRENCH

Six months after fighting broke out between the French and Viet Minh, Ho Chi Minh issued an appeal to his countrymen asking that they back the Viet Minh banner and declaring that they would win because "we use the strategy of a protracted war of resistance." In September, 1947, Truong Chinh fleshed out this strategy in *The Resistance Will Win*, the first major Vietnamese formulation of its military doctrine of what he explicitly called a people's war. In seconding Ho's appeal for support, Truong Chinh sought to legitimize Ho's call by linking the war against the French to the Vietnamese tradition of heroic resistance. Thus Truong

17. Turley, "Civil-Military Relations in North Viet Nam," 880.

Chinh vowed that the Viet Minh would emulate the clever strategems and ruses of the Trans, the perseverance and endurance of the Les, and the speed and ferocity in attack of the Quang Trung emperor.[18]

Despite this appeal to tradition, Truong Chinh was clearly influenced by the thought of Mao Tse-tung, which he nevertheless failed to acknowledge. He echoed Mao's call for a protracted war against a superior force and reiterated Mao's emphasis on self-reliance. He also repeated Mao's conviction that the people's war depended on a strategic defensive posture and a tactical offensive one of rapid settlement engagements. Further, he borrowed Mao's idea that the three levels of armed forces flowed into each other from the basic source of the people. He even clinched this point by repeating Mao's analogy, "The people are the water and our army the fish."[19]

Mao's most important influence on Truong Chinh, of course, was the three stages of the protracted war, which Truong Chinh simply renamed the stage of contention, the stage of equilibrium, and the stage of the general counteroffensive. He agreed with Mao that "there are no clear dividing lines between the three stages. The later stage originates in the former. The former stage creates conditions for the later stages." Nevertheless, Truong Chinh pressed upon the stages the stamp of orthodoxy characteristic of this period: "The long-term resistance war of our people must pass through three stages. That is *a necessity*." On this point Truong Chinh was even more orthodox about people's war than Mao, who felt that victory was possible without a full development of the third stage.[20]

In spite of the fact that *The Resistance Will Win* was mainly an application of Mao's strategy of people's war to Viet Nam, Truong Chinh did add some distinctive Vietnamese touches. His third stage went well beyond that of Mao, who was vague on this stage, in recommending that a rapid concentration of forces launch lightning attacks on the cities to annihilate the final enemy positions. Here is perhaps the first clue of the Vietnamese preference for go-for-broke attacks that Mao repeatedly warned against.[21]

18. Ho Chi Minh, *Selected Writings*, 73; Truong Chinh, *Primer for Revolt: The Communist Takeover in Vietnam*, Introduction and notes by Bernard B. Fall (New York, 1963), 88–89, 109.
19. Truong Chinh, *Primer for Revolt*, 113, 116–17, 168, 193.
20. *Ibid.*, 146–54, 213.
21. *Ibid.*, 154.

The Resistance War represented a genuine attempt to follow Truong Chinh's theoretical formulation. One exception, or at least one note of hypocrisy, was the stress on self-reliance that Ho reiterated as late as 1952 at a conference on guerrilla warfare, even while the Vietnamese were receiving a steady, large flow of Chinese supplies. But adherence to the three stages of protracted war remained a matter of great importance throughout the war. The platform of the Lao Dong party's second Congress of 1951 declared, "The War of Resistance of the people of Viet-Nam is a people's war, with the characteristic of a nation-wide, all-out and protracted war. It must pass through three stages." In his political report at the same Congress, Ho made a point of outlining them. In the first stage, which went from September, 1945, to the autumn and winter of 1947, the party aimed at preserving and building up its main forces. The second stage lasted from the autumn and winter of 1947 until the Congress of 1951, during which time the party contended with the enemy and prepared for the general counteroffensive. The continued belief in the three stages for the Resistance War was underscored by the subsequent official party history, which summarized arguments of an intraparty dispute over the actual starting date of the third stage.[22]

Following the successful conclusion of the Resistance War against the French in 1954, the next major statement of Vietnamese military doctrine was Giap's *People's War, People's Army*, which was published in 1959. It was as much a historical recapitulation of the Resistance War as a theoretical exposition of people's war. It was a very orthodox statement, borrowing heavily from Truong Chinh. Like Truong Chinh, Giap made no mention or recognition of Mao Tse-tung, though the book's very title almost begs for a footnote. What is significant about this work is not its theoretical originality but the fact that its publication coincided with the Lao Dong party's decision to launch armed struggle in the South. Much like Truong Chinh's *The Resistance Will Win*, Giap's *People's War, People's Army* can be seen as a theoretical blueprint for the struggle to come.[23]

22. Ho Chi Minh, *Selected Writings*, 114–15, 146; Tran Van Dinh (ed.), *This Nation and Socialism Are One*, 229; *An Outline History of the Viet Nam Workers' Party*, 73.
23. Vo Nguyen Giap, *People's War, People's Army*, Foreword by Roger Hilsman and Profile by Bernard B. Fall (New York, 1962), 153.

First, Giap respected the necessity of the three phases of contention, equilibrium, and general counter-offensive, though he acknowledged the execution could be more complex in practice. Second, he stressed the invaluable role of resistance bases in the countryside and the political benefits of linking the anti-imperialist revolution with the antifeudal revolution. Third, he asserted that victory was possible only through a united front based on a worker-peasant alliance. Fourth, he insisted that a people's war must be waged under the sole leadership of the Communist party. Fifth, he admitted that in the resistance war victory was due to the support of progressive peoples throughout the world, even though self-reliance remained a guiding principle of people's war.[24]

In light of the coming struggle in the South against the American-backed regime of Ngo Dinh Diem, Giap's approach was neither startling nor original. The only departure from official, people's war orthodoxy was a waffling on the issue of self-reliance. In *People's War, People's Army*, Giap continued to stress the interlocking relationship between guerrilla warfare and more conventional forms of warfare. In fact he elevated the importance of the relationship, calling it a general law. He held up the offensive in the winter and spring of 1953–1954, which culminated in Dienbienphu, as the prime example of coordination between mobile warfare and guerrilla warfare.[25] The fight against Diem, then, was to be a textbook campaign.

KHOI NGHIA AND DIENBIENPHU

The very mention of Dienbienphu, along with the August revolution of 1945, however, stirs up discordant notes in any "orthodox" statement of people's war. These were distinctively Vietnamese occurrences and do not fit in well with the Chinese pattern. Yet the nationalistic pride of the Vietnamese prompted them to Vietnamize the Chinese people's war with these two domestic ingredients in their subsequent war against the Americans.

Douglas Pike contends that the Vietnamese Communist doctrine of *khoi nghia* (usually translated as "general uprising," though it can also be rendered as "popular uprising" or "righteous revolt") is an adapta-

24. *Ibid.*, 22–30, 85.
25. *Ibid.*, 93–95.

tion of the central Communist myth of the general strike. The sterling example of *khoi nghia* to Vietnamese Communists was the August revolution, which Truong Chinh also called the August general insurrection, suggesting that it was similar to the Russian October revolution.[26]

Yet the Communists did not invent *khoi nghia*. In Viet Nam the idea of a general uprising has been around as long ago as the thousand years of Chinese domination, during which Vietnamese noblemen attempted to rouse the people against the Chinese. When the French came, fiery waves of scholar-patriots called for general uprisings against the foreigners. The Yen Bay mutiny of 1930, carried out by the Vietnamese Nationalist party (VNQDD), was also an attempt at general uprising. Thus, David Marr observes, the theme of *khoi nghia* has been adopted by the Communists from a proud and enduring nationalist tradition of popular revolt against outside interventionists.[27]

In the form it has taken under the Communists, *khoi nghia* comes as the result of simple anarchy created by terrorism or other means of violence and intimidation, combined with the party's fanning and channeling of revolutionary hatreds toward an ultimate takeover of political power. In a sense, *khoi nghia* represents the solidly Leninist notion of organizing the spontaneous emotional outbursts of the masses toward the rational end of revolution. But there is also the distinctive Vietnamese element of the miraculous in *khoi nghia*. As Douglas Pike explains, "Once the people were organized, their revolutionary spirit would be fanned until—the social myth ran—some morning it would explode into the *Khoi Nghia* and the people would seize power."[28]

Truong Chinh thought of the August revolution as the perfect example of *khoi nghia*, calling it a powerful uprising of the masses. Bernard Fall, however, describes Truong Chinh's account as showing a well-planned Communist coup of three ingredients: the creation of a united front with non-Communist nationalists, the outflanking of these Nationalists with better organization and greater maneuverability, and an astute eye for seizing upon opportunities of the moment (in the case of the August revolution, the defeat of the Japanese and the momentary absence of the French). These ingredients are certainly not antithetical

26. Pike, *Vietnam War*, 20; Truong Chinh, *Primer for Revolt*, 6.
27. Marr, *Vietnamese Anticolonialism*, 185.
28. Pike, *Vietnam War*, 2.

to the principles of people's war; but the Vietnamese themselves distinguished people's war, which they saw in essence as a combination of military and political struggle, from the August revolution, which was basically won by the political force of the masses and the party alone.[29]

While the August revolution was an example of *khoi nghia* at the national level, a 1969 article in the Hanoi journal *Nghien Cuu Lich Su* (*Historical Research*) asserted that *khoi nghia* was also naturally effective as a grass roots political movement. The writer told of a case of a *khoi nghia* on Minh Island in the Mekong Delta. It happened in 1959 and 1960 during a period of nationwide Communist demonstrations in which party cadres succeeded in rousing unarmed villagers to scare away a government army battalion.[30]

Khoi nghia and the August revolution represent the Vietnamese political supplement to people's war. Dienbienphu, a classic case of the big gamble a people's war is supposed to avoid, represents the military supplement. As Chalmers Johnson puts it, the tradition of Dienbienphu is the military shock attack that, in a single stroke, so bloodies the enemy in the field that his political superiors at home lose their will to continue.[31] The Tet offensive of 1968 and the Easter invasion of 1972 were both launched in this tradition. Dienbienphu was the crowning moment of Giap's career, and it was a tradition he clung to even after the ashes of the Tet offensive. In an interview in the spring of 1969, when asked how the Americans would be defeated, he responded: "Dienbienphu, madame . . . Dienbienphu . . . history doesn't always repeat itself. But this time it will. We won a military victory over the French, and we'll win it over the Americans, too. Yes, madame, their Dienbienphu is still to come. And it will come. The Americans will lose the war on the day when their military might is at its maximum . . . we'll beat them at the moment when they have the most men, the most arms, and the greatest hope of winning."[32] Spectacular as the triumph in 1975 was, however, it was not a Dienbienphu.

---

29. Truong Chinh, *Primer for Revolt*, 19; Bernard B. Fall, Introduction, *ibid.*; Woodside, *Community and Revolution in Modern Vietnam*, 225.
30. To Minh Trung, "Materials for Study: Leading Flag of General Uprising Movement in the South," *Nghien Cuu Lich Su*, I (January, 1969), 47–54.
31. Johnson, *Autopsy on People's War*, 50.
32. Stetler (ed.), *The Military Art of People's War*, 331.

THE SEARCH FOR A STRATEGY AGAINST THE AMERICANS

As far as the basic principles of revolutionary struggle are concerned, the introduction of *khoi nghia* and Dienbienphu were simply measures for victory at the culmination of the third stage of protracted war. For the correct implementation of a people's war, though, these doctrinal "novelties" created complications. But, as long as the war was in a guerrilla warfare stage, these introductions posed no problems. In late 1964, however, when consideration of a lunge for victory became possible, the marriage of these supplements to people's war became difficult. To such believers in the Chinese version of people's war as Truong Chinh, general offensive–general uprising (a Communist term that put the traditions of *khoi nghia* and Dienbienphu together) was left-wing opportunism pure and simple, while to others the simple people's war formula was too slow. The advent of significant numbers of American ground combat troops further complicated matters, all of which prompted a full-fledged debate over military strategy.

The elements introduced by the Americans were disturbing. First, there was the military challenge of the tremendous, superior mobility of allied forces, which was due in large part to the ubiquitous helicopter transports, and their massive firepower on the ground, which was multiplied by overlapping artillery fans. And in the air, helicopter gunships, low-flying ground support planes, and tactical fighter-bombers were poised to respond almost instantly to a ground commander's call. This made frontal assaults on the most isolated of Allied positions suicidal, and even lightning surprise attacks in the middle of the night could be broken up. How, then, was one to progress through the three stages of protracted war, if the enemy possessed greater numbers, firepower, and mobility? Further, long-range air strikes made it very difficult to establish secure base areas, and the thought of permanently liberated zones seemed vainglorious indeed. Pike asked the question that surely must have struck the Hanoi leadership as well: "What defense does a people's war have against long range air strikes?" Even more disturbing was the fact that largely because of the air strikes and the terrorism in the countryside, by 1965 security had replaced land as the dominant concern of the peasant masses. With land as the concern, the Communists could reach the peasantry with their old agrarian policies and formulas, but with security as the focus, there were no ready answers.[33]

The debate lasted from 1964 to 1968 and was conducted both by the leadership in Hanoi and by senior commanders of the southern battlefield. While the debate was largely a function of the complexity of the battlefield situation, it also reflected the fact that this was a period in which Giap's military authority may not have been absolute. From 1959 to 1961 Giap shared power with Nguyen Chi Thanh, and despite the latter's departure to command forces in the South, reverberations of their differences may well have persisted until Thanh's untimely death in 1967. The chief participants, at least in terms of published writings, were Giap, Le Duan, and Van Tien Dung in Hanoi, and Nguyen Chi Thanh, Truong Son, and Cuu Long (the latter two being *nommes des guerres*) in the South. Essentially, the debate revolved around the question of whether, in addition to protracted guerrilla warfare, pressure should be put on the Americans through continual frontal assaults and large-scale battles. By the summer of 1967 the debate was shelved, probably because of Nguyen Chi Thanh's death, a more immediate concern over whether to hold negotiations, and preparations for the Tet offensive. The arguments of this debate, however, shed light on the evolving definition of people's war.[34]

It must be emphasized at the outset that there were clear doctrinal limits to the debate. Any thought of formally abandoning people's war or the strategy of general offensive–general uprising was definitely beyond the pale. While the principals wrote and obliquely criticized each other, other articles in official journals were restating the fundamental tenets of people's war as if to say, whatever it is that the leaders are debating, the basics remain sacrosanct. Among these untouchables were the overall strategy of people's war relying principally on protracted war and self-reliance, the necessity of both political and armed struggle, an army drawn from the masses, a broad-based united front that is placed under the leadership of the workers and a Marxist-Leninist party, and the combination of rural struggle and urban struggle through legal,

33. Pike, *Vietnam War*, 10; Robert L. Sansom, *The Economics of Insurgency*, 236–40.

34. JUSPAO, *VNDRN*, No. 106–II, p. iii; Patrick J. McGarvey (ed.), *Visions of Victory: Selected Vietnamese Communist Military Writings, 1964–1968* (Stanford, Calif., 1969), 3–24.

semilegal, and illegal methods. As late as July, 1965, there was a re-statement of the three stages of people's war in straight Maoist terms, though they were given new names: defense, resistance, and counteroffensive. Nevertheless, despite these constraints, there remained plenty of latitude for discussion.[35]

In a January, 1966, article in *Hoc Tap*, "Once Again We Will Win," Giap confidently declared the fundamental soundness of the weapon of "invincible people's war," which he described as a closely coordinated revolution of the masses through both armed and political struggle. William Turley argues, however, that in the existing situation, Giap felt that the Viet Cong should revert to guerrilla tactics and avoid set-piece battles with the Americans, because even though they lacked a political base in Viet Nam, the Americans' superior firepower made it impossible to push them into the sea. For this Giap was accused of harboring "rightist tendencies," but it was his firm view, according to Patrick McGarvey, that only the combination of a grueling, protracted war of attrition and morale-shattering attacks on urban centers would induce the United States to seek a withdrawal.[36]

Giap's views were later supported by the more general exposition of Le Duan, who provided a comprehensive overview of the war, which he termed "a people's war developed to a very high level." Presumably the high level was due to the addition of the strategy of the general offensive–general uprising. In his treatise, Le Duan's invocation of the tradition of Dienbienphu and *khoi nghia* was clearest when he talked about the opportunities of revolutionary leaps: "If we strike at the right moment, pick the right target and . . . couple . . . armed assaults with popular uprisings, then we can make very important leaps apt to change . . . the face of war." Thus, Le Duan, too, favored a reliance on protracted guerrilla tactics coupled with carefully timed shock assaults on key targets. Continual big-unit battles would only drain away resources needed for these attacks.[37]

Opposing this view as much as was possible in the confines of this

35. Hoang Van Thai, "The Strategy of People's War and the Building of the People's Armed Force," *Hoc Tap*, VII (July, 1965), 44–45; "The Problem of National Liberation in This Era," *Hoc Tap*, III (March, 1964), 9–15.

36. Stetler (ed.), *The Military Art of People's War*, 263–65; Turley "Civil-Military Relations in North Viet Nam," 890; McGarvey (ed.), *Visions of Victory*, 41.

37. Le Duan, *The Vietnamese Revolution*, 67, 74.

debate was General Nguyen Chi Thanh. He favored continuing frontal assaults on American forces, no matter how bloody, over more protracted forms of guerrilla warfare. He also chided unnamed critics (presumably Giap) for preoccupation with the number of phases in a guerrilla war and with which phase the Communists were in presently. To Thanh this offered no guidance to the current situation, since history can never be repeated exactly. He knew better than to formally disavow people's war, and Patrick McGarvey suggests that Thanh left it to his deputy Truong Son to square his views with people's war.[38]

While acknowledging that "guerrilla warfare is the magic wand of any liberation war" and that the lesson of the 1966–1967 dry season was that small- and large-scale attacks must be closely combined, Truong Son still argued that in fighting the Americans, big-unit battles must be pursued, because the Americans must be kept off-balance and because without these large-scale operations guerrilla warfare would get nowhere. In this connection, Turley contends that one of those who carried on Thanh's views after his death was Van Tien Dung, the army's chief of staff and the field commander of the final campaign of liberation in 1975.[39]

Another participant in the debate, Cuu Long, was probably a COSVN commander in the Mekong Delta. (Cuu Long is the classic Vietnamese name for Mekong.) Reflecting the typical frustrations of a field commander wanting to be heard, he felt that the relevance of people's war could be recaptured if the leaders paid attention to certain points. He stressed that a people's war, as opposed to a conventional war, depended on an all-around struggle: armed and political struggle, and military proselyting, through the efforts of all three forces—local, regional, and main forces. However, the central fact to be grasped, in his opinion, was that the basic forces for carrying out a people's war were the guerrillas and "people's militia," or regional forces. Despite Cuu Long's obvious bias in favor of protracted guerrilla war, he was unwilling to abandon the principle of stages. Instead he proposed a new scheme of four stages that traced the succession of a people's war from a low to a high

38. Turley, "Civil-Military Relations in North Viet Nam," 892; McGarvey (ed.), *Visions of Victory,* 11.
39. McGarvey (ed.), *Visions of Victory,* 21, 148; Turley, "Civil-Military Relations in North Viet Nam," 893.

degree. In short, Cuu Long did not favor large-scale or concentrated attacks until the guerrilla forces had built themselves up to capable, large-unit formations.[40]

In the debate Giap had the last word with the publication of his major work, *Big Victory, Great Task,* in September, 1967, just after Thanh's death and just before the Tet offensive. The tone of the book was that of a relaxed, "all is well" review of past progress. He concluded, "A glance at all aspects of the anti–U.S. national-salvation resistance war of our people shows that the war situation has never been so favorable as it is now." This was partly because, in perhaps the first major Vietnamese review of the American global strategy of flexible response, Giap contended the Vietnamese had discredited the strategy of local war (which he linked to the Kennedy administration's new military principle of flexible response) by pushing the Americans past the limits envisioned for this type of war, thereby proving it to be impractical. He said that a local war at a maximum should only tie up six American divisions, and nine were already in Viet Nam with no victory in sight. Naturally, he ascribed the victory to the strategy and tactics of people's war. "Relying mainly on their own strength, our people in the South successfully conducted a general uprising and defeated the special war of the American and the puppets."[41]

Emphasizing the balanced nature of the struggle, Giap recounted the progress made in the three prongs of attack. In the armed struggle he boasted that the Binh Gia victory in January, 1965, marked the defeat of the Americans' "special war strategy" (fighting through proxies), forcing them into an undesirable local war and driving the puppet troops into a state of collapse. In the political struggle he claimed that in 1965 and 1966, thirty cities seethed with the demonstrations of urbanites rising up against the Thieu-Ky clique and creating an unstable political situation. As for military proselyting, he pointed to the military crisis in I Corps, which required five changes in commanders in five months.[42]

40. McGarvey (ed.), *Visions of Victory,* 101, 107–112.

41. Vo Nguyen Giap, "The Big Victory, the Great Task," in McGarvey (ed.), *Visions of Victory,* 206–208, 223, 228–29, 235.

42. *Ibid.,* 200–202. While on the mark in the first prong, he offered no evidence to support Communist responsibility for progress in the other two.

The upshot of this debate over military strategy, which was linked to the larger attempt to develop a more mature phase of revolutionary theory, was basically a reaffirmation of people's war as the party's military doctrine, albeit with some changes. The necessity of stages was dropped, though some continued to display a lingering affection for them. There were also some distinctive Vietnamese additions, primarily the incorporation of the strategy of general offensive–general uprising as a tribute to *khoi nghia* and Dienbienphu, and also such concepts as revolutionary leaps, the three strategic areas, the three prongs, and the three methods of legal, semilegal, and illegal activities, the latter two having been mentioned by Ho as far back as the 1920s.

POST-TET OFFENSIVE FORMULATIONS

Although numerous Communist documents indicate that the Tet Offensive was a go-for-broke bid for political power, its true objective remains controversial.[43] In any case, it was a watershed in the Viet Nam War. Ho Chi Minh, in a July, 1968, speech (barely two months after the conclusion of the offensive), remarked that the war had reached a new stage. Indeed in recognition of this, the Communists introduced two new organizations to their war effort. In April, 1968, in the midst of the offensive, they announced the creation of the Vietnam Alliance of National Democratic and Peaceful Forces to broaden the base of their united front, perhaps in response to Lin Piao's criticism that the National Liberation front had too narrow a social base. A year later, the Provisional Revolutionary Government was established to make demands for a coalition government credible and to show that the prong of political struggle, too, had reached a high level.[44]

The Tet offensive required some theoretical rethinking as well. Shortly after the offensive Truong Chinh delivered a major speech, ostensibly on Karl Marx. The Hanoi press hailed it as a "new contribution to the treasury of theoretical works on the Vietnamese Revolution," although it admitted that its presentation was followed by "several sessions of heated debate." This was no doubt an understatement. The speech was

43. See, for example, JUSPAO, *VNDRN*, No. 22; *VNDRN*, Nos. 28–29.
44. Ho Chi Minh, *Selected Writings*, 340; JUSPAO, *VNDRN*, No. 42, p. 1; *VNDRN*, No. 101–III, p. 1.

a quite explicit rejection of the strategy of all-out offensives advocated by his politburo colleagues Le Duan and Giap. For example, he said: "We must . . . grasp the motto of 'long-drawn out fight and relying mainly on one's self,'" and "Our strategy is to protract the war; therefore, in tactics, we should avoid unfavorable fights to the death."[45]

The rejoinders were relatively tame. In an article in *Nhan Dan* (*People's Daily*) in February, 1970, Le Duan, in effect, equivocated by pleading for flexibility in military strategy and decrying the invocation of standard formulas: "There has never been nor will there ever be a single formula for carrying out the revolution that is appropriate to all circumstances and times. . . . The whole question depends on the concrete conditions of history." He further insisted that despite what happened during Tet, one cannot succeed without attempting such uprisings, although he did admit that a victorious revolution depended on a balanced, judicious step-by-step process. He did not comment on whether or not the Tet offensive fit into such a process.[46]

Giap's response was another book, *Banner of People's War, The Party's Military Line*, published in December, 1969. The book was more somber in tone than his previous writings, but the title bespoke his continued devotion to people's war. He wrote, "Our Party's military line is the people's war line." He continued to stress the importance of coordinating guerrilla warfare with regular warfare and that "only in the situation where guerrilla war grows and thrives does the regular war have favorable conditions for developing its powerful force and for advancing incessantly."[47]

Giap's central effort in this book was to set forth a new "people's war waging formula," which was really another attempt at integrating people's war with the strategy of general offensive–general uprising. He laid down six new requirements. First, his formula was that of a comprehensive, all-people's war associating military forces with political forces in a grand armed and political revolution. Second, he called for closely coordinated attacks in the three strategic areas. Third, he demanded a thorough understanding of the ideology of the strategic offensive in a revolutionary war. (The implications here were that Tet-like

45. JUSPAO, *VNDRN*, No. 51, pp. 1–2.
46. *Ibid.*, No. 77, pp. ii, 20.
47. *Ibid.*, No. 70, pp. 13, 61.

offensives were an integral part of people's war, but they should be launched only after careful analysis of the concrete conditions.) Fourth, the new form still required a protracted war strategy that nevertheless displayed a willingness to exploit opportunities for larger victories. Fifth, while attriting enemy forces continued to be an objective, the new formula called for equal attention to building up an administrative power. (This may be regarded as a revival of the principle of developing base and liberated areas.) And sixth, he insisted on a rule of self-reliance while simultaneously seeking international assistance.[48]

In this book Giap also gave greater prominence to the tactic of fighting the many with the few, or fighting strength with weakness. This no doubt reflected a recognition that in purely conventional terms the Vietnamese could never hope to reach a superior balance of forces against the Americans. Mao reached a similar conclusion earlier vis-à-vis the Japanese, but unlike the Chinese, the Vietnamese were not willing to abandon large-scale attacks for an indefinite protracted war. They lacked the patience. Consequently, Van Tien Dung, in a companion piece to Giap's book, proclaimed, "We have eliminated every military formula according to which attacks can only be launched when we possess more numerous and more powerful weapons and technical means than does the enemy."[49] Thus, after Tet, the Vietnamese still clung to people's war as their military line, but with a restated formula that permitted them to continue large offensives in the Dienbienphu, *khoi nghia* tradition along with "classical" protracted war. Once again, though, they stressed the necessity of balance between armed struggle and political struggle, and between guerrilla warfare and regular warfare.

THE SOUNDS OF SILENCE

The period roughly from the signing of the Paris Peace Agreement in January, 1973, until the liberation of Saigon on April 30, 1975, and on to the present has been a time of eloquent silence on the subject of people's war. Even at the time of the liberation of Saigon, a much-feted triumph, there were no expressions of gratitude to the theory of people's war.

48. *Ibid.*, 40–53. The comments in parentheses are mine.
49. *Ibid.*, i; No. 71, p. 17.

In early 1972, Giap came out with a series of articles in *Nhan Dan* under the general title, "Arm the Revolutionary Masses and Build the People's Army." This work, however, was mainly a recapitulation of Vietnamese military history and does not replace *The Party's Military Line* as a statement of his miliary thought. The only new note in these articles was a recognition of the need to modernize the army and to introduce a more direct form of conscription.[50]

Significantly, it was Van Tien Dung, the field commander of the "great spring victory," who was called upon to write the official account. Modestly he started out by saying that fuller versions of the liberation would be forthcoming in books and articles for years to come, but, despite his promise, so far there have been very few. Further, he called the campaign a general offensive and uprising, yet at no point does he refer to any concrete examples of uprisings. Although he did make occasional references to the people's war strategy, he neglected to show where or how the strategy was carried out. In fact, what is striking about Dung's account is its totally conventional military tone. It reads as a pure and simple narrative of a major conventional military campaign by the regular North Vietnamese army overwhelming the army of the South Vietnamese government.[51]

One point of interest in Dung's account that becomes clear is the absolute command of the North Vietnamese Communist party over the campaign. This was particularly evident with the arrival of politburo member Le Duc Tho in Loc Ninh (a small district town thirty miles north of Saigon) in April to establish a party forward headquarters and issue directives personally in behalf of the Hanoi leadership. Thus, at the victory celebrations, Le Duc Tho could honestly say that the triumph was due to "the correct and talented leadership of the party."[52]

In a subsequent article under the joint authorship of Giap and Dung, there were more references to people's war. The campaign was referred to as a balanced people's war offensive, and the stock formula was repeated: "Another outstanding success of our party consisted in creating and developing to a very high level the combined strength of people's war, of revolutionary war, using military attacks by mobile strategic army columns as main striking forces, combining military attacks with

50. *Ibid.*, No. 106–III, pp. v, 3–4.
51. Van Tien Dung, *Our Great Spring Victory*, pp. 2–3, 13–14.
52. *Ibid.*, 119, 152, 184, 256.

popular uprisings, combining military struggle with political struggle and agitation among enemy troops . . . and winning total victory by means of a general offensive and uprising right in the 'capital city.'" The article continued with assertions that guerrilla forces and regional forces participated wholeheartedly, and uprisings by the masses burst out everywhere. It is strange that in his account Dung mentioned none of this. In fact, one suspects that the Hanoi leadership had this article published under the authorship of both chief military leaders to expressly correct Dung's theoretical oversight. The article itself offered no new concrete example of any of this activity. Instead it proceeded with a purely military analysis of such topics as the space factor, time factor, and mobility and rapid deployment, applying various forms of combat (with some minimal references to people's war), and the surprise factor.[53] What was significant was that despite the obvious gap between theory and the reality of the conduct of the final campaign, it appeared viscerally impossible for the Vietnamese to abandon the people's war formula—as if to do so might vitiate the legitimacy of thirty years of struggle.

The Minimal Definition of a Marxist People's War of National Liberation

This journey to a minimal definition of a Marxist people's war of national liberation has been designed to show two things. First, Communist concepts develop and change in response to new events and ideas, and these changes are supposed to improve the usefulness of the concepts to furthering the revolutions at hand. Hence, one must be flexible in approaching definitions and sensitive to the time and phase to which one is applying a definitional standard. It is not fair, for example, to use a 1940 formulation of people's war to judge the actions of Vietnamese revolutionaries in the 1970s. Second, minimal definitions are nevertheless possible, and in fact crucial to the legitimacy of a Communist revolution. In the Communist world individual careers and entire revolutions are made or broken on the basis of following the proper line or strategy. In the eyes of comrades or fraternal Socialist parties, what the

53. Vo Nguyen Giap and Van Tien Dung, *How We Won the War* (Ypsilanti, Mich., 1976), 40–54.

leadership of a revolutionary movement says it is doing is important, and its legitimacy depends on actually accomplishing what it has staked out as its theoretical task.

In their revolution, the Vietnamese claimed to have achieved liberation against both the French and the Americans through a Marxist, people's war of national liberation. Further, they have contended time and again that their experience stands as a great beacon and lesson for other revolutionary movements to follow and learn from. In determining the degree of universal relevance of the Vietnamese victory, whatever concessions they must make for flexibility, the Vietnamese have to be true at least to their own terms, and to the extent that they consider their struggle to be a people's war of worldwide significance, they must meet the standards of the Chinese formulation as well. It is hardly unreasonable to levy on the Vietnamese the definitional requirement that the practice of their people's war be in accord with their own theoretical formulations, as they have been unwavering since 1941 in their insistence that their struggle was a people's war. However much the strategy was rephrased, reformulated, and reargued, and whatever the changes in practice, people's war is a term they have always stuck with.

The most universal definition is Lin Piao's. It has five requirements for a people's war. First, it must be led by a Leninist party. Second, it must be based on mass support and a united front. Third, it must have an army controlled by the Leninist party. Fourth, it must develop rural revolutionary base areas. Finally, it must be a protracted war based on the following points: a mass line, a self-reliant effort with only supplemental amounts of foreign assistance, and, though regular stages may not be necessary, the war should develop from guerrilla into conventional war and be sustained by these irregular forces and their popular and local sources of recruitment.

The Vietnamese have not refuted the Chinese formulation but have added to it. Most fundamentally, they have added their traditions of *khoi nghia* and Dienbienphu in the general offensive–general uprising strategic supplement, which comes close to overturning Mao's caution against risking all-out attacks. In essence, the Vietnamese theoretical approach to people's war and revolution in general has been one of balance—balance between armed struggle and political struggle, between town and country, between men and weapons, and between guerrilla forces and conventional forces. While the Vietnamese, too, have abandoned the three stages, the kernel of the idea remains in the continued insistence that the different types of warfare and forces are all necessary and flow into and renew one another.

Taking these two definitions together, it appears that Lin Piao's is the fundamental one, although a few caveats and comments are in order. The creation of a revolutionary base area, though certainly helpful in aiding self-reliance, is not critical, since such a requirement would limit people's wars to very large or sparsely populated countries. Both the Chinese and Vietnamese have, in practice, been hypocritical about self-reliance, though the Vietnamese have been so to a greater degree than the Chinese. Yet the essence of self-reliance is that it ties people's war to the people. The less one relies on the people, the less one has a people's war, so the point is still a crucial one. This is especially true in considering the Vietnamese penchant for large offensives. It seems that such a strategy can only be squared with the requirements of a people's war if the effort occurs as a result of a balanced growth of forces *within* the country of struggle and is tangibly supported by efforts of the movement's mass base. In other words, it must be essentially a self-reliant effort, although international support in the form of weapons is probably necessary and doctrinally permissible.

Looking at all these definitional ingredients together, and comparing them with the actual performance of the Communists, the conclusion is simple: in their victory they were not true to their own strategy. Thus, although they won, they also lost. Just as the Americans were flying blind in a cloud of numbers, the Communists, after the Tet offensive, were also flying blind without a revolutionary strategy to serve as a compass. Despite continued lip service to people's war, the strategy had been broken and the path to liberation descended to the pedestrian and unillumining route of conventional warfare. The Communist triumph, when it finally came, was devoid of any elevating revolutionary theory to legitimize the seizure of power. Although this may not have mattered in the first flush of victory in 1975, events since then have proven the wisdom of Lin Piao's warning that if the precepts of a people's war are not faithfully followed, "no victory can be won, or be consolidated even if it is won."[54]

54. Lin Piao, *Long Live the Victory of People's War!*, 42. Even though in context this quote pertains to self-reliance, it is no travesty of Lin Piao's meaning to apply it to a more general application of people's war as a whole.

CONCLUSION

To most Americans, the war in Viet Nam seems to have been a great defeat for the United States, a triumph for the Communist forces in Viet Nam, and a vindication of the revolutionary strategy of people's war. It was not so simple. Viet Nam was the war everyone lost—and won. Thus before any lessons can be proclaimed, the question of what actually happened needs to be reexamined. Those who contend, for example, that the lesson of Viet Nam is that the United States should adopt a policy of total nonintervention are obviously basing this view on the perception that the United States failed in its intervention and therefore should not try again. Granted, the United States failed, but the crucial point is not so much the failure itself as it is the nature and extent of this failure.

The war in Viet Nam is best seen from two vantage points: as a struggle for national legitimacy in Viet Nam and as an attempted demonstration of the revolutionary strategy of people's war. In terms of relative importance, the former contest was more crucial to the Vietnamese (Communists and nationalists) and the latter of greater consequence to the Americans. In my analysis of these two struggles, my conclusions suggest very different lessons from those based glibly on the general fact of the American failure.

National Legitimacy

The immediate struggle in Viet Nam was the competition between the Communists and the Saigon government for the mantle of national legitimacy. This struggle, in turn, divided into a contest both for traditional legitimacy and modern legitimacy. With respect to traditional legitimacy, while the Communists essentially desired to impose an entirely different basis of legitimacy (Marxism) as their goal, they were careful to behave according to the dictates of traditional legitimacy on their way to this goal. Correct hierarchical relations were preserved by

Bao Dai's abdication in favor of Ho Chi Minh in 1945; and when the French tried to return after World War II, the Viet Minh played the part of national protector of the fatherland.

In the second war, with the Americans, the United States committed a grave mistake in dispatching large numbers of ground combat troops to Viet Nam. The presence of these troops made it difficult for the Saigon government to hold onto its claims of traditional legitimacy, and correspondingly easy for the Communists to depict themselves as champions against yet another foreign intervenor and to link themselves with all the heroes of the past who had fought against the intrusions of outsiders. If the Americans thought they were very different from Frenchmen, they did not appear to be to the villagers. The Viet Cong, of course, did everything they could to keep these differences blurred.

What made the situation even worse was that the South Vietnamese leaders had very few claims of their own to national legitimacy. Although Ngo Dinh Diem was a nationalist, he did very little to show his sentiments during the struggle against the French. The subsequent leaders, Nguyen Cao Ky and Nguyen Van Thieu, both served in the French armed forces; thus, whatever sympathies they had for independence did not come into public view. Naturally, these facts and the presence of the American troops redounded to the credit of the Communists. They also played a useful role in deflecting attention from the fundamental incompatibility between Marxism and the nature of traditional Vietnamese legitimacy. The Communists might not have gotten away with this if American troops had not been so conspicuously present.

Admittedly, there is a "catch-22" quality to this *ex post facto* counsel. Whatever the ultimately fatal effects of the large injection of American GI's into the stream of Vietnamese society, it is also clear that the whole effort would have been lost from the very beginning without such an infusion. The Communists themselves have repeatedly affirmed that the South would have been theirs in 1964 and 1965 were it not for the dispatch of these troops. Yet the point remains that this infusion created a dependency that made the South Vietnamese too vulnerable to stand on their own in the last crisis.

Nevertheless, in a tragic sense, the South Vietnamese had been trying. The story of this dependency is akin to J. R. R. Tolkien's dramatic trilogy, *The Lord of the Rings*. The humanlike hobbits, Bilbo and then Frodo, stumble onto a magical ring that gives them the power to become invisible. Yet with each use of the ring they lose something of their visible, material substance. The drama of this trilogy lies in whether Frodo can destroy the ring before it destroys him. He barely makes it. The South Vietnamese, in invoking the ring of American power, did not. In 1964 and 1965 the massive American intervention on all fronts saved the South Vietnamese government for another day. The cost in substance, of course, was the native legitimacy of this regime. Again in the Tet offensive American power was invoked, although this time the South Vietnamese displayed some political leadership and the army at least did not disintegrate. But again there was a further cost to Saigon's legitimacy. Once more, in the Easter invasion, it was necessary to call in American power. This time the South Vietnamese were able to handle the situation on the ground, but not without the crucial ingredient of American air power. The cost to South Viet Nam, though, was the toll on the nerves of its leader, Nguyen Van Thieu, who by now was convinced that he could only exercise his leadership by resorting to military force. Finally, in 1975 the ring of American power could no longer be summoned and the South Vietnamese government disappeared, having sacrificed too much of its substance to this ring.

From an American perspective, the commitment of these ground combat troops linked the American destiny too closely to that of the Vietnamese. This raised the stakes of the conflict far out of proportion to its worth to any of the international patrons. In response, both the Soviets and Chinese provided more aid more faithfully than they had for any other people's war. That such revolutionary constancy may not have been worth it to the Soviets is suggested by their failure to respond to Nixon's unprecedented mining and bombing of Hanoi and Haiphong on the eve of the Moscow summit meeting in May, 1972. Instead the summit was held, the participants all smiles, almost as if there were no war raging in Viet Nam.

In addition to the struggle for traditional legitimacy, both sides sought to lead the country into the modern world. In this contest for modern legitimacy, both were hindered by their lack of self-reliance. In the 1960s the South Vietnamese government did make some definite strides toward national legitimacy. Fair elections were held. Thanks to American aid, government services began to reach the countryside. In 1970 a sweeping land reform bill was finally implemented. But the whole system was underwritten by American aid. The government never developed the ability to collect its own taxes, and the temptation of relying on the Americans rather than facing hard political choices seriously undermined the independence and legitimacy of the basic political order.

Although it was not apparent during the war, the record of the Communists with respect to modern legitimacy has been almost worse. Politically, however repressive the Saigon regime may have appeared, there was still more freedom in the South than in the North. The Communists have been as inept at economics as they are adept at fighting. Today the former territory of South Viet Nam is less prosperous than it was in the days of Nguyen Van Thieu. With economic prosperity one of the prime goals of modern development and legitimacy, the Communist rulers are in a difficult position that cannot all be blamed on the destruction of the war. Since "liberation" in 1975, Vietnamese from all ethnic backgrounds and social classes have fled the fatherland in historically unprecedented numbers. Further, in a backhanded tribute to the former regime's land reform bill, official Communist spokesmen admit that a *cause célèbre* of the war, the idea of land to the tiller, is now passé because the power of the landlord class has already been broken.[1] Interestingly, this happy arrival of rural justice has not been accompanied by any dramatic rise in agricultural production. Although bumper crops were turned in by Mekong Delta peasants after the 1970 land reform bill, since liberation economic mismanagement and peasant resistance to attempted price controls have severed the link between rural justice and agricultural prosperity.

Indeed, despite everyone's showy interest in their welfare throughout the war, the peasants must have regarded both nationalists and Communists as strange. South Vietnamese government officials, by their dress, demeanor, and social background, were largely viewed as cosmopolitan snobs. In sharp contrast, the humble origins, appearance, and social proximity of most Communist cadres made them far more credible to the peasantry because the Communists appeared far less in-

---

1. William J. Duiker, *Vietnam Since the Fall of Saigon*, Ohio University Southeast Asia Series, LVI (Athens, Ohio, 1980), 8.

terested in self-aggrandizement.[2] Moreover, appeals by government officials to nationalism and the inauguration of government-designed development projects evoked little enthusiasm or support. The patriotic appeals were rarely linked to issues of village politics, and the development projects were fashioned without much knowledge of communal needs.

The Communists, on the other hand, were closer to the people, and their cadres became adroit at adapting the program of the National Liberation front to the local needs of villagers. Nevertheless, however satisfactory the performance of the Communists at the local level, the larger national objectives of the Viet Cong were as strange as the Western airs of visiting Saigon bureaucrats. Dictatorships of the proletariat and collective farms do not enjoy a rich history in the legends and traditions of the Vietnamese peasantry. As long as there was an incumbent government at the top closely identified with the highly visible American "dominators," the foreignness of communism could be hidden by traditional calls to save the fatherland. With the removal of the incumbent superstructure and its foreign protectors, there was nothing to hide behind.

It can be argued that at the time of the signing of the Paris peace agreement in January, 1973, the South Vietnamese government had attained passive legitimacy. Despite all the American aid, this was not an insignificant achievement. The sudden collapse of the former government of South Viet Nam two years after the peace agreement, however, demonstrated that the larger goal of transforming its tenuous writ of passive legitimacy to an active form had never been attained. The Americans had "let it down" before this could happen. But just as the Americans cannot take all the credit for the apparent stability in 1973, they cannot be entirely blamed for Saigon's collapse either.

Turning to the Communists' side, their seizure of power in 1975 has not automatically guaranteed them a claim to the Mandate of Heaven and national legitimacy, either active or passive. While the Communists continue to hold onto the power they won in 1975, at this writing the question of the national legitimacy of their regime remains unresolved, much in the same way, though for different reasons, that the question remained unresolved during years of the American involvement. As in

2. Popkin, *The Rational Peasant*, 261.

many other underdeveloped countries, Heaven's jurors have yet to return with the verdict of who shall be the next emperor to pick up the fallen mandate of the toppled precolonial order of the past. Although the Americans and South Vietnamese have lost, national legitimacy in Viet Nam has not yet been won by anyone.

The "achievement" of this stalemate perhaps entitles the United States to recoup some self-respect from its involvement in Viet Nam, but the luster of this accomplishment is dimmed by the Americans' basic ignorance of what they were doing. Unsure of itself in a French colonial environment, the United States grasped at whatever analagous experiences it could think of (except, of course, that of the French) and relied too heavily on all the numbers flowing from its computers. While these numbers told many tales, they said very little about national and revolutionary legitimacy.

The Americans' ignorance showed up most clearly in the failures in human intelligence. In other counterinsurgency operations against Communist guerrillas, intelligence operations often provided critical breakthroughs. Early in the Malayan emergency (from 1948 to 1960), the British flushed out and killed the Communist military commander. Later they penetrated the courier system of the insurgents. In the 1940s repeated raids on party hideouts kept the Communist guerrilla leadership in Greece on the run and off-balance. During the campaign against the Huks in the Phillippines, a raid in 1950 netted the entire Communist party politburo. There were no such dramatic coups in Viet Nam.

In fact, in Viet Nam the intelligence advantages lay in the hands of the Communists. Achieving these advantages, of course, is the primary military objective of a people's war strategy. Despite the fact that American military units had a virtually undefeated record in the field, they repeatedly failed to clinch their engagements by their inability to carry out the classic mission of the infantry, "to close with and destroy the enemy." In failing to do this, it was for a lack, not of prowess or firepower, but of intelligence. Truong Nhu Tang, who was a founding member of the National Liberation front in 1960 and who defected and now resides in Paris, told Al Santoli that Viet Cong units frequently operated within three hundred meters of unsuspecting American GI's and that they had advance knowledge of allied operations.[3] In retaining

3. Al Santoli, "Why Viet Cong Flee," *Parade*, July 11, 1982, p. 5.

such advantage until the very end of the war, one important objective of a people's war was achieved.

If the main focus of the war was on the legitimacy crisis in Viet Nam, offstage it was nevertheless true that the war itself had become a legitimacy crisis to the Americans. After all, it was not unreasonable for the American public to expect and insist on concrete results from an investment of a half-million men. As the troop numbers rose to this level, confident promises rained down like manna from administration spokesmen. "The boys will be home by Christmas" and "the light is at the end of the tunnel" were some of the more reassuring ones. The promises ended with the Tet offensive in 1968. After Tet, both sides were floundering in the dark, one in ignorance and the other without a legitimating revolutionary strategy. The American command, however, was correct in claiming a major victory at Tet, both militarily and politically. This time, though, in finally bringing the Communist wolf to bay, almost no one would listen because of all the rosy-hued cries in the past. And the war dragged on to a much different conclusion.

Revolutionary Legitimacy

Adhering to the definitional criteria of people's war was crucial to the Communists' claim that the Vietnamese revolution had wider application. The Vietnamese were faithful to this strategy in the Resistance War against the French and also in the war against the Americans until the Tet offensive. Tet was supposed to be the culmination of the people's war strategy, but the offensive was beaten back. More than just a military defeat, the Tet offensive shattered the revolutionary strategy. After some groping, the Communists thereafter essentially abandoned people's war and took another road, leaving the strategy and path of people's war unillumined by the Vietnamese experience and even somewhat discredicted for future use.

The full extent of the Communists' failure stands out in starkest relief when their performance is measured by their own definitional criteria. The final definition of people's war for the Vietnamese was a typical mix of something orthodox from China supplemented by the Vietnamese traditions of *khoi nghia* and Dienbienphu, as well as an overall Vietnamese concern for balance.

In two respects the Vietnamese revolutionaries *were* faithful to Mao and Lin Piao's 1965 formulation of people's war. The Communists were led by a Leninist party serving as a vanguard. The point to note, though, is that this Leninist party was the Lao Dong party of Hanoi and not the fictitious party in the South, the People's Revolutionary party, that supposedly guided the National Liberation front. Also, Communist military forces—North Vietnamese regulars and Viet Cong guerrillas—were controlled by a Leninist party. General Giap in all his theoretical and historical writings, was dutifully subservient to a commanding role for the party. That the party controlled the gun and not vice versa also stands out in Van Tien Dung's account of the final triumphant campaign of 1975. Whatever else it may not have been, the seizure of power in Saigon was the triumph of a Communist party and revolution.

From this point on, though, the case for a Communist claim of successfully waging and proving the efficacy of a strategy of people's war begins to unravel and finally fall apart.

A small country like Viet Nam, where the fighting was "cheek to jowl," simply lacked the space for accommodating the Chinese requirement of revolutionary base areas, and long-range American bombers eliminated the necessary security to show the fence-sitting public what alternative models of society might be possible under communism. Still, it is noteworthy that the Communists repeatedly tried, without much success, to carve out base areas and "liberated zones" within South Viet Nam. Until 1970, however, the press of allied operations always made it more convenient to establish these areas in Cambodia and Laos, despite the difficulties of building a Vietnamese people's war among foreigners. During 1970 the war expanded to all of Indochina, and there no longer were any sanctuaries from Allied depredations. Throughout the war, the Communist base areas remained at a rudimentary level, though they radiated (mainly to foreign journalists) something of a Sherwood Forest allure. Never were any of them economically viable, nor were they ever able to provide enough resources or manpower to sustain the war effort independently. They were, in short, a far cry from Mao Tse-tung's Kiangsi and Yenan Soviets.

Politically, Lin Piao required a people's war to be launched by the vehicle of a united front and to build mass support by promoting a mass line. While the Viet Minh did have the trappings of a united front during the resistance war against the French, this is decidedly not true in the case of the National Liberation front of the Viet Cong. The two other non-Marxist parties in the NLF, the Radical Socialist party and the South Viet Nam Democratic party, existed only on paper, as did the supposed vanguard of the front itself, the People's Revolutionary party. Nevertheless, hypocritical organization though it was, the NLF, with over 300,000 members in the mid-1970s, was the largest, most effective political organization in the country next to, and perhaps including, the cumbersome machinery of the Saigon bureaucracy and military.

Lin Piao's speech is best interpreted as a stinging criticism of the Viet Cong and North Vietnamese for too many requests for foreign aid and too little development of a mass support base among the South Vietnamese people. On this score the sins of comission and omission of the NLF were numerous. The purpose of the mass line is to champion genuinely popular causes, programs, and issues that will broaden the support base of the resistance so that it indeed may become largely self-supporting except for the provision of heavy weaponry. One way *not* to do this is to launch a campaign of indiscriminate terror. Unlike the Chinese and the Viet Minh earlier, the NLF engaged in a major effort of terror and assassination. While some of it was highly selective, the random rocket attacks and shelling of populated areas were not. To the Chinese such a reliance on terror was an unacceptable shortcut that revealed the paucity of the NLF's support base. According to the precepts of people's war, it was, in a word, cheating.

This led to some serious political failures that have received scant attention. It is incredible, for example, that the Communists were not able to forge an effective alliance with the Buddhists, given the venomous and anti-Western feelings of some of the Buddhist sects. The Communists failed to capitalize on the protests against Diem in 1963, and though they were successful in partially taking over the Buddhist demonstrations in 1965 and 1966, they proved unable to ignite the people's passions, as the Buddhist clerics had so successfully done, after the sects decided to rein in their demonstrators. Shocked by the near takeover of their movement in these protests and genuinely frightened by the Tet offensive, most Buddhist groups remained cool to further Communist overtures. Efforts to court ties with the other religious sects, the Cao Dai and the Hoa Hao, did occassionally produce splinter groups, but their memories of previous Communist terror, plus intermittent repeat performances, never really allowed any significant support to develop in these quarters either.

Further, the Communists failed to make inroads in other important sectors. Ironically, as in the case of the pro-Kuomintang syndicalist labor unions in China, South Vietnamese labor, such as it was, owed its main loyalty to the Confederation of Vietnamese Workers, which was led by Tran Quoc Buu, an independent-minded Catholic whose ultimate loyalty nevertheless remained with the government. Intellectuals, as well, for all their grumbling, never really flocked to the banner of the NLF. An organization designed especially for them, and also perhaps to still Chinese criticism, the Viet Nam Alliance of National, Democratic and Peaceful Forces, proclaimed in the midst of the Tet offensive in April, 1968, never really got off the ground. In general, the links of the Communists to the cities and their cosmopolitan culture were always tenuous.

In fact, both sides relied too much on a straight military approach to the essentially political problem between them. Neither side was forced to depend on self-reliance to the extent it had to rely primarily on local sources of support. In the struggle for national legitimacy, this was damaging to both sides, but in the struggle for revolutionary legitimacy it made waging a true people's war all but impossible.

Although Mao and Lin Piao no longer insisted on the three stages of guerrilla, mobile, and regular war by 1965, the orthodox Vietnamese Communists were reluctant to accede to this dispensation. In pragmatically jettisoning the three stages, what remained was the necessity of developing a people's war from guerrilla forms and local sources of recruitment and support, which would form the base for larger military formations and maneuvers and sustain the war even in its last conventional assaults. As a legacy to the three stages, both the Chinese and Vietnamese maintain three levels of forces (village, district, and main force units) in their militaries. Both cite the indispensability of developing all three levels of forces all the way through a people's war. A people's war cannot continue its expansion from a local base unless it simultaneously maintains ties with that base. The Chinese Communists followed such a path to their liberation in 1949 and commended it to revolutionary comrades elsewhere. The Vietnamese followed it faithfully in their Resistance War with the French, and again with the Americans, until the Tet offensive.

The disastrous setback of the Tet offensive sent the Communists into a tailspin. Indigenous southerners manned the first wave of the Communist assaults, and they suffered heavy casualties. According to the script, popular uprisings and defections from ARVN units brought about by this first wave were to be followed by a second wave of regular North Vietnamese troops, catapulting the Communists to power. When the uprisings and defections did not occur, the second wave held back. After Tet, in addition to providing organization and leadership, the northern comrades assumed most of the responsibility for the manpower and resources to carry on the fight. The Easter invasion of 1972 and the "great spring victory of 1975" were conventional assaults by North Vietnamese forces with insignificant participation and support from guerrilla units and organizations of the National Liberation front. Quite simply, after Tet the Communists were no longer fighting a protracted war.

To make the Chinese strategy of people's war more relevant to Viet Nam, the Vietnamese Communists added the homespun ingredients of *khoi nghia* and Dienbienphu, as well as a general concern for balance in the actual waging of the war. Although the August revolution of 1945 was a stellar modern incarnation of the traditional *khoi nghia*, a repetition has not so far occurred. Throughout the war against the Americans, the Communists sought to stir up the people into spontaneous acts against the authorities with the hope that the resultant climate of unrest could build to the point where the government could no longer function. Such was the goal, for example, in capitalizing on the Buddhist protests in 1965 and 1966. In the Tet offensive the military assaults did stun the Saigon bureaucratic apparatus to the point where, if massive popular uprisings had sprung up, they could have brought about the revolutionary deluge. But they did not—not in 1968, 1972, or 1975.

In a negative sense a *khoi nghia*, the paralysis of a political order through popular disturbance, was achieved in the great spring victory of 1975. The waves of popular panic that set in during the last fifty-five days in the Central Highlands, Hue, and Danang made it impossible for the government to function or military resistance to form against the dam-bursting gush of Hanoi's legions. In a sense, then, perhaps Hanoi can justly claim to have waged at least half of a general offensive–general uprising, that is, a general offensive–general panic. Suffice it to say, though, a case for a strategy of people's war based on a proof of anarchy is antithetical to everything Marxism-Leninism stands for. Communists are certainly not squeamish about outbursts of spontaneous violence, but this violence must always be channeled, controlled, and organized by the Leninist party. And, in any case, the NLF can take very little credit for the panic of 1975.

Rebelling against Mao's censure of adventurist, go-for-broke offensives, the Viet Minh seized the bait of an elite French force of paratroopers in the remote hills of Dienbienphu, and turned the French lure into perhaps the most humiliating defeat in the history of France. The difference in opinion between the Chinese and Vietnamese over such daring ventures may have reflected the difference between China, the "semicolony," and Viet Nam, the colony. The Chinese Communists did not think it profitable to indulge in costly efforts for the sake of shaking up domestic opinion in several European countries whose colonial links were not clearly understood by the man in the street. But in Viet Nam, where the colonial ties were clear to the people in both the colony and the metropole, a spectacular military venture, even if it went down to defeat, might so demoralize domestic French opinion that the practical effect of the defeat would still be as a victory. Thus the Vietnamese enshrined the success of Dienbienphu in the canon of their revolutionary doctrine.

Although a departure from Mao's advice, Dienbienphu still represented a genuine culmination to a strategy of people's war. In fact, General Giap, in his account of the siege, is careful to describe it in terms of Mao's three stages of protracted war. The siege itself would never have been successful if the whole country had not been aflame with a carefully developed campaign of people's war. At the time of the siege, local guerrillas had taken control of most of the villages in the Tonkin Delta, regional forces in the Central Highlands were destroying French columns in skillful ambushes, and French positions were subject to hit-and-run attacks in Cochinchina. Far from being an isolated conventional battle, Dienbienphu was the diamond set in a crown of people's war.

But against the Americans, General Giap never got his Dienbienphu. He said that the American defeat would come when the Americans were at their strongest. The equivalent of Dienbienphu in the American war was Tet, not the final campaign in 1975. Although it was Giap who went down to defeat, the American public mistakenly transformed Tet into something of a political Dienbienphu. Tet, however, destroyed the whole crown of people's war. And as spectacular as was the great spring victory—fashioned after Tet—it, too, was not a Dienbienphu.

What was missing from this last campaign was balance. It has always been more important to the Vietnamese than to the Chinese to square their revolution with the dictates of Marxist-Leninist orthodoxy, despite the virtual impossibility of reconciling Vietnamese realities with Communist theory. Mao Tse-tung, in discovering the near uselessness of the urban proletariat as a revolutionary class, offered no apologies for turning to the peasantry. The Vietnamese were constitutionally incapable of breaking the doctrinal umbilical cord to the proletariat and throughout the war always tried to maintain at least some presence in the cities in order to give the proletariat a chance to join in.

Everywhere in Vietnamese Communist writings, a world of symmetry and balance was depicted. According to them, the three stages of the protracted war were flowing into and renewing each other. The war was being waged with equal vigor in the hills, forest, and plains. Efforts in the city and countryside were proceeding in tandem. The method of fighting by three prongs (armed struggle, civilian struggle, and proselyting of ARVN troops) was well integrated. The three levels of forces played mutually reinforcing roles, all in a grand, beautifully orchestrated strategy of people's war. It was a world of dreams.

Obviously the validity of this discussion hinges on what is meant by the term *people*. My definition of *people* has been confined to the people within the territory of the former state of South Viet Nam. Since this was the territory being fought over, it seems logical to confine the definition of people to the residents of this territory and exclude all outsiders, even the North Vietnamese, from inclusion in the term. This, I think, is a fair representation of the meaning of relying on local forces. Nevertheless, the North Vietnamese are, as they frequently said, "kith and kin brothers" of their South Vietnamese compatriots. Hence, why cannot what the North Vietnamese did in 1975 be compared with what the northern Chinese did in 1949? In that campaign Mao raised a force of northerners from his base areas and overran southern China, and no one has accused Mao of not waging a true people's war. If such an expanded territorial definition of the people can be accepted, then the Vietnamese do not end up looking too bad. Still, even with this expanded definition, the Vietnamese case did not represent a protracted war after Tet, nor did it retain its balance after this debacle.

A resolution of this rather crucial definitional puzzle can best come from the North Vietnamese themselves. Despite the fact that the war was orchestrated and controlled by Hanoi from the very outset of the armed struggle, maintaining the fiction that Hanoi was scrupulously adhering to the Geneva accords while the Americans were shamefully violating them was an important plank in Hanoi's appeal to the larger, international audience. The State of North Viet Nam was being violated by dastardly American air attacks while the southerners were waging a legitimate people's war of liberation against the puppets of American neocolonialism. Throughout the war, Hanoi depicted their southern compatriots as being in the vanguard of the fighting front, with the Democratic Republic of [North] Viet Nam serving as the "great socialist rear." Clearly, then, in all Hanoi's official pronouncements, local forces meant southern forces. After the Tet offensive, when local forces were rather plainly sitting on their hands, Hanoi insisted it had no forces in the South. Thus, when Hanoi's forces alone struck in 1972 and triumphed in 1975, according to their own definition of the term *people*, the victory came by a revolution from without.

I have measured the performance of the revolutionaries in terms of their own theory, and from my analysis, one central conclusion is inescapable. Unlike Lenin, Mao, and even Ho Chi Minh, Truong Chinh, and General Giap during their own resistance war, the Vietnamese Communists were no longer doing what they said they were doing after the Tet offensive. Although I have been somewhat exacting in my scrutiny of the revolutionary legitimacy of the Vietnamese demonstration of people's war strategy, I readily concede that following the revolutionary script may not be vital to a successful seizure of power. Certainly the triumph of 1975 demonstrated this. But following the script is important for the broader significance of this victory as a model for the world revolutionary tide of socialism. In virtually abandoning people's war after Tet for the more immediate goal of political power, the significance of the liberation of Saigon in 1975 descended from the general to the merely unique. As a people's war the Vietnamese revolution was a fraud.

As for the Americans, in 1975 the North Vietnamese overwhelmed the South Vietnamese in a conventional invasion that is just the type of assault the American military is so well-equipped and trained to withstand. This was convincingly demonstrated in the repulse of the Tet offensive and the Easter invasion. Thus, the United States succeeded where it was supposed to fail, in suppressing guerrilla warfare, and chose not to participate in a battle it could have won. In misinterpreting the meaning of the Tet offensive, in failing to take military measures, such as supplying the close air support that proved decisive in the Easter invasion, that could clearly have staved off defeat in 1975, the Americans did a far better job of defeating themselves than the Communists ever did.

Wider Implications

An analysis of the war in Viet Nam from the perspectives of both revolutionary and national legitimacy demonstrates that the United States should keep its involvements in Marxist, people's wars, short of a commitment of ground combat troops. Yet it is dangerous to generalize from the single case of Viet Nam and from a definition of national legitimacy specific to Viet Nam. In Greece, for example, the traditional link of Greek politics to external forces and political issues allowed the British to dispatch combat troops to Athens with little stigma. In Malaya the British were able to employ their own troops without the adverse effects experienced by the French and Americans in Viet Nam, and in Laos the presence of foreigners "trampling their grass" was viewed as part of the natural order of life.

These observations illustrate a central point: the answer to the optimal degree of Western intervention in a Marxist, people's war (or other types of rebellion) must come from an analysis of the fundamental components of national legitimacy in a specific country, and of the effects of the various levels of intervention being contemplated on this legitimacy. If, instead of merely applying a global policy without regard to local conditions, a thorough analysis of the nature of legitimacy in

Vietnamese society had been performed, it is doubtful that a case for such a massive involvement as was actually undertaken could have been sustained.

A wider implication to Viet Nam is that the record of the American involvement there should caution against the American penchant for developing global or even regional policies that gloss over analyses specific to a country. An example of this continued predilection for glib uniformities is the catchy phrase, "arc of crisis," used during the Carter administration to describe what once was called the "northern tier" (Greece, Turkey, Iraq, Iran, and Afghanistan). If the nature of this crisis is not differentiated from country to country, the type of mistakes committed in the Viet Nam era will only perpetuate themselves. The transferral of lessons derived from Iran to Saudi Arabia, for example, would be hazardous without careful analysis of both societies. Thus, in the pursuit of global policies, foreign policy decision-makers could profit from applying the "strategic tailoring" of military units to perform missions in a variety of specific environments, to a "political tailoring" of American policies to national political cultures.

This cautionary note is especially salient for the Reagan administration as it promotes its Caribbean Basin plan and attempts to respond simultaneously to insurgencies in most of Central America. While there are many factors that bind the region together, differences among these countries can be crucial. Communist insurgencies raged side by side in Viet Nam, Cambodia, and Laos in Indochina, and though to the Communists and, alas, to the Americans they may have been seen as part of the same revolutionary tide, the three waves had distinct differences. Just because the Cambodian and Vietnamese capitals fell with such forceful drama in April, 1975, there was no reason for the United States to completely give up in Laos. In Laos, Washington was backing a government and leader with widely perceived legitimacy, and a steadier American hand might have achieved a workable stalemate. Similarly, the successful campaign of liberation led by the Sandinistas in 1979 against the Somoza regime in Nicaragua does not necessarily mean that the only possibility for reform in neighboring El Salvador is through revolutionary violence.

Another broad implication of Viet Nam is the revelation of a curious vulnerability of communism as a grounds for the legitimacy of a political order. It has shown itself in China and, in a less pristine fashion, in Viet Nam to be an excellent ideology for seizing power. But, as the repudiation of the legacy of Mao Tse-tung in China and the paralysis and the inability of the Socialist Republic of Viet Nam to manage its economy have proven, communism is far less efficacious as an ideology for development or national legitimacy. In China today people openly wonder if the current "four modernizations" campaign is possible without the unstated fifth modernization, democracy. As Le Duan today contemplates the shambles of his bold theorizing about "three revolutions" in 1967, could it be that he is agonizing over the possibility that to create a socialist man he must first allow a democratic man to rise up and discover his inalienable rights to be free from, among other things, communist theory?

Although my analysis of Viet Nam is confined to an investigation of what happened from the vantage points of national legitimacy and revolutionary legitimacy, it should prove useful for those choosing to define the area of investigation differently. An investigation of the effect of Viet Nam on the international system, for example, could profit from an appreciation of the significance of domestic or internal developments to events in the international arena. Also, ethical analyses and perspectives on the war generally have produced quick denunciations of American actions in the war but a curious silence on the behavior of the Communists, often leaving an impression of Communist rectitude. The attempt here has been to set up a pattern of analyzing the conduct of both sides with equal rigor. I would be very pleased to see ethicists follow this same approach.

The United States is not the only country to have drawn lessons from Viet Nam. The Soviet Union obviously has, too. Studies systematically delineating the lessons of both countries would serve as invaluable counterpoints to each other. The enthusiastic adoption of the helicopter into the Soviet military and the series of Soviet interventions in Africa after the Viet Nam War imply that Viet Nam was a source of some inspiration to the Russians. Interestingly, however, they now seem to be playing more of the role of the Western interventionist, propping up incumbent regimes rather than aiding revolutionary freedom fighters (as both their intervention in Afghanistan and their abandonment of the Eritrean rebels in favor of supporting the new "revolutionary" Ethiopian government illustrates). That American helicopters and tactics were also a source of inspiration elsewhere became ironically clear in the replication of these tactics by the Vietnamese in their invasion and occupation of Cambodia in 1978 and 1979.

For most Americans, the memory of Viet Nam festers as a haunting nightmare of failure. Far from being a simple and abject failure, though, the American intervention in Viet Nam was one of rich variegation. As in the case of Mark Twain's cat drawing the wrong lesson from sitting on a hot stove and therefore unquestioningly assuming that stoves are at all times and places hot, the burners of Viet Nam were hot and cold from time to time and place to place. In Viet Nam places just five miles distant could yield diametrically opposite lessons. Recalling the story of the officers and the adviser, the adviser in the district town had a situation too hot to handle, in bringing national legitimacy to his South Vietnamese counterparts; but the officers in the hills had the North Vietnamese running, and stopped their strategy of people's war cold.

Thus, in losing a people's war, the Communists went on to win the war itself. But in adopting a conventional war strategy, they won by a means they should have lost. The United States, on the other hand, won a war it thought it lost, and lost by default what it could have won.

BIBLIOGRAPHY

Books

Barnet, Richard J. *Intervention and Revolution*. New York, 1968.

Baskir, Lawrence M., and William A. Strauss. *Chance and Circumstance: The Draft, the War, and the Vietnam Generation*. New York, 1978.

Binder, Leonard, et al. *Crises and Sequences in Political Development*. Princeton, N.J., 1971.

Braestrup, Peter. *Big Story: How the American Press and Television Reported and Interpreted the Crisis of Tet 1968 in Vietnam and Washington*. 2 vols. Boulder, Colo., 1977.

Bradford, Zeb B., Jr. "The Lessons of the Vietnam Experience." In *American Defense Policy*, edited by Richard G. Head and Ervin J. Rokke. 3rd ed. Baltimore, 1973.

Brodulina, T., comp. *K. Marx, F. Engels, V. Lenin: A Collection on Historical Materialism*. Moscow, 1972.

Brown, Weldon A. *The Last Chopper: The Denouement of the American Role in Vietnam, 1963–1975*. Port Washington, N.Y., 1976.

Buttinger, Joseph. *Vietnam: A Political History*. New York, 1968.

Carr, Edward Hallett. *Studies in Revolution*. London, 1950.

Chai, Winberg, ed. *Essential Works of Chinese Communism*. Rev. ed. New York, 1972.

Chen, King C. *Vietnam and China, 1938–1954*. Princeton, N.J., 1969.

Commission for the Study of the History of the Viet Nam Workers' Party. *An Outline History of the Viet Nam Workers' Party (1930–1975)*. Hanoi, 1976.

Cooper, Chester L. *The Lost Crusade: America in Vietnam*. New York, 1970.

Dawson, Alan. *55 Days: The Fall of South Viet Nam*. Englewood Cliffs, N.J., 1977.

Devillers, Philippe, and Jean Lacouture. *End of a War: Indochina, 1954*. New York, 1969.

Duiker, William J. *The Comintern and Vietnamese Communism*. Papers in International Studies Southeast Asia Series No. 37. Athens, Ohio, 1975.

———. *The Rise of Nationalism in Vietnam, 1900–1941*. Ithaca, N.Y., 1976.

———. *Vietnam Since the Fall of Saigon*. Ohio University Southeast Asia Series, LVI. Athens, Ohio, 1980.

Duncanson, Dennis J. *Government and Revolution in Vietnam*. New York, 1968.

Easton, David. *A Systematic Analysis of Political Life*. New York, 1965.

Fall, Bernard B. *Street Without Joy*. New York, 1972.

———. *The Two Viet-Nams: A Political and Military Analysis*. 2nd rev. ed. New York, 1968.

———, ed. *Ho Chi Minh on Revolution: Selected Writings, 1920–66*. New York, 1967.

FitzGerald, Frances. *Fire in the Lake: The Vietnamese and the Americans in Vietnam*. New York, 1972.

Frizzell, Donaldson D., and Ray L. Bower, eds. *Air Power and the 1972 Spring Invasion*. USAF Southeast Asia Monograph Series. Vol. II, Monograph 3. Washington, D.C., 1976.

Gelb, Leslie H., and Richard K. Betts. *The Irony of Vietnam: The System Worked*. Washington, D.C., 1979.

George, Alexander L., David K. Hall, and William E. Simon. *The Limits of Coercive Diplomacy*. Boston, 1971.

Gettleman, Marvin E., ed. *Viet Nam: History, Documents, and Opinions on a Major World Crisis*. New York, 1965.

Goodman, Allan E. *The Lost Peace: America's Search for a Negotiated Settlement of the Vietnam War*. Stanford, Calif., 1978.

Graff, Henry F. *The Tuesday Cabinet: Deliberation and Decision on Peace and War Under Lyndon B. Johnson*. Englewood Cliffs, N.J., 1970.

Hersh, Seymour M. *My Lai 4*. New York, 1970.

Herz, Martin F. *Beginnings of the Cold War*. New York, 1966.

Hilsman, Roger. *To Move a Nation: The Politics of Foreign Policy in the Administration of John F. Kennedy*. Garden City, N.Y., 1967.

Ho Chi Minh. "The Party's Military Work Among the Peasants: Revolutionary Guerrilla Methods." In *Armed Insurrection*, edited by A. Neuberg. London, 1970.

———. *Selected Writings (1920–1969)*. Hanoi, 1973.

Hoang Van Chi. *From Colonialism to Communism: A Case History of North Vietnam*. New York, 1964.

Hoopes, Townsend. *The Limits of Intervention*. New York, 1969.

Hosmer, Stephen T., Brian M. Jenkins, and Konrad Kellen. *The Fall of South Vietnam*, Santa Monica, Calif., 1977.

Johnson, Chalmers A. *Autopsy on People's War*. Berkeley, Calif., 1973.

———. *Peasant Nationalism and Communist Power*. Stanford, Calif., 1962.

Johnson, Lyndon Baines. *The Vantage Point: Perspectives of the Presidency, 1963–1969*. New York, 1971.

Joint United States Public Affairs Office. *Viet-Nam Documents and Research Notes*. Nos. 1–114. Saigon, 1967–73.

Kahin, George McTurnan, and John W. Lewis. *The United States in Vietnam*. New York, 1967.

Kalb, Marvin, and Elie Abel. *Roots of Involvement: The U.S. in Asia, 1784–1971*. New York, 1971.

Kinnard, Douglas. *The War Managers.* Hanover, N.H., 1977.

Klare, Michael. *War Without End: American Planning for the Next Vietnams.* New York, 1972.

Lacouture, Jean. *Ho Chi Minh: A Political Biography.* Translated by Peter Wiles. Edited by Jane Clark Seitz. New York, 1968.

———. *Vietnam: Between Two Truces.* Translated by Konrad Kellen and Joel Carmichael. New York, 1965.

Lake, Anthony, ed. *The Vietnam Legacy: The War, American Society, and the Future of American Foreign Policy.* New York, 1976.

Lancaster, Donald. *The Emancipation of French Indochina.* London, 1961.

Lansdale, Edward Geary. *In the Midst of Wars.* New York, 1972.

Le Duan. *On the Socialist Revolution in Viet Nam.* 3 vols.; Hanoi, 1965–67.

———. *The Vietnamese Revolution: Fundamental Problems, Essential Tasks.* Hanoi, 1970.

Lenin, Vladimir Ilyich. *"Left-Wing" Communism: An Infantile Disorder.* New York, 1934.

———. *Selected Works in Three Volumes.* Vol. III. New York, 1967.

Lewy, Guenter. *America in Vietnam.* New York, 1978.

Liska, George. *War and Order: Reflections on Vietnam and History.* Baltimore, 1968.

Littauer, Raphael, and Norman Uphoff, eds. *The Air War in Indochina.* Rev. ed., Boston, 1972.

McAlister, John T., Jr. *Viet Nam: The Origins. of Revolution.* New York, 1969.

McAlister, John T., Jr., and Paul Mus. *The Vietnamese and Their Revolution.* New York, 1970.

McGarvey, Patrick J., ed. *Visions of Victory: Selected Vietnamese Communist Military Writings, 1964–68.* Stanford, Calif., 1969.

Marr, David G. *Vietnamese Anticolonialism 1885–1925.* Berkeley, Calif., 1971.

Marx, Karl, and Friedrich Engels. *The Communist Manifesto.* 1848; rpr. New York, 1964.

May, Ernest R. *"Lessons" of the Past: The Use and Misuse of History in American Foreign Policy.* New York, 1973.

Mitrany, David. *Marx Against the Peasant: A Study in Social Dogmatism.* Chapel Hill, N.C., 1951.

Mozingo, David P., and T. W. Robinson. *Lin Piao on "People's War": China Takes a Second Look at Vietnam.* Santa Monica, Calif., 1965.

Neuberg, A. [pseud.]. *Armed Insurrection.* Translated by Quinton Hoare. London, 1970.

Nguyen Cao Ky. *Twenty Years and Twenty Days.* New York, 1976.

Nighswonger, William A. *Rural Pacification in Vietnam.* New York, 1966.

Nixon, Richard Milhous. *RN: The Memoirs of Richard Nixon.* New York, 1978.

Oberdorfer, Don. *Tet!* New York, 1971.

Osborne, Milton E. *Strategic Hamlets in South Viet-Nam: A Survey and Comparison.* Ithaca, N.Y., 1965.

Osgood, Robert E. *Limited War Revisited.* Boulder, Colo., 1979.

Packenham, Robert A. *Liberal America and the Third World: Political Development Ideas in Foreign Aid and Social Science.* Princeton, N.J., 1973.

Palmer, Dave Richard. *Summons of the Trumpet: U.S.–Vietnam in Perspective.* San Rafael, Calif., 1978.

Pfeffer, Richard M., ed. *No More Vietnams?* New York, 1968.

Pike, Douglas. *History of Vietnamese Communism, 1925–1976.* Stanford, Calif., 1978.

———. *Viet Cong: The Organization and Techniques of the National Liberation Front of South Vietnam.* Cambridge, Mass., 1966.

———. *War, Peace and the Viet Cong.* Cambridge, Mass., 1969.

Popkin, Samuel L. *The Rational Peasant: The Political Economy of Rural Society in Vietnam.* Berkeley, Calif., 1979.

Porter, D. Gareth. *A Peace Denied: The United States, Vietnam, and the Paris Agreement.* Bloomington, Ind., 1975.

Race, Jeffrey. *War Comes to Long An: Revolutionary Conflict in Vietnamese Province.* Berkeley, Calif., 1972.

Ravenal, Earl C. *Never Again: Learning From America's Foreign Policy Failures.* Philadelphia, 1978.

Reischauer, Edwin O. *Beyond Vietnam.* New York, 1967.

Rogowski, Ronald. *Rational Legitimacy: A Theory of Political Support.* Princeton, N.J., 1974.

Sabine, George H. *A History of Political Theory.* 3rd ed. New York, 1961.

Sansom, Robert L. *The Economics of Insurgency in the Mekong Delta of Vietnam.* Cambridge, Mass., 1970.

Schram, Stuart R. *The Political Thought of Mao Tse-tung.* Rev. ed. New York, 1969.

Schwartz, Benjamin I. *Chinese Communism and the Rise of Mao.* Cambridge, Mass., 1979.

Scott, James C. *The Moral Economy of the Peasant.* New Haven, Conn., 1976.

Seton-Watson, Hugh. *From Lenin to Khrushchev: The History of World Communism.* New York, 1960.

Shaplen, Robert. *The Last Revolution: The U.S. in Vietnam, 1946–1966.* Rev. ed. New York, 1966.

———. *The Road from War: Vietnam, 1965–71.* Rev. ed. New York, 1971.

Sharp, Ulysses S. Grant. *Strategy for Defeat: Vietnam in Retrospect.* San Rafael, Calif., 1978.

Shawcross, William. *Sideshow: Kissinger, Nixon, and the Destruction of Cambodia.* New York, 1979.

Sheehan, Neil, *et al*. *The Pentagon Papers as Published by the New York Times*. New York, 1971.

Snepp, Frank. *Decent Interval*. New York, 1977.

South Vietnam: A Political History, 1954–1970. Keesing's Research Report, No. 5. New York, 1970.

Spanier, John. *American Foreign Policy Since World War II*. 7th ed. New York, 1977.

Stetler, Russell, ed. *The Military Art of People's War: Selected Writings of General Vo Nguyen Giap*. New York, 1970.

Tanham, George K. *Communist Revolutionary Warfare: From the Viet-Minh to the Viet-Cong*. New York, 1961.

Taylor, Maxwell D. *Swords and Plowshares*. New York, 1972.

Terzani, Tiziano. *Giai Phong! The Fall and Liberation of Saigon*. Translated by John Shepley. New York, 1975.

Thich Nhat Hanh. *Vietnam: Lotus in a Sea of Fire*. New York, 1967.

Thompson, Virginia. *French Indochina*. New York, 1937.

Thompson, W. Scott, and Donaldson D. Frizzell, eds. *The Lessons of Vietnam*. New York, 1977.

Tran Van Dinh, ed. *This Nation and Socialism Are One: Selected Writings of Le Duan*. Chicago, 1976.

Tran Van Don. *Our Endless War: Inside Vietnam*. San Rafael, Calif., 1978.

Truong Chinh. *Primer for Revolt: The Communist Takeover in Viet Nam*. Introduction and notes by Bernard B. Fall. New York, 1963.

Truong Chinh and Vo Nguyen Giap. *The Peasant Question (1937–1938)*. Translation and Introduction by Christian Pelzer White. Data Paper, Number 94: Southeast Asia Program. Ithaca, N.Y., 1974.

Tucker, Robert C. *The Marx-Engels Reader*. New York, 1972.

———. *The Marxian Revolutionary Idea*. New York, 1969.

———, ed. *The Lenin Anthology*. New York, 1975.

Turner, Robert F. *Vietnamese Communism: Its Origins and Development*. Stanford, Calif., 1975.

U.S. Department of the Army. *Report of the Department of the Army Review of the Preliminary Investigations into the My Lai Incident, 14 March 1970*. Vol. I of 4 vols. Washington, D.C., 1970.

Van Tien Dung. *Our Great Spring Victory: An Account of the Liberation of South Vietnam*. Translated by John Spragens, Jr. New York, 1977.

Vo Nguyen Giap. "The Big Victory, the Great Task." In *Visions of Victory: Selected Vietnamese Communist Military Writings, 1964–1968*, edited by Patrick J. McGarvey. Stanford, Calif., 1969.

———. *People's War, People's Army*. Foreword by Roger Hilsman. Profile by Bernard B. Fall. New York, 1962.

Warner, Denis. *Certain Victory: How Hanoi Won the War*. Kansas City, Kan. 1978.

————. *The Last Confucian: Vietnam, South-East Asia, and the West.* Baltimore, 1964.

Westmoreland, William Childs. *A Soldier Reports.* Garden City, N.Y., 1976.

White, Ralph K. *Nobody Wanted War: Misperception in Vietnam and Other Wars.* New York, 1968.

Windchey, Eugene G. *Tonkin Gulf.* Garden City, N.Y., 1971.

Woodside, Alexander B. *Community and Revolution in Modern Vietnam.* Boston, 1976.

————. *Vietnam and the Chinese Model: A Comparative Study of Nguyen and Ch'ing Civil Government in the First Half of the Nineteenth Century.* Cambridge, Mass., 1971.

Zasloff, Joseph J., and MacAlister Brown, eds. *Communism in Indochina: New Perspectives.* Lexington, Mass., 1975.

Articles

Adams, Sam. "Vietnam Cover-up: Playing with Numbers." *Harpers*, CCL (May, 1975), 41–45, 62–70.

Ahmad, Eqbal. "Revolutionary War and Counter-Insurgency." *Journal of International Affairs*, XXV, No. 1, 1–47.

Bennet, John T. "Political Implications of Economic Change." *Asian Survey*, VII (August, 1967), 581–91.

Bundy, William P. "Path to Viet Nam: Ten Decisions." *Orbis*, XI (Fall, 1967), 647–63.

Chang Jin Park. "American Foreign Policy in Korea and Vietnam: Comparative Case Studies." *Review of Politics*, XXXVII (January, 1975), 20–47.

Chen, King C. "Hanoi vs. Peking: Politics and Relations—A Survey." *Asian Survey*, XII (September, 1972), 806–17.

Chesneaux, Jean. "The Historical Background of Vietnamese Communism." *Government and Opposition*, IV (Winter, 1969), 118–41.

Collins, John M. "Vietnam Postmortem: A Senseless Strategy." *Parameters: Journal of the U.S. Army War College*, VII (March, 1978), 8–15.

Duc Thuan. "Understanding: On the Historical Mission of the Working Class in the National Liberation Revolution in Vietnam (before 1930)." *Nghien Cuu Lich Su*, CXXXI (March–April, 1970), 7–20.

Elliott, David W. P. "North Vietnam Since Ho." *Problems of Communism*, XXIX (July–August, 1975), 35–52.

Falk, Richard A. "Vietnam: The Final Deceptions." *Nation*, May 17, 1975, pp. 582–84.

Fall, Bernard. "The Agonizing Reappraisal." *Current History*, XLVIII (February, 1965), 95–102.

Fifield, Russell H. "The Thirty Years War in Indochina: A Conceptual Framework." *Asian Survey*, XVII (September, 1977), 857–80.

Galbraith, John Kenneth. "Plain Lessons of a Bad Decade." *Foreign Policy*, I (Winter, 1970–71), 31–45.

Gilster, Herma L. "Air Interdiction in Protracted War: An Economic Evaluation." *Air University Review*, XXVII (May–June, 1977), 2–18.

Ginsburgh, Robert N. "Strategy and Air Power: The Lessons of Southeast Asia." *Strategic Review*, II (Summer, 1973), 18–25.

Goodman, Allan E. "Conflict and Accommodation Within Legislative Elite in South Vietnam." *Pacific Affairs*, XLIV (Summer, 1971), 211–28.

———. "South Vietnam: Neither War Nor Peace." *Asian Survey*, X (February, 1970), 107–33.

Grinter, Lawrence E. "How They Lost: Doctrines, Strategies and Outcomes of the Vietnam War." *Asian Survey*, XV (December, 1975), 114–32.

Hasdorf, James E. "Vietnam in Retrospect: An Interview with Ambassador Frederick E. Nolting, Jr." *Air University Review*, XXV (January–February, 1974), 2–10.

Hoang Van Thai. "The Strategy of People's War and the Building of the People's Armed Force." *Hoc Tap*, VII (July, 1965), 44–51.

Holsti, Ole R., and James N. Rosenau. "Does Where You Stand Depend on When You Were Born? The Impact of Generation on Post-Vietnam Foreign Policy Beliefs." *Public Opinion*, XLIV (Spring, 1980), 1–22.

Hunt, David. "Organizing for Revolution in Vietnam: Study of a Mekong Delta Province." *Radical America*, VIII, (January–April, 1974), 1–184.

Johnson, Chalmers A. "The Third Generation of Guerrilla Warfare." *Asian Survey*, VII (June, 1968), 435–47.

Kahin, George McTurnan. "Political Polarization in South Vietnam: U.S. Policy and the Post Diem Period." *Pacific Affairs*, LII (Winter, 1979–80), 647–73.

Kirk, Donald. "The Thieu Presidential Campaign: Background and Consequences of the Single-Candidacy Phenomenon." *Asian Survey*, XII (July, 1972), 609–27.

Kissinger, Henry A. "U.S. Foreign Policy: Finding Strength Through Adversity." *Department of State Bulletin*, May 5, 1975, pp. 557–66.

Le Duc Binh. "The Party Theory of Lenin and the Development of Our Party." *Hoc Tap*, IV (April, 1970), 63–75, 81.

Le Ngoc. "Engels: Teacher of World Proletarian Revolution and Scholar." *Hoc Tap*, XI (November, 1970), 43–52 (JPRS No. 52,165, pp. 53–64).

"Learn from President Ho's Book, 'Forever Follow the Great Lenin's Road.'" *Hoc Tap*, IV (April, 1970), 76–81.

"Legality of U.S. Participation in the Defense of Viet-Nam." *American Journal of International Law*, LX (July, 1966), 565–85.

Lustig, Jeff. "On Organization: The Question of the Leninist Party." *Politics and Society*, VII, No. 1, 27–69.

Makinin, G. E. "Economic Stabilization in Wartime: A Comparative Study of Korea and Vietnam." *Journal of Political Economy*, LXXIX (November–December, 1971), 1216–44.

Moise, Edwin E. "Land Reform and Land Reform Errors." *Pacific Affairs*, XLIX (Spring, 1976), 70–93.

Moore, J. N. "Lawfulness of Military Assistance to the Republic of Vietnam." *American Journal of International Law*, LXI (January, 1967), 1–35.

Nguyen Khac Vien. "Traditional Vietnam: Some Historical Stages." *Vietnamese Studies*, XXI [1969?], 1–56.

O'Ballance, Edgar O. "Sino-Soviet Influence on the War in Vietnam." *Contemporary Review*, CCX (February, 1967), 70–76.

"Party Congress in Hanoi." *Indochina Chronology*, I (January–March, 1982), 7.

Powell, Ralph L. "Maoist Military Doctrines." *Asian Survey*, VIII (April, 1968), 239–63.

Race, Jeffrey. "How They Won." *Asian Survey*, X (August, 1970), 628–51.

Ravenal, Earl C. "Was Vietnam a Mistake?" *Asian Survey*, XIV (July, 1974), 589–607.

Reischauer, Edwin O. "Back to Normalcy." *Foreign Policy*, XX (Fall, 1975), 199–208.

Roskin, Michael. "From Pearl Harbor to Vietnam: Shifting Generational Paradigms and Foreign Policy." *Political Science Quarterly*, LXXXIX (Fall, 1974), 563–88.

Sacks, Milton I. "Restructuring Government in South Vietnam." *Asian Survey*, VII (August, 1967), 515–27.

Santoli, Al. "Why Viet Cong Flee." *Parade*, July 11, 1982, pp. 4–6.

Silverman, Jerry Mark. "The Domino Theory: Alternatives to a Self-fulfilling Prophecy." *Asian Survey*, XV (November, 1975), 915–39.

———. "Local Government and National Integration in South Viet Nam." *Pacific Affairs*, XLVII (Fall, 1974), 305–26.

Smith, Melden E., Jr. "The Strategic Bombing Debate: The Second World War and Viet Nam." *Journal of Contemporary History*, XII (October, 1976), 175–93.

Starr, John Bryan. "Conceptual Foundations of Mao Tse-tung's Theory of Continuous Revolution." *Asian Survey*, XI (June, 1971), 620.

Tao, J. "Mao's World Outlook: Vietnam and the Revolution in China." *Asian Survey*, VIII (May, 1968), 416–32.

Taylor, Milton C. "Local Government Finance in South Vietnam." *Journal of Developing Areas*, VI (April, 1972), 399–411.

"The Problem of National Liberation in This Era." *Hoc Tap*, III (March, 1964).

To Minh Trung. "Materials for Study: Leading Flag of General Uprising Movement in the South." *Nghien Cuu Lich Su*, I (January, 1969), 47–54.

Truong Buu Lam. "Patterns of Vietnamese Response to Foreign Intervention: 1858–1900." *Yale University Southeast Asia Studies*, XI (1967), 1–151.

Turley, William S. "Civil-Military Relations in North Viet Nam." *Asian Survey*, IX (December, 1969), 879–900.

Warner, Geoffrey. "The U.S. and Vietnam, 1945–65: Part I, 1945–54." *International Affairs*, XLVII (July, 1972), 379–95.

White, Ralph K. "Attitudes of the South Vietnamese." *Papers of the Peace Research Society*, X (June, 1968), 46–57.

———. "Misperception and the Vietnam War." *Journal of Social Issues*, XXII (July, 1966), 1–54.

Wolf, Charles, Jr. "The Logic of Failure: A Vietnam 'Lesson.'" *Journal of Conflict Resolution*, XVI (September, 1972), 397–403.

Woodside, Alexander B. "Ideology and Integration in Post-Colonial Vietnamese Nationalism." *Pacific Affairs*, XLIV (Winter, 1971), 487–511.

Wylie, Raymond F. "Mao Tse-Tung, Ch'en Po-Ta, and the 'Sinification of Marxism,' 1936–1938." *China Quarterly*, LXXIX (September, 1979), 447–81.

X [George F. Kennan]. "Sources of Soviet Conduct." *Foreign Affairs*, XXV (July, 1947), 566–82.

Zasloff, Joseph J. "Rural Resettlement in South Viet Nam: The Agroville Program." *Pacific Affairs*, XXXV (Winter, 1962–63), 327–40.

Newspapers

"Arms Policy: Farewell to Nixon Doctrine." Washington *Post*, December 13, 1979, Sec. A, p. 33.

"DeGaulle's Warning to Kennedy: An 'Endless Entanglement' in Vietnam." New York *Times*, March 15, 1972, Sec. L, p. 47.

"Jackson, in Beirut, Urges P.L.O. to Halt Terrorism." New York *Times*, September 19, 1979, Sec. A, p. 4.

Lacouture, Jean. "A Bittersweet Journey to Vietnam." New York *Times*, August 23, 1976, Sec. L, p. 23.

Sterba, James P. "'Friendship Pass' No Longer Links Peking to Hanoi." New York *Times*, February 5, 1979, Sec. 1, p. A3.

Pamphlets

DRVN Commission for Investigation of the U.S. Imperialists' War Crimes in Viet Nam. *The Late December 1972 U.S. Blitz on North Viet Nam.* Hanoi, 1973.

Engels, Friedrich. *The Revolutionary Act: Military Insurrection or Political and Economic Action.* New York, 1933.

Furniss, Edgar S., Jr. *Counterinsurgency: Some Problems and Implications.* New York, 1966.

Lin Piao. *Long Live the Victory of People's War!* Peking, 1965.

Mao Tse-Tung. *Problems of Strategy in China's Revolutionary War.* 1936; rpr. Peking, 1967.

————. *On Protracted War.* 1938; rpr. Peking, 1967.

Pike, Douglas. *Vietnam War: View From the Other Side.* Saigon, 1967.

Second Congress of the Communist International. *National and Colonial Questions.* London, 1920.

Vo Nguyen Giap and Van Tien Dung. *How We Won the War.* Ypsilanti, Mich., 1976.

Unpublished Works

Boudarel, Georges. "Military Line of the ICP." Paper presented at the Vietnam Studies Group Conference on Vietnamese Marxism in Comparative Perspective, Washington, D.C., October 27, 1978.

Brocheux, Pierre. "The ICP and the Peasant Question in Comparison with the CCP and PKI." Paper presented at the Vietnam Studies Group Conference on Vietnamese Marxism in Comparative Perspective, Washington, D.C., October 27, 1978.

————. "Vietnamese Revolutionary Doctrine." Paper presented at the Vietnam Studies Group Conference on Vietnamese Marxism in Comparative Perspective, Washington, D.C., October 28, 1978.

Duiker, William J. "Vietnamese Revolutionary Doctrine." Paper presented at the Vietnam Studies Group Conference on Vietnamese Marxism in Comparative Perspective, Washington, D.C., October 28, 1978.

Eldridge, A. "The Crisis of Authority: The President, Kissinger, and Congress, 1969–74." Paper presented at the International Studies Association Meeting, Toronto, Canada, February, 1976.

Holsti, Ole R., and James N. Rosenau. "The 'Lessons' of Vietnam: A Study of American Leadership." Paper presented at the Seventeenth Annual Convention of the International Studies Association, Toronto, Canada, February, 1976.

INDEX

Adams, Sam, 71
Advisers, numbers of, 60
Afghanistan, 86, 175
Agroville Plan, 59
Aid, American, 86–87
Air armada, American, 69
Allied forces, numbers of, 68
An Loc, siege of, 89
An Quang sect, 61, 86–87. *See also*
  Buddhists; Thich Tri Quang
Angola, 1
Ap Bac, battle of, 57
Army of the Republic of Viet Nam
  (ARVN): battle of Ap Bac, 57; recruit-
  ment, 64; desertions and defections,
  74, 86, 169; Tet offensive, 79; Cam-
  bodia, 84; size, 87–88; morale, 86,
  96–97; and Easter invasion, 89–90;
  ammunition supplies, 97; and prose-
  lyting of, 171
August revolution: account of, 33–35;
  right of revolution, example of, 102;
  Vietnamese contribution, 102; as
  case of *khoi nghia*, 144–46; mentioned, 80, 100, 120, 123, 141. *See
  also Khoi nghia*; People's war

Ball, George, 61
Ban Me Thuot, fall of, 98
Bao Dai, 34, 40, 43, 49
BARRELL ROLL, Operation, 66. *See also*
  Ho Chi Minh Trail
Base area: in people's war, 158, 166
Bidault, Georges, 47
Big-unit war, 68–69
Binh Gia, battle of, 64, 151
Binh Xuyen, 38–39, 50–51
Body count, 69–71
Blum, Leon, 121
Bolshevik Revolution, 126
Bourgeois revolution, 112
Buddhists: early uprisings, 17–18, 26;
  Diem protests, 58, 60–61; during
  interregnum, 62; Struggle Force,

73–74; political blocs, 87; Communist failure with, 167

Cambodian incursion, 69, 83–85
Can Lao party, 58, 62
Can Vuong faction, 24, 26–27, 29
Cao Dai sect, 28, 32, 38–39, 50, 87,
  167–68
Caravelle manifesto, 58
Carter, Jimmy, 2
Catholics, 28, 41, 54, 87
Central Intelligence Agency (CIA), 60
Champa, 18–19
Chiang Kai-shek, 118, 133
Chinese: domination, period of, 17; as-
  sistance to Viet Minh, 41–42, 45; at
  the Geneva conference, 46; as-
  sistance to Viet Cong, 75–76; revolu-
  tion unacknowledged, 126
Chou En'lai, 47, 87
Christianity, 22–23
Christmas bombing, 92–94
Clifford, Clark, 79
Cold war, 108–109
Communist International (Comintern),
  116, 120–22
Communist Manifesto, 112, 116
Communist party. *See also* Lao Dong
  party; Indochinese Communist party;
  Viet Cong; Viet Minh Communism:
  Vietnamese, 120–32
—history: founding Indochinese Communist party, 29–30; activities until
  World War II, 29–31; during World
  War II, 32–33; immediate postwar
  period, 33–36; during Franco-Viet
  Minh war, 37–46; at the Geneva
  Conference, 46–48; from 1955 to
  1960, pp. 50–52; armed struggle decision, 56; during interregnum (1964),
  63–64; ability to replace losses, 68;
  role in Struggle Force, 73; during Tet
  offensive, 76–81; low point for,
  81–82; Cambodian incursion plans,